Bond Investing For Dummies®

Cheat Sheet

Understanding Bond Ratings

Before you buy a corporate bond, get an idea of how much financial muscle the issuing corporation has. Bond ratings are available through any brokerage house. Three of the most popular rating services are Moody's, Standard & Poor's, and Fitch.

Corporate Bond Credit Quality Ratings

Credit risk ratings	Moody's	Standard & Poor's	Fitch
Investment grade			
Tip-top quality	Aaa	AAA	AAA
Premium quality	Aa	AA	AA
Near-premium quality	A	A	A
Take-home-to-Mom quality	Baa	BBB	BBB
Not investment grade			
Borderline ugly	Ba	BB	BB
Ugly	B	B	B
Definitely don't-take-home-to-Mom quality	Caa	CCC	CCC
You'll be extremely lucky to get your money back	Ca	CC	CC
Interest payments have halted or bankruptcy is in process	C	D	C
Already in default	C	D	D

Asking a Broker All the Right Questions

Ring ring. There's a broker on the line, and, oh boy, does he have a bond for you! Don't buy so fast. First, ask the following:

- **Who is the bond issuer?** Is it the U.S. Treasury? General Electric? Dade County, Florida? The Russian Federation? Moe's Hardware Store? A bond is an IOU, and an IOU is only as good as the entity that owes U. In addition, different kinds of bonds have different characteristics, such as tax-ability, callability, and volatility.

- **How is the bond rated?** Especially among corporate bonds (more likely to default than municipal or agency bonds), you want to know whether the company issuing the bond is financially stable. Ratings are readily available through any brokerage house.

- **What is the maturity date?** Long-term bonds tend to pay higher rates of interest, but your money is tied up for longer and the price of the bond, should you wish to sell it before maturity, tends to be more volatile.

- **What is the yield-to-maturity?** There are many ways of measuring a bond's return. Yield-to-maturity (see Chapter 4) is perhaps the most important measure. (Bond funds, which have no maturity, can be more difficult to compare.)

- **Is the bond callable?** Can the issuer of the bond hand you back your money at any time? All things being equal, a callable bond is not desirable, and you should get more interest in compensation for the call feature.

- **What's the worst-case yield?** Suppose the bond does get called. What would be your yield on the bond at that point? When comparing callable bonds, this figure is very important.

- **May I please have the CUSIP?** The CUSIP number allows you to go to www.investingin bonds.com or www.finra.org to see what recent trades have been made on any particular bond. Doing so gives you a very good idea of what a fair price would be for the bond you are being offered.

For Dummies: Bestselling Book Series for Beginners

Bond Investing For Dummies®

Cheat Sheet

The Most Important Online Bond Tools

These seven Web sites serve as your navigation guide through the vast universe of bonds and bond funds:

- ✔ **www.investinginbonds.com**: Run by the Securities Industry and Financial Markets Association, this is the place to go to find out overall bond market yields and, perhaps more importantly, what individual bonds (which you can look up by their CUSIP number or issuer) are selling for.

- ✔ **www.finra.org**: This is the Web site of the Financial Industry Regulatory Authority, formed in July 2007 when the National Association of Securities Dealers merged with the New York Stock Exchange Member Regulation. Find scores of information on bond yields, prices, and trends.

- ✔ **www.treasurydirect.gov**: Find out what your savings bonds are worth. Buy and sell U.S. Treasury bills and bonds at no cost.

- ✔ **www.bloomberg.com**: Go to <u>Market Data: Rates and Bonds</u> for up-to-date information on multiple bond markets.

- ✔ **finance.yahoo.com/bonds**: Find scads of information on individual bonds and bond funds. Go to <u>Bond Screener</u> for a complete bond shopping guide.

- ✔ **www.moneychimp.com/calculator/bond_yield_calculator.htm**: Complicated URL, simple calculator. You put in the price of the bond, the coupon rate, and the maturity date, and out comes the all-important yield-to-maturity.

- ✔ **www.morningstar.com**: Click the <u>Funds</u> icon on the blue bar at the top of the screen. Find lots of information on any bond fund you can imagine, including Morningstar's exclusive rating system. (Avoid one-star funds; shoot for five stars.)

Choosing Between a Taxable and a Tax-Free Municipal Bond

If you want to know which kind of bond will leave you with more money at the end of the day, grab your calculator and apply the following rather simple formula:

1. **Start with 100.**

2. **Subtract your tax bracket.** If you are in the 28 percent bracket, for example, subtract 28 from 100. That number — 72 — is called the *reciprocal* of your tax bracket.

3. **Divide the municipal yield by the reciprocal.** The result tells you what you would have to earn on the taxable bond to equal the amount you would get on the tax-exempt municipal bond.

Using these numbers, consider a muni paying 5 percent:

5 / 72 = 6.94 percent

That number, 6.94, represents your *tax-equivalent yield,* or your break-even between taxable and tax-exempt bond investing. If you can get 5 percent on a muni versus 6.94 percent on a taxable bond, it won't matter which you choose, as far as take-home pay. (Of course, other factors may matter, such as the quality or the maturity of the bond.) If the taxable bond is yielding greater than 6.94 percent, it will likely be your best bet. If the taxable bond is yielding less than 6.94 percent, you're likely better off with the tax-free bond.

For Dummies: Bestselling Book Series for Beginners

Bond Investing FOR DUMMIES®

by Russell Wild, MBA

Wiley Publishing, Inc.

Bond Investing For Dummies®

Published by
Wiley Publishing, Inc.
111 River St.
Hoboken, NJ 07030-5774
www.wiley.com

Copyright © 2007 by Wiley Publishing, Inc., Indianapolis, Indiana

Published by Wiley Publishing, Inc., Indianapolis, Indiana

Published simultaneously in Canada

For general information on our other products and services, please contact our Customer Care Department within the U.S. at 800-762-2974, outside the U.S. at 317-572-3993, or fax 317-572-4002.

For technical support, please visit www.wiley.com/techsupport.

Wiley also publishes its books in a variety of electronic formats. Some content that appears in print may not be available in electronic books.

Library of Congress Control Number: 2007935019

ISBN: 978-0-470-13459-7

Manufactured in the United States of America

10 9 8 7 6 5 4 3 2 1

WILEY

About the Author

Russell Wild is a NAPFA-certified financial advisor and the principal of Global Portfolios, an investment advisory firm based in eastern Pennsylvania. He is one of few wealth managers in the nation who is both fee-only (takes no commissions) and welcomes clients of both substantial *and* modest means. Wild, in addition to the fun he has with his financial calculator, is also an accomplished writer who helps readers understand and make wise choices about their money. His articles have appeared in many national publications, including *AARP The Magazine, Consumer Reports, Details, Maxim, Men's Journal, Men's Health, Cosmopolitan, Reader's Digest,* and *Real Simple.* He also contributes regularly to professional financial journals, such as *Wealth Manager* and *Financial Planning.*

The author or coauthor of two dozen nonfiction books, Wild's last work, prior to the one you're holding in your hand, was *Exchange-Traded Funds For Dummies* (Wiley, 2007). Before that was *The Unofficial Guide to Getting a Divorce* (Wiley, 2005), coauthored with attorney Susan Ellis Wild, his ex-wife — yeah, you read that right. No stranger to the mass media, Wild has shared his wit and wisdom on such shows as *Oprah, The View, CBS Morning News,* and *Good Day New York,* and in hundreds of radio interviews.

Wild holds a Master of Business Administration (MBA) degree in international management and finance from Thunderbird, the Garvin School of International Management, in Glendale, Arizona (consistently ranked the #1 school for international business by both *U.S. News and World Report* and *The Wall Street Journal*); a Bachelor of Science (BS) degree in business/economics *magna cum laude* from American University in Washington, D.C.; and a graduate certificate in personal financial planning from Moravian College in Bethlehem, Pennsylvania (America's sixth-oldest college). A member of the National Association of Personal Financial Advisors (NAPFA) since 2002, Wild is also a long-time member and currently serves as vice president of the American Society of Journalists and Authors (ASJA).

The author grew up on Long Island and now lives in Allentown, Pennsylvania with his two children, Adrienne and Clayton, along with Norman, the killer poodle. His Web site is www.globalportfolios.net.

Dedication

To the handful of people I've known in this crazy society who somehow manage to keep proper perspective on money, and have helped me to do the same: Arun, Auggie, Marc, Michael, Robert, Susan, and Vicki and Joe.

Author's Acknowledgments

This being my second *Dummies* book, I'd like to thank for a second time all the good people at Wiley, many of whom were involved in my first *Dummies* project, *Exchange-Traded Funds For Dummies*. We're becoming like old friends! I'm so glad that you guys assigned Joan Friedman once again as the project editor. If Moody's gave editors ratings, as it does bonds, Joan would certainly be rated Aaa.

Thanks to some of my colleagues in the investment world, especially Marilyn Cohen, official tech consultant on this book, who knows bonds better than anyone on the planet and provided me with invaluable insight into the behind-the-curtains world of bond trading. And my great appreciation to Michael Pace, an extremely sharp certified financial planner, fellow member of the National Association of Personal Financial Advisors (NAPFA), and excellent catcher of errors and inserter of added good information.

Thanks to Brenda Lange and David Kohn, fellow writers and members of the American Society of Journalists and Authors (ASJA), for their literary input. I also appreciate the help of all the number crunchers and media liaisons at Morningstar, as well as some very helpful folks at the U.S. Treasury, the Securities Industry and Financial Markets Association, and the Financial Industry Regulatory Authority. Special thanks go to Rebecca Cohen at Vanguard.

And thanks to my literary agent, Marilyn Allen, for her continued good representation in the tangled and complicated world of book publishing.

Some others who provided very helpful input are mentioned throughout the pages of the book. I appreciate your help, one and all. Oh, I almost forgot . . . Thank *you*, Little Pepper (my daughter), for your illustrations!

Publisher's Acknowledgments

We're proud of this book; please send us your comments through our Dummies online registration form located at www.dummies.com/register/.

Some of the people who helped bring this book to market include the following:

Acquisitions, Editorial, and Media Development

Project Editor: Joan Friedman

Acquisitions Editor: Stacy Kennedy

Technical Consultant: Marilyn Cohen

Editorial Supervisor: Carmen Krikorian

Editorial Manager: Michelle Hacker

Editorial Assistants: Erin Calligan Mooney, Joe Niesen, David Lutton, Leeann Harney

Cover Photos: © Royalty-Free/Corbis

Cartoons: Rich Tennant (www.the5thwave.com)

Composition Services

Project Coordinator: Erin Smith

Layout and Graphics: Brooke Graczyk, Joyce Haughey, Stephanie D. Jumper, Julie Trippetti

Anniversary Logo Design: Richard Pacifico

Proofreaders: John Greenough, Susan Moritz, Evelyn W. Still

Indexer: Potomac Indexing LLC

Publishing and Editorial for Consumer Dummies

Diane Graves Steele, Vice President and Publisher, Consumer Dummies

Joyce Pepple, Acquisitions Director, Consumer Dummies

Kristin A. Cocks, Product Development Director, Consumer Dummies

Michael Spring, Vice President and Publisher, Travel

Kelly Regan, Editorial Director, Travel

Publishing for Technology Dummies

Andy Cummings, Vice President and Publisher, Dummies Technology/General User

Composition Services

Gerry Fahey, Vice President of Production Services

Debbie Stailey, Director of Composition Services

Contents at a Glance

Table of Contents

Introduction

- -

Chances are that right now you're standing in the Personal Finance section of your favorite bookstore. Take a look to your left. You see that pudgy, balding guy in the baggy jeans perusing the book on getting rich by day-trading stock options? Look to your right. You see that gal with the purple lipstick and the hoop earrings thumbing through that paperback on how to make millions in foreclosed property deals? I want you to walk over to them. Good. Now I want you to take this book firmly in your hand. Excellent. And now I want you to smack each of them over the head with it.

Nice job!

Wiley (the publisher of this book) has lawyers who are going to want me to assure you that I'm only kidding about smacking anyone. So in deference to the attorneys, and because I want to get my royalty checks . . . I'm kidding! I'm only kidding! Don't hit anyone!

But the fact is that *someone* should knock some sense into these people. If not, they may wind up — as the vast majority of people who try to get rich quick do — with nothing but big holes in their pockets.

Those who make the most money in the world of investments possess an extremely rare commodity in today's world — something called patience. At the same time they're looking for handsome returns, they are also looking to protect what they have. Why? Because a loss of 75 percent in an investment (think tech stocks 2000–2002) requires you to earn *400 percent* to get back to where you started. Good luck getting there!

In fact, garnering handsome returns and protecting against loss are pretty much the same thing, as any financial professional should tell you. But only the first half of the equation — the handsome return part — gets the lion's share of the ink. Heck, there must be 1,255 books on getting rich quick for every one book on limiting risk and growing wealth slowly but surely.

Welcome to that one book: *Bond Investing For Dummies.*

So just what are bonds? The word *bond* basically means an IOU. You lend your money to Uncle Sam, to General Electric, to Procter & Gamble, to the city in which you live — to whatever entity issues the bonds — and that entity promises to pay you a certain rate of interest in exchange for borrowing your money. This is very different from stock investing, where you purchase shares in a company, become an alleged partial owner of that company, and then start to pray that the company churns a profit and the CEO doesn't pocket it all.

Stocks (which really aren't as bad as I just made them sound) and bonds complement each other like peanut butter and jelly. Bonds are the peanut butter that can keep your jelly from dripping to the floor. They are the life rafts that can keep your portfolio afloat when the investment seas get choppy. Yes, bonds are also very handy as a source of steady income, but, contrary to popular myth, that should not be their major role in most portfolios.

Bonds are the sweethearts that may have saved your grandparents from selling apples on the street during the hungry 1930s. (Note that I'm not talking about high-yield "junk" bonds here.) They are the babies that may have saved your 401(k) from devastation during the three growly bear-market years on Wall Street that started this century. Bonds belong in nearly every portfolio. Whether they belong in *your* portfolio is something I help you to decide in this book.

About This Book

Allow the next 340 or so pages to serve as your guide to understanding bonds, choosing the right bonds or bond funds, getting the best buys on your purchases, and achieving the best prices when you sell them. You also find out how to work bonds into a powerful, well-diversified portfolio that serves your financial goals much better (I promise) than day-trading stock options or attempting to make a profit flipping real estate in your spare time.

I present to you, in easy-to-understand English (unless you happen to be reading the Ukrainian or Korean translation), the sometimes complex, even somewhat mystical and magical world of bonds. I explain such concepts as bond maturity, duration, coupon rate, callability, and yield, and I show you the differences between the many different kinds of bonds, such as Treasuries, agency bonds, corporates, munis, zeroes, convertibles, strips, and TIPS.

You discover the mistakes that many bond investors make, the traps that some wily bond brokers lay for the uninitiated, and the heartbreak that can befall those who buy certain bonds without first doing their homework. (Don't worry — I walk you through how to do your homework.) You find out how to mix and match your bonds with other kinds of assets, such as stocks and real estate, taking advantage of the latest in investment research to help you maximize your return with minimal risk.

Here are some of the things that you need to know before buying any bond or bond fund — things you'll know *cold* after you read *Bond Investing For Dummies*:

- ✔ **What's your split gonna be?** Put all your eggs in one basket, and you're going to wind up getting scrambled. A key to successful investing is diversification. Yes, you've heard that before — so has everyone — but you'd be amazed how many people ignore this advice!

  Unless you're working with really exotic investments, the majority of a portfolio is stocks and bonds. The split between those stocks and bonds — whether you choose a 90/10 (aggressive) portfolio (composed of 90 percent stocks and 10 percent bonds), a 70/30 (balanced) portfolio, or a 35/65 (conservative) portfolio — is very possibly *the single most important investment decision you'll ever make*. Stocks and bonds are very different kinds of animals, and their respective percentages in a portfolio can have a profound impact on your financial future. Chapter 12 deals with this percentage issue directly, but the importance of mixing and matching investments pops up in other chapters, as well.

- ✔ **Exactly what kind of bonds do you want?** Depending on your tax bracket, your age, your income, your financial needs and goals, your need for ready cash, and a bunch of other factors, you may want to invest in Treasury, corporate, agency, or municipal bonds. Within each of these categories, you have other choices to make: Do you want long-term or short-term bonds? Higher quality bonds or higher yielding bonds? Freshly issued bonds or bonds floating around on the secondary market? Bonds issued in the United States or bonds from Mexico or Brazil? I introduce many different bond types in Part II, and I discuss which may be most appropriate for you — and which are likely to weigh your portfolio down.

- ✔ **Where do you bond shop?** Although bonds have been around more or less in their present form for hundreds of years (see a brief history of bonds in Chapter 3), the way they are bought and sold has changed radically in recent years. Bond traders once had you at their tender mercy. You had no idea what kind of money they were clipping from you every time they traded a bond on your alleged behalf. That is no longer so.

Whether you decide to buy individual bonds or bond funds (Chapter 14 helps you make that thorny decision), there are now ways to know almost to the dime how much the hungry middlemen intend to nibble — or have nibbled from your trades in the past. Part IV is your complete shopper's guide.

✔ **What kind of returns can you expect, and what is your risk of loss?** Here is the part of bonds that most people find most confusing — and, oh, how misconceptions abound! (You can't lose money in U.S. government bonds? Um . . . How can I break this news to you gently?) In Chapter 4, I explain the tricky concepts of duration and yield. I explain why the value of your bonds is so directly tied to prevailing interest rates — with other economic variables giving their push and pull. I give you the tools to determine just how much money you can reasonably expect to make off a bond, and under what circumstances you may lose money.

If you've ever read one of these black and yellow *Dummies* books before, you have an idea what you're about to embark on. This is not a book you need to read from front to back, or (if you're reading the Chinese or Hebrew edition) back to front. Feel free to jump back and forth and glean whatever information you think will help you the most. No proctor with bifocal glasses will pop out of the air, Harry-Potter style, to test you at the end. You needn't put it all to memory now — or ever. Keep this reference book for years to come as your little acorn of a bond portfolio grows into a mighty oak.

Conventions Used in This Book

To help you navigate the text of this tome as easily as possible, I use the following conventions:

✔ Whenever I introduce a new term, such as, say, *callability* or *discount rate,* it appears (as you can clearly see) in *italics.* You can rest assured that a definition or explanation is right around the corner.

✔ If I want to share some interesting tidbit of information that isn't essential to your successful investing in bonds, I place it in a *sidebar,* a grayish rectangle or square with its own heading, set apart from the rest of the text. (See how this whole italics/definition thing works?)

✔ All Web addresses appear in `monofont` so they're easy to pick out if you need to go back and find them.

Keep in mind that when this book was printed, some Web addresses may have needed to break across two lines of text. Wherever that's the case, rest assured that we haven't put in any extra characters (hyphens or other doohickeys) to indicate the break. So, when using one of these Web addresses, just type in exactly what you see in this book. Pretend as if the line break doesn't exist.

What You're Not to Read

Unless you're going to become a professional bond trader, you probably don't need to know everything in this book. Every few pages, you'll undoubtedly come across some technical stuff that you really don't have to know to be a successful bond investor. Read through the technical stuff if you wish, or, if ratios and percentages and such make you dizzy, feel free to skip over it.

Most of the heavy technical matter in this book is tucked neatly into the grayish sidebars. But if any technicalities make it into the main text, I give you a heads up with a Technical Stuff icon. That's where you can skip or speed read — or choose to get dizzy. Your call!

Foolish Assumptions

If you feel you truly need to start from scratch in the world of investments, perhaps the best place would be *Investing For Dummies* by Eric Tyson (published by Wiley). But the book you're holding in your hands is only a smidgen above that one in terms of assumptions of investment savvy. I assume that you are intelligent, that you have a few bucks to invest, and that you have a basic education in math (and a maybe a very, very rudimentary knowledge of economics) — that's it.

In other words, even if your investing experience to date consists of opening a savings account, balancing a checkbook, and reading a few Suze Orman columns, you should still be able to follow along. Oh, and for those of you who are already buying and selling bonds and feel completely comfortable in the world of fixed income, I'm assuming that you, too, can learn something by reading this book. (Oh? You know it all, do you? Can you tell me what a *sukuk* is, or where to buy one, huh? See Chapter 9!)

How This Book Is Organized

Here's a thumbnail sketch of what you'll be seeing in the next 340 or so pages.

Part I: Bond Appetit!

In this first part, you find out what makes a bond a bond. You discover the rationale for their being. I take you through a portal of time to see what bonds looked like dozens, even hundreds, of years ago. You get to see how bonds evolved and what makes them so very different from other investment vehicles. I give you a primer on how bonds are bought and sold. And I introduce you to the sometimes very helpful but sometimes misleading world of bond ratings.

Part II: Numerous and Varied Ways to Make Money in Bonds

Anyone, well practically anyone, who wants to raise money can issue a bond. The vast majority of bonds, however, are issued by the U.S. Treasury, corporations, government agencies, or municipalities. This section examines the advantages and potential drawbacks of each and looks at the many varieties of bonds that each of these entities may offer. I also introduce you to some rather unusual breeds of bonds — not the kind your grandfather knew!

Part III: Customizing and Optimizing Your Bond Portfolio

Different investments — including bonds — bring various promises of return and various measures of risk. Some bonds are as safe as bank CDs; others can be as wildly volatile as tech stocks. In this part of the book, I help you assess just how much investment risk you should be taking at this point in your life, and how — largely using a mix of different bonds — to minimize that risk for optimal return.

Part IV: Bonds Away! Navigating the Fixed-Income Marketplace

In this part, I address the role of bond brokers, discuss the pros and cons of owning individual bonds as opposed to bond funds, explain how to buy and sell bonds without getting clipped, and offer ways to protect yourself so that you don't get stuck with any fixed-income dogs. I reveal ways for you to blow away the black smoke that has long shrouded the world of bond trading.

Part V: Bonds As Replacements for the Old Paycheck

Many people think of bonds as the ultimate retirement tool. In fact, they are — and they aren't. In this section, I discuss bonds as replacements for your paycheck. As you discover, many retirees rely too heavily on bonds — or on the wrong kinds of bonds. Reading this section, you may discover that your nest egg needs either a minor tune-up or a major overhaul and that your bond portfolio needs beefing up or paring down.

Part VI: The Part of Tens

In this final section — a standard feature in all *Dummies* books — we wrap up the book with some practical tips and a few fun items.

Part VII: Appendix

The Web offers much in the way of additional education on bonds, as well as some excellent venues for trading bonds. Let the appendix serve as your Web guide.

Icons Used in This Book

Throughout the book, you find little cartoons in the margins. In the *Dummies* universe, they are known as *icons,* and they signal certain exciting (or possibly not-so exciting) things going on in the accompanying text.

Although this is a how-to book, you also find plenty of whys and wherefores. Any paragraph accompanied by this icon, however, is guaranteed to be at least 99.99 percent how-to.

Read twice! This icon indicates that something important is being said and is really worth putting to memory.

The world of bond investing — although generally not as risky as the world of stock investing — still offers pitfalls galore. Wherever you see the bomb, know that there is a risk of your losing money.

If you don't really care how to calculate the after-tax present value of a bond selling at 98, yielding 4.76 percent, maturing in 9 months, and subject to AMT, and you're just looking to get a broad understanding of bonds, feel free to skip or skim the more dense paragraphs with this icon.

The world of Wall Street is full of people who make money at other people's expense. Where you see the pig face, know that I'm about to point out an instance where someone (most likely calling himself a bond broker or perhaps a bond mutual-fund manager) will likely be sticking a hand deep in your pocket.

Where to Go from Here

Where would you like to go from here? If you wish, start at the beginning. If you're mostly interested in municipal bonds, hey, no one says that you can't jump right to Chapter 8. Global bonds? Go ahead and jump to Chapter 9. It's entirely your call. Maybe start by skimming the index at the back of the book.

Part I
Bond Appetit!

"Treasuries? Munis? Zeroes? I say we stick the money in the ground like always, and then feed this guy to the sharks."

In this part . . .

In the first three chapters of this section, you find out what makes a bond a bond. You discover the rationale for their being and what makes them different from other investment types. You can begin to assess whether bonds belong in your portfolio (chances are they do!). I take you on a trip back in time to see how bonds looked in yesteryear and show you how and why they evolved into the most popular investment vehicle on earth today. You also find out how the bond markets work, and about some relatively recent developments that have turned those markets more or less on their pointed heads.

In Chapter 4, you get a preliminary education on the complicated pricing of bonds and the myriad (and often confusing) ways that bond returns are measured. You'll pick up some very important bond concepts (and much of the bond jargon) that could help you to operate more effectively as an investor in the bond market.

Chapter 1

So You Want to Be a Bondholder

*L*ong before I ever knew what a bond was (it's essentially an IOU), I lent five dollars to Tommy Potts. This was the first time that I ever lent money to anyone. Tommy was a blond, goofy-looking kid in my seventh-grade class. I can't recall why he needed the five dollars so much, but he was my pal, and he promised to repay me, so I acquiesced.

Weeks went by, and I couldn't get my money back, no matter how much I bellyached. Finally, I decided to go to a higher authority. So I approached Tommy's dad.

I figured that Mr. Potts would give Tommy a stern lecture on the importance of maintaining his credit and good name, and that Mr. Potts would then either make Tommy cough up my money, or he would make restitution himself.

"Er, Mr. Potts," I said, "I lent Tommy five bucks, and . . ."

"You lent *him* money?" Mr. Potts interrupted, pointing his finger at his deadbeat 12-year-old son, who, if I recall correctly, at that point had turned over one of his pet turtles and was spinning it like a top. "Um, yes, Mr. Potts — five dollars." At which point, Mr. Potts neither lectured nor reached for his wallet. Rather, he erupted into savage laugher. "You lent *him* money!" he bellowed repeatedly, laughing, slapping his thighs, and pointing to his turtle-torturing son. "You lent *him* money! *HA . . . HA . . . HA . . . HA . . .*"

And that, dear reader, was my very first experience as a creditor. I never saw a nickel in either interest or returned principal, not to this very day.

Oh, yes, I've learned a lot since then.

Understanding What Makes a Bond a Bond

Now supposing that Tommy Potts, instead of being a goofy kid in the seventh grade, were the United States government. Or the city of Philadelphia. Or Procter & Gamble. Tommy, in his new powerful incarnation, needs to raise not five dollars but $50 million, for whatever reason. So Tommy decides to issue a bond. A bond is really not much more than an IOU with a serial number. People in suits, to sound impressive, sometimes call bonds *debt securities* or *fixed-income securities.*

A bond is always issued with a certain *face amount,* also called the *principal,* also called the *par value* of the bond. Most often, simply because it is convention, bonds are issued with face amounts of $1,000. So in order to raise $50 million, Tommy would have to issue 50,000 bonds each selling at $1,000 par. Of course, he would then have to go out and find investors.

Every bond pays a certain rate of *interest,* and typically (but not always) that rate is fixed over the life of the bond (hence *fixed-income* securities). The life of the bond, in the parlance of financial people, is known as the bond's *maturity.* (The bond world is full of jargon.) The rate of interest is a percentage of the face amount and is typically (again, simply because of convention) paid out twice a year.

So if a corporation or government issues a $1,000 bond, paying 6 percent, that corporation or government promises to fork over to the bondholder $60 a year — or, in most cases, $30 twice a year. Then, when the bond matures, the corporation or government gives the bondholder his or her $1,000 back.

In some cases, you can buy a bond directly from the issuer and sell it back directly to the issuer, but in most cases, bonds are bought and sold through a brokerage house or a bank. Oh, yes, these brokerage houses take a piece of the pie, sometimes a quite sizeable piece — more on that (and how to limit broker gluttony) in Part IV.

So far, so good?

In short, dealing in bonds isn't really all that different from the deal I worked out with Tommy Potts. It's just a bit more formal, the issuance of bonds is regulated by the Securities and Exchange Commission (and other regulatory authorities), and most (but not all) bondholders — unlike me — wind up getting paid back!

Choosing your time frame

Almost all bonds these days are issued with life spans (maturities) of up to 30 years. Few people are interested in loaning their money for longer than that, and people young enough to think more than 30 years ahead rarely have enough money to lend. In the parlance of bond people, any bond with a maturity of less than five years is called a *short bond*. Bonds with maturities of 5 to 12 years are called *intermediate bonds*. Bonds with maturities of 12 years or more are called *long bonds*.

In general (sorry, but you're going to read those words a lot in this book; bond investing comes with few hard-and-fast rules), the longer the maturity, the greater the interest rate paid. That's because bond buyers generally (there I go again) demand more compensation the longer they agree to tie up their money. At the same time, bond issuers are willing to fork over more interest in return for the privilege of holding onto your money longer.

It's exactly the same theory and practice with bank CDs: Typically the two-year CD pays more than the one-year CD, which pays more than the six-month CD.

The difference between the rates you can get on short bonds versus intermediate bonds versus long bonds is known as the *yield curve*. *Yield* simply refers to the annual interest rate. In Chapter 4, I provide an in-depth discussion of interest rates, bond maturity, and the all-important yield curve.

Determining who you trust to hold your money

Let's consider again the analogy to bank CDs. Both bonds and CDs tend to pay higher rates of interest the longer the time period you're willing to lend your money. But that's where the similarity ends.

When you give your money to a savings bank to plunk into a CD, that money — your principal — is guaranteed (up to $100,000 per account) by the Federal Deposit Insurance Corporation (FDIC). For that reason, all savings bank CDs — all those that carry FDIC insurance — are pretty much the same. You can choose your bank because it is close to your house or because it gives lollipops to your kids, but if solid economics be your guide, you should open your CD where you're going to get the highest rate of interest. End of story.

Things aren't so simple in the world of bonds. A higher rate of interest isn't always the best deal. When you fork your money over to buy a bond, your principal is guaranteed only by the issuer of the bond, so that guarantee is only as solid as the issuer itself. (Remember my seventh-grade experience?)

That's why U.S. Treasury bonds (guaranteed by the United States government) pay one interest rate, General Electric bonds pay another rate, and General Motors bonds pay yet another rate. Can you guess where you'll get the highest rate of interest?

You would expect the highest rate of interest to be paid by General Motors (currently a somewhat shaky company). Why? Because lending your money to GM involves some risk. If GM were to go bankrupt, you might lose a good chunk of your principal. That risk requires GM to pay a higher rate of interest. Without paying some kind of *risk premium,* the manufacturer of gas-guzzling cars simply would not be able to attract any people to lend it money to make more gas-guzzling cars.

Conversely, the United States government, which has the power to levy taxes and print money (despite the cries of a few anarchistic nutcases) is not going bankrupt any time soon. Therefore, U.S. Treasury bonds, which are said to carry no risk of default, tend to pay relatively modest interest rates.

If Tommy Potts were to come to me for a loan today, needless to say, I wouldn't loan him money. Or if I did, I would require a huge risk premium, along with some kind of collateral (more than his pet turtles). Bonds issued by the likes of Tommy Potts or General Motors — bonds that carry a relatively high risk of default — are commonly called *high-yield* or *junk* bonds. Bonds issued by solid companies and governments that carry very little risk of default are commonly referred to as *investment-grade* bonds.

There are many, many shades of gray in determining the quality and nature of a bond. It's not unlike wine tasting in that regard. In Chapter 4, and again in Chapter 14, I give many specific tips for "tasting" bonds and choosing the finest vintages for your portfolio.

Recognizing the difference between bonds, stocks, and Beanie Babies

Aside from the maturity and the quality of a bond, other factors could weigh heavily in how well a bond purchase treats you. In the following chapters, I introduce you to such bond characteristics as *callability, duration,* and *correlation,* and I explain how the winds of the economy, and even the whims of the bond-buying public, can affect the returns of your bond portfolio.

For the moment, I simply wish to point out that, by and large, bonds' most salient characteristic — and the one thing that most, but not all bonds share — is a certain stability and predictability, well above and beyond that of most other investments. Because you are, in most cases, receiving a steady stream of income, and because you expect to get your principal back in one piece, bonds tend to be more conservative investments than, say, stocks, commodities, or collectibles.

The bond market is HUMONGOUS

How much is invested in bonds worldwide? Are you holding onto your seat? According to 2006 figures compiled by the Securities Industry and Financial Markets Association, the total value of all bonds outstanding worldwide is now slightly over $61 *trillion.* That's equal to about five times the current gross domestic product of the United States — the dollar value of all goods and services produced in this country in an entire year.

Given that the stock market gets so much more attention than the bond market, you may be surprised to know that the total value of all stocks outstanding worldwide is a mere $50 trillion.

Is conservative a good thing? Not necessarily. It's true that many people (men, mostly) invest their money too aggressively, just as many people (women, mostly) invest their money too conservatively. The appropriate portfolio formula depends on what your individual investment goals are. I help you to figure that out in Chapters 12 and 13.

By the way, these are not my personal gender stereotypes. Some solid research shows that males of the human species do tend to invest (and drive) much more aggressively than do women.

Why Hold Bonds? (Hint: You'll Likely Make Money!)

In the real world, plenty of people own plenty of bonds — but often the wrong bonds in the wrong amounts and for the wrong reasons. Some people have too many bonds, making their portfolios too conservative; some have too few bonds, making their portfolios too volatile; some have taxable bonds where they should have tax-free bonds; others have tax-free where they should have taxable bonds. Others are so far out on the limb with shaky bonds that they may as well be lending money to Tommy Potts.

The first step in building a bond portfolio is having clear investment objectives. (Although I hear it from clients all the time, "I want to make money" is *not* a clear investment objective!) I help you to develop clear objectives in Chapter 2. In the meantime, I want you to consider some of the typical reasons people buy and hold bonds . . . both good and bad.

Identifying the best reason to buy bonds: Diversification

Most people buy bonds because they perceive a need for steady income, and they think of bonds as the best way to get income without risking principal. This is one of the most common mistakes investors make: compartmentalization. They think of principal and interest as two separate and distinct money pools. They are not.

Let me explain: Joe Typical buys a bond for $1,000. At the end of six months, he collects an interest payment (income) of, say, $25. He spends the $25, figuring that his principal (the $1,000) is left intact to continue earning money. At the same time, Joe buys a stock for $1,000. At the end of six months, the price of his stock, and therefore the value of his investment, has grown to, say, $1,025. Does he spend the $25? No way. Joe reckons that spending any part of the $1,025 is spending principal and will reduce the amount of money he has left working for him.

In truth, whether Joe spends his "interest" or his "principal," whether he spends his "income" or generates "cash flow" from the sale of stock, he is left with the *very same* $1,000 in his portfolio.

Thinking of bonds, or bond funds, as the best — or only — source of cash flow or income can be a mistake.

Bonds are a better source of steady income than stocks because bonds, in theory (and usually in practice), always pay interest; stocks may or may not pay dividends and may or may not appreciate in price. Bonds also may be a logical choice for people who may need a certain sum of money at a certain point in the future — such as college tuition or cash for a new home — and can't risk a loss.

But unless you absolutely need a steady source of income, or a certain sum at a certain date, bonds may not be such a hot investment because over the long haul, they tend to return much less than stocks. I revisit this issue, and talk much more of the differences between stocks and bonds, in Chapter 12.

For now, the point I wish to make is that the far better reason to own bonds, for most people, is to *diversify* a portfolio. Bonds tend to zig when stocks zag. The key to truly successful investing, as I outline in Chapter 11, is to have at least several different *asset classes* — different investment animals with different characteristics — all of which can be expected to yield positive long-term return, but which do not all move up and down at the same time.

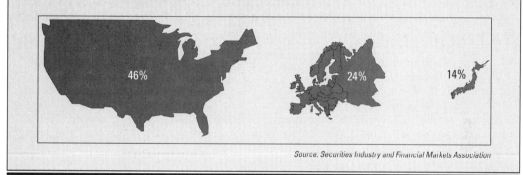

Bond map of the world: Where are most bonds issued?

Approximately 84 percent of all the world's bonds created in 2006 were issued in the United States, Europe, or Japan.

46%   24%   14%

Source: Securities Industry and Financial Markets Association

Going for the cash

Bonds are not very popular with the get-rich-quick crowd — for good reason. The only people who get rich off bonds are generally the insiders who trade huge amounts and can clip the little guy. Nonetheless, certain categories of bonds — high-yield corporate bonds, for example — have been known to produce impressive gains.

High-yield bonds may have a role — a limited role — in your portfolio, as I discuss in Chapter 6. But know up front that high-yield bonds do not offer the potential long-run return of stocks, and neither do they offer the portfolio protection of investment-grade bonds. Rather than zigging when the stock market zags, many high-yield bonds zag right along with your stock portfolio. Be careful!

There are some high-yield bonds that I prefer over others — bonds that are held by few people. I recommend those in Chapter 9.

Even high quality, investment-grade bonds are often purchased with the wrong intentions. Note: The safest bond of all, a U.S. Treasury bond, *will not guarantee your return of principal unless you hold it to maturity.* In other words, if you buy a 20-year bond and you want to know for sure that you're going to get your principal back, you had better plan to hold it for 20 years. If you sell it before it is fully ripe, you may lose a bundle. Bond prices, especially on long-term bonds — yes, even Uncle Sam's bonds — can fluctuate greatly! I discuss the reasons for this fluctuation in Chapter 4.

I also discuss the very complicated and often misunderstood concept of bond returns. You may buy a 20-year U.S. Treasury bond yielding 6 percent, and you may hold it for 20 years, to full maturity. And yes, you'll get your principal back, but you may actually get far more or far less than 6 percent interest on your money! It's complicated, but I explain this variation in a way you can understand — I promise! — in Chapter 4.

Introducing the Major Players in the Bond Market

Every year, millions — yes, literally millions — of bonds are issued by thousands of different governments, government agencies, municipalities, financial institutions, and corporations. They all pay interest. In many cases, the interest rates aren't all that much different from each other. In most cases, the risk of the issuer *defaulting* — not paying back your principal — is minute. So why, as a lender of money, would you want to choose one type of issuer over another?

Glad you asked!

Following are some important considerations about each of the major kinds of bonds, categorized by who issues them. I'm just going to scratch the surface right now. For a more in-depth discussion, see the five chapters in Part II.

Supporting (enabling?) your Uncle Sam with Treasury bonds

Politicians like raising money by selling bonds, as opposed to raising taxes, because voters hate taxes. Of course, when the government issues bonds, it promises to repay the bond buyers over time. The more bonds the government issues, the greater its debt. Voters don't seem to care much about debt.

The current debt of the United States government is slightly more than $8.6 trillion: almost $30,000 per every man, woman, and child.

The interest payments on that debt, combined with the steady repayment of principal, are an enormous burden. Of every dollar spent by the U.S. government in 2006, approximately eight cents went to the interest payments on Treasury bonds. In my mind, that's a bit too much cash, but this is not a political book, so I'm not going to tell you how to vote. (Not that you would listen to me anyway.) From here on, I address only the role that Treasury bonds may play in your portfolio.

In Chapter 5, I explain all the many, many kinds of Treasury bonds — from EE Bonds to I Bonds to TIPS — and the unique characteristics of each. For the moment, I merely wish to point out that all of them are backed by the "full faith and credit" of the federal government. Despite its huge debt, the United States of America is not going bankrupt any time soon. And for that reason, Treasury bonds are often referred to as "risk-free." Careful! That does *not* mean that the price of Treasury bonds does not fluctuate.

When bonds experts speak of Treasury bonds as having no risk, what they mean is that the bonds have no *credit* risk. But Treasury bonds are very much subject to the other kinds of risk that most other bonds are subject to: interest rate risk, inflation risk, and reinvestment risk. I discuss these risks in Chapter 10.

Collecting corporate debt

Bonds issued by for-profit companies are riskier than government bonds but tend to compensate for that added risk by paying higher rates of interest. (If they didn't pay higher rates of interest, why would you or anyone else want to take the extra risk?) In recent history, corporate bonds in the aggregate have tended to pay about a percentage point higher than Treasuries of similar maturity.

As you'll discover, I am a huge fan of diversification. It is especially important to diversify when dealing with riskier investments. For that reason, I hate to see anyone plunk too great a percentage of his or her portfolio into any individual corporate bond. Wealthier investors — those with portfolios of $1 million or more — can diversify by buying a collection of bonds. Savvy investors can temper their risks by familiarizing themselves with bond ratings and researching the issuing companies' bottom lines. But I generally advocate bond ownership — especially where it comes to corporate bonds — in bond funds. I discuss these funds at the end of this chapter and again, in greater depth, in Chapter 16.

Oh, one more little thing about corporate bonds for the moment: They tend to get *called* a lot. That means that the corporation changes its incorporated mind about wanting your money and suddenly throws it back at you, canceling the bond. Bond calls can be no fun! They add a heavy dose of unpredictability to what should be a predictable investment. Read all about calls and other peculiarities of the corporate bond world in Chapter 6.

Demystifying those quasi-governmental agencies

Federal agencies such as Federal Home Loan Mortgage Corporation (Freddie Mac), Federal National Mortgage Association (Fannie Mae), and Small Business Administration issue a good chunk of the bonds on the market — together, about 18 percent of the bonds held by individual households. Such agencies aren't quite government and aren't quite private concerns. They are government "sponsored," and in theory, Congress and the Treasury would serve as protective big brothers if one of these agencies were to take a financial beating and couldn't pay off its debt obligations.

Because of their quasi-governmental status, agencies' bond offerings are generally considered the next-safest thing to Treasury bonds. As such, the interest paid on these bonds is typically just a smidgen higher than the interest rate you would get on Treasuries of similar maturity.

I discuss federal agency bonds — the traditional kind of bonds these agencies offer — in Chapter 7. Some bonds issued or guaranteed by the federal agencies are distinctly nontraditional in that they represent an ownership interest in pools of mortgages. These are more complicated than traditional bonds, and I'm sorry to say that many people who invest in them haven't the foggiest idea what they're investing in. More about these babies in Chapter 9.

Going cosmopolitan with municipal offerings

The bond market, unlike the stock market, is overwhelmingly institutional. In other words, the vast majority of bonds are held by insurance companies, pension funds, endowment funds, and mutual funds. The only exception is the municipal bond market.

Municipal bonds (*munis*) are issued by cities, states, and counties. They are used to raise money either for general day-to-day needs of the citizenry (schools, roads, sewer systems) or for specific projects (a new bridge, a sports stadium).

Munis' popularity with individual investors may be due in small part to the warm and fuzzy feelings to be had by investing in local infrastructure. But my guess is that their popularity comes much more from their special tax status.

The household bond market pie

Among the kinds of traditional bonds most popular with individual investors in the United States are Treasuries, corporate bonds, bonds issued by federal agencies, and municipal bonds. According to the Securities Industry and Financial Markets Association and the United States Treasury, as of 2006, U.S. households held more than $15 trillion of these four kinds of bonds alone:

- ✔ $5.2 trillion in corporate bonds (see Chapter 6)
- ✔ $4.9 trillion in Treasuries (see Chapter 5)
- ✔ $2.8 trillion in agency bonds (see Chapter 7)
- ✔ $2.3 trillion in municipal bonds (see Chapter 8)

Interest on most municipal bonds is exempt from federal income tax. And even though the interest rates paid are modest, many individual investors, especially those in the higher tax brackets, can often get a better after-tax return on municipal bonds than on comparable taxable bonds.

Like corporate bonds, but unlike Treasuries, municipal bonds are often subject to call. You may *think* you're buying a ten-year investment, but you may be forced to relinquish the bond in two years. (Bond brokers often fail to advertise this fact to buyers.)

Municipal bonds tend to be less risky than corporate bonds but not as safe as Treasuries and agency bonds. Just as corporate bonds are given ratings, so are municipal bonds. It's important to know before investing whether the local government issuing the bond has the wherewithal to pay back your principal. Cities don't go bankrupt often, but it does happen. I reveal much, much more on munis in Chapter 8.

Buying Solo or Buying Bulk

One of the big questions about bond investing that I help you to answer later in this book is whether to invest in individual bonds or bond funds.

I'm a big advocate of bond funds — both bond mutual funds and exchange-traded funds. Mutual funds and exchange-traded funds both represent baskets of securities (usually stocks or bonds, or both) and allow for instant and easy portfolio diversification.

I outline the pros and cons of owning individual bonds versus bond funds in Chapter 14. Here, I give you a very quick sneak preview of that discussion.

Picking and choosing individual bonds

Individual bonds offer investors the opportunity to really fine-tune a fixed-income portfolio. With individual bonds, you can choose exactly what you want in terms of bond quality, maturity, and taxability.

For larger investors — especially those doing their homework — investing in individual bonds may also be more economical than investing in a bond fund. That's especially true for those investors up on the latest advances in bond buying and selling.

Once upon a time, any buyer or seller of individual bonds had to take a giant leap of faith that his or her bond broker wasn't trimming too much meat off the bone. No more. In Chapter 15, I show you how to find out exactly how much your bond broker is making off you — or trying to make off you. I show you how to compare comparable bonds to get the best deals. And I discuss some popular bond strategies, including the most popular and potent one, *laddering* your bonds, which means staggering the maturities of the bonds you buy.

Going with a bond fund or funds

Investors now have a choice of more than 5,000 bond mutual funds or exchange-traded funds. All have the same basic drawback: management expenses. But even so, some make for very good potential investments, particularly for people with modest portfolios.

Where to begin your fund search? I promise to help you weed out the losers and pick the very best. As you'll discover (or as you know already if you have read my *Exchange-Traded Funds For Dummies*), I'm a strong proponent of buying *index funds* — mutual funds or exchange-traded funds that seek to provide exposure to an entire asset class (such as bonds or stocks) with very little trading and very low expenses. I believe that such funds are the way to go for most investors to get the bond exposure they need. I suggest some good bond index funds, as well as other bond funds, in Chapter 16.

If you would like to know more about funds in general, I would advise you to pick up copies of *Exchange-Traded Funds For Dummies* and the latest edition of Eric Tyson's *Mutual Funds For Dummies,* both published by Wiley.

Chapter 2

Developing Your Investment Game Plan

Do you remember the great auto-rental scene in *Get Shorty?* Mobster Chili Palmer (John Travolta) travels to L.A., shows up at the auto rental place, and discovers, to his chagrin, that the only vehicle to be had is an Oldsmobile minivan.

"What is that?" he asks the rental car attendant, pointing to the curb.

"It's an Oldsmobile Silhouette."

"I ordered a Cadillac."

"Oh, well," says the attendant, "you got the Cadillac of minivans."

And off drives the pistol-packing gangster, out to collect mob debt money, driving the streets of L.A. in a boxy vehicle with built-in child seats and a rooftop luggage carrier. It's as incongruous as, well, a pistol-packing gangster aiming to make the big score by investing in Fannie Mae bonds.

Portfolios, like Cadillacs and minivans, suit certain kinds of personalities. In order to choose the most appropriate investments — be they bonds, stocks, or pork-belly futures — it helps to know what kind of person you are. I'm not talking about knowing yourself in a grand, metaphysical, Freudian or Socratic sense, but knowing yourself, and perhaps your spouse, at least to the point that you can formulate some reasonable household financial goals.

Unlike all the other chapters in this book, this chapter does not focus squarely on bonds. Rather, it sets the stage for a full discussion of bonds by helping you first figure out what kind of investor you are (Chili Palmer, Warren Buffett, or Nervous Nelly?) and whether a Fannie Mae bond portfolio may suit you better than, say, dropping your savings into casino stocks, uranium futures, or hush money. I also discuss some very fundamental investment principles, such as reversion to the mean and the cold-clay link between risk and return.

The investment principles I present in this chapter pertain to all financial investments, bonds included. If you're a seasoned investor, you may already be familiar with these market truths. But a quick review certainly couldn't hurt.

Focusing on Your Objectives

Investing in a portfolio of Fannie Mae bonds is a moderately conservative way to go. (See Chapter 7 for more on Fannie Maes, Ginnie Maes, and various other federal agency bonds.) You very likely won't get rich investing in these — or most other kinds of bonds. But at 2 a.m., when you get up to go to the bathroom, you'll know where your money is, and you can go back to sleep with ease.

On the other hand, investing your savings in the stock of a single, small technology company can indeed make you rich. (Think Microsoft back when a nerdy, young Bill Gates was working out of his garage.) But you may also wake up Thursday morning and find that your investment is worth a fraction of what it was on Wednesday. (Think any great number of tech stocks, both large and small, in the dark and financially dismal days of 2001 and 2002.)

For most people, some kind of in-between portfolio, perhaps with Fannie Mae bonds *and* tech stocks, would make the most sense. But you need to decide whether you want to be smack in the middle of the continuum or whether you care to hang your hat more toward the mild side or the wild side. That decision will have a great bearing on just how much you wind up stocking up on bonds or bonding with stocks.

Deciding what you want to be when you grow up

The kind of portfolio you want to build depends on what you want to get out of it, be it immediate income, slow and steady appreciation, or pop-goes-the-weasel kind of growth.

Are you looking to quit your day job as soon as possible and start a second career writing haiku poetry? Are you seeking to pay the kids' college bills and worry about building your retirement nest egg after that point? Do you want to drop out of society after the kids are grown, buy a 52-foot sailboat, and travel the Caribbean from island to island? These are the kinds of questions you need to ask yourself.

Fortunately, you don't need to be all that specific in your future goals to formulate a fairly good financial plan. You merely need to be somewhat clear about how much you and your partner will likely be earning (if anything) and how much you will likely be spending over a certain period of time.

Our society has changed much in the last generation, and very many Boomers nearing traditional retirement age aren't looking for anything even closely resembling a traditional retirement. Me, I love what I do and hope to continue doing it for as long as I'm capable. (However, I wouldn't mind clocking fewer hours and, after the kids have grown, taking a few more trips to places like Greece and Morocco.)

Picturing your future nest egg

In Chapter 12, I give you the tools to help you fine-tune your retirement goals and figure out what lump sum you will likely need, given the kind of lifestyle you envision, to replace your weekly paycheck. But for now, I'm just going to share some very loose guidelines.

It doesn't much matter whether you are like me and intend to keep working past traditional retirement age or whether you want a more old-fashioned retirement (complete with checkered pants, green golf shirts, blue hair, and mah-jongg games). Most financial planners suggest that your ultimate savings goal be something in the order of 20 times your annual anticipated expenses, minus any income from Social Security, pension, or part-time employment.

In other words, if you think you'll need $50,000 a year to live on at age 65 or so, and you anticipate yearly income of $20,000 from a combination of Social Security payments and, say, hobby income, your goal should be to grow a nest egg worth at least $600,000. ($50,000 − $20,000 = $30,000. $30,000 × 20 = $600,000.)

Understanding the Rule of 20

Before I explain the (rough . . . very rough) Rule of 20, let me first say that that number may scare the heck out of you if you haven't put much away so far, but it shouldn't scare you all that much.

Remember that compound interest is a very, very powerful force. Someone starting to save at age 30, investing wisely in a diversified portfolio, would likely have to put aside only about $250 a month to have a darned good chance of building a $600,000 nest egg by age 65. If the 30-year-old had a job where the employer matched his 401(k) contributions by kicking in 50 percent on top of whatever he put in, $167 a month would do the trick.

Okay, so where does the multiplier of 20 come from? It simply gives an approximation of what you should have by age 65 to spend what you need every year, live an average lifespan (mid 80s), and have a pretty good chance of not running out of money before you die. Obviously, if you can save more, so much the better.

 If you think that you may live longer than the average lifespan, or if you're planning to quit work before age 65, you should plan to save more than 20 times your annual living expenses. The longer you plan a life of ease, the more money you'll need to tap.

For those of us who would like to keep working as long as we can, there's still nothing whatsoever wrong with financial independence, so I would advocate the same financial goal. Again, I'm talking rough estimate here, and I can't emphasize that enough. But I need to throw out some kind of estimate so as to illustrate how your nest egg goals have everything to do with how heavily you invest in bonds.

Choosing your investment style

Okay, what does the Rule of 20 have to do with your choice of investments and the wisdom of holding bonds? Simple: The further away you are from achieving that financial goal, the higher the rate of savings you need or the higher the rate of return you require from your portfolio — or both.

 In Chapter 12, I try to answer the very difficult question, "What percent of your portfolio should be in bonds?" For now, I simply want to point out that people who need a higher rate of return generally don't want too bond-laden a portfolio. A heavy position in bonds is more appropriate for investors who don't need a lot of growth but, rather, can sit back and enjoy steady but slow growth.

Say, for example, you are 55 or 60 years old and, thanks to your good savings habits, you are now on the cusp of having your "20x" portfolio. If much of that portfolio is now in stocks or stock mutual funds, it may be time for you to start shifting a good chunk of your portfolio into bonds. Why take much risk with things like stocks or commodities if you don't need to?

Be aware, however, that simple portfolio-construction formulas (that typically use age as a main determinant) often don't work! I'm giving you some very rough rules just to get you thinking about how I think in terms of investment allocation. As I explain in Chapter 12, that same 55- or 60-year-old investor who may want to shift more of his or her portfolio to bonds may actually want to shift back to stocks 20 years later if the portfolio is worth millions.

Making Your Savings and Investment Selections

Yes, you can shove your money under the mattress, but with inflation currently running about 3 percent a year, $1,000 in today's dollars will have only about $940 in purchasing power two years from now and $860 in purchasing power five years from now. Economists call that loss in purchasing power *inflation risk,* and it is indeed a very real kind of risk. Moral of the story: Don't keep money under the mattress. You have to do *something* with it.

In my mind, *savings* refers to money socked away that is perhaps growing fast enough to keep up with inflation, or slightly more. *Investments* refers to money socked away that is projected to grow significantly faster than the rate of inflation.

The whole point of investing is to earn a *real return,* which is to say the rate of return after inflation. If your nominal return is 8 percent but inflation is 5 percent, your real return is approximately 3 percent (8% − 5% = 3%). Getting a nominal return of 2 percent when there is no inflation is much better than getting a 15 percent return when the inflation rate is 20!

Different types of bonds can fall into either category: savings or investments. Some bonds — like U.S. savings bonds — generally keep about even with inflation. Other bonds, such as high-yield corporate bonds, usually keep you well ahead of the game.

In general, money that may be needed in the upcoming months, or even a few years down the pike, should be kept in safe savings; you can't risk a loss of principal. (Yes, loss of principal is possible with most bonds, especially long-term bonds. You discover why in Chapter 4.) Money that you most likely won't need for many years to come should be invested for growth; even if there is a loss of principal, you will likely make that back, and then some, before you require any withdrawals.

Following are some of the most popular options for saving and investing, which I briefly compare and contrast with bond investing.

Home sweet home

Yes, of course, home equity represents a form of savings. It is also your most *illiquid* savings. (*Liquidity* refers to the ease with which you can cash out on an investment, if you need to.) You need a place to live . . . and you always will. So for your home to ever do you much good as a store of value, you'll need to downsize. At that point, you can sell the more expensive home, pick up a cheaper abode (or rent one), and pocket the difference.

Home values don't often drop appreciably, but they certainly can. I had an aunt who once had an expensive home in Northridge, California — epicenter of the huge 1994 earthquake. Overnight, it lost its status as an expensive home!

Saving your money in safety

With the following savings options, the principal is guaranteed (or close to guaranteed), and the rate of return should keep you even with or slightly ahead of the inflation game:

✔ **Your local savings bank:** There's something to be said for keeping at least a small balance at the neighborhood bank. I do. Need a loan someday? It may be easier if you are a regular customer. Local businesses are also more likely to accept a check drawn on a local bank. Then there's the "bank experience," which may be especially important if you're a parent. Each of my two children has a saving account at the corner bank, and they love going there for the free plate of cookies.

At all savings banks in the United States, deposits are insured up to $100,000 by the Federal Deposit Insurance Corporation (FDIC). Even if the bank goes under, you're covered. The interest rates paid by local banks tend to be very modest, more modest than those paid by most bonds.

✔ **Certificates of Deposit (CDs):** The longer you're willing to commit your money to the bank, the higher the interest rate. Generally a 6-month CD may pay an interest point more than passbook savings, a 12-month CD may pay a bit more, and an 18-month CD yet a wee bit more. If you have one to several thousand dollars sitting around, perhaps you might put one-third into each. That way, you're not tying up all your money for the entire time, and if interest rates go higher in six months, you'll be free to take part of your money and upgrade to a higher-yielding CD.

Shop for the best rates at www.bankrate.com or www.money-rates.com. And especially if you're dealing with a local bank, ask to talk to the

manager and see if you can negotiate something higher than the advertised rate. CD rates are usually comparable to very short-term bonds but
are not on a par with longer-term bonds.

✔ **Internet banking:** Consider opening an account with a Web-based,
FDIC-insured savings bank, such as www.emigrantdirect.com or
www.ingdirect.com. The rates on savings accounts are often comparable to one-year CDs, and you don't need to tie up your money at all.

✔ **Money market funds:** Money market mutual funds are not insured by
the FDIC so they aren't quite as safe as bank accounts or U.S. savings
bonds, but they are almost as safe. They tend to offer a slightly higher
return than bank accounts but not as much as a bond portfolio. If you
hold one of these funds outside of your retirement account, you may
want to choose a tax-free money market fund, especially if you are in a
higher tax bracket.

Note that with money market funds, your principal is secure but the
interest rate is not; it can, and often does, vary from day to day. That's
just the opposite of a bond, by the way: With a bond, your interest rate
is fixed, but the value of your principal can vary day to day. (I explain
this in Chapter 4.)

✔ **Short-term, high quality bonds:** Short-term bond mutual funds and
exchange-traded funds, both taxable and tax-free, are similar to money
market funds and often pay a bit more. Read all about them, and how to
choose the best one for your portfolio, in Chapters 13 and 16.

Investing your money with an eye toward growth

By sinking your savings into investments such as the ones I list here —
carefully! — your payoff can be handsome. But, of course, you can also lose
money.

✔ **Company stocks:** Whereas bonds represent a loan you are making to a
company or government, stocks represent partial ownership in a company. Over the long run, few investments pay off as well as stocks, which
have an 80-year track record of returning about 10 percent a year —
about twice the return of bonds.

The problem with stocks is that they can be extremely volatile, perhaps
going up 20 percent one year and tumbling 20 percent the next. You can
somewhat reduce that volatility by holding a wide variety of different

kinds of stocks, most easily done with stock mutual funds or *exchange-traded funds* (which, like mutual funds, represent baskets of securities but, unlike mutual funds, trade like stocks). You can also temper the volatility of a stock portfolio by blending into that portfolio certain other kinds of investments — such as bonds — that tend to hold their own, or may even head north, when stocks head south.

✔ **Gold and other commodities:** In the past, commodities — gold, silver, oil, wheat, coffee — have been very difficult to invest in and extremely volatile. The volatility is still there, but commodities have lately become very easy to invest in. Barclays Bank, for example, offers something called *exchange-traded notes* (ETNs), which are similar to exchange-traded funds and track a broad index of commodities. (For more information, see www.ipathetn.com.)

Like bonds, commodities tend to hold their own, or even go up, when stocks go down. Over the past 35 years, commodity investors overall have seen slightly higher returns than have stock investors. Commodities tend to increase value over time because the world is becoming an awfully crowded place, with more and more people consuming limited resources.

✔ **Investment real estate:** Whether you invest in apartments to rent, or shopping centers, or office space, there's money to be made in investment real estate. (Like commodities, real estate is a limited resource.) However, tending to real estate, as any landlord knows, can be a lot of work. And some tenants tend to be real pains in the butt — calling you at midnight to fix a leaky faucet! *Real estate investment trusts* (REITs) operate much like stocks and let you enjoy the fruits of others' labors, profiting merely by depositing your money. (No leaky faucets!) Of course, as with stocks, there's risk involved — more so than there is with most bond offerings. REITs, like stocks, are best purchased in the form of a mutual fund or exchange-traded fund. Dozens of REIT funds are offered by most brokerage houses. See Chapter 17 for more info.

✔ **Entrepreneurial ventures:** Open a restaurant . . . a dry cleaning shop . . . a dance studio . . . a gas station. Several million Americans have the bulk of their savings invested in small businesses. You're in control that way, and there's a chance that your small business could go big. But running a business requires tons of work, and there's always a risk that profits won't materialize. When small businesspeople come into my office, I certainly try not to discourage them from growing their businesses, but I also advise funneling some money toward other investments, such as bonds and stocks. Yes, diversification is good for the entrepreneur as well as the employee.

What about whole life insurance, variable annuities, and such?

I've seen insurance salespeople so good that they could sell sand to a Saudi. I've been pitched all kinds of insurance products, and they sound great — absolutely wonderful — until I actually get back to my office, start punching numbers, and look for cracks in the salesperson's pitch. Those cracks are always there. I'm not saying that insurance people are bad or insurance companies are bad — not at all. Insurance is a necessary part of modern life. As a general rule, however — and a very *good*

general rule — insurance products and investment products should remain separate and distinct. Is a variable annuity or a whole life insurance policy ever a good thing? Yes, I suppose. But very rarely. More often, purchasers of such hybrid investment/insurance products wind up angry and upset with their purchases — especially when they find out that there's no going back without forfeiting a good chunk of their original investment in exorbitant *surrender fees.*

Understanding Five Major Investment Principles

When I first became a serious student of investments, I was amazed at how much hard, academic research existed. Most of it contradicts anything and everything you've ever been told about investments by the magazines and books that shout "Get Rich Now!" or "Five Hot Stocks for the New Year!" If you know nothing else about investing, know the following five eternal, essential investment truths — all real-world tested — and you'll be way, way ahead of the game.

1. Risk and return are two sides of the same coin

If you see an investment that has gained 50 percent in the last year, sure, at least consider taking a position. But know this: Any investment that goes up 50 percent in a year can just as easily go down 50 percent in a year. That's the nature of the investment world.

Risk and return go together like fire and oxygen. Short-term, high quality bonds bring modest returns but bear little risk. Long-term, low quality bonds bring more handsome returns but bear considerable risk. Lower quality bonds *must* offer greater potential for return or no one but maybe a few loonies would invest in them. Higher quality bonds *must* offer lower rates of return or so many investors would flock to them that the price would be bid up (which would effectively lower the rate of return).

2. Financial markets are largely efficient

If someone says to you that a certain investment is "guaranteed" to return 30 percent a year with no risk, you are being lied to. Financial markets are *efficient,* which means that thousands upon thousands of buyers, sellers, fund managers, and market analysts are constantly out there looking for the best deals. If a truly safe investment were to offer a guaranteed return of 30 percent, so many people would make offers to buy that investment that the price would surely be bid up . . . and the return would then drop.

The efficiency of the markets is why even so few professional investors can beat the indexes. In numerous studies — each supporting the findings of the others — actively managed mutual funds (funds whose managers try to pick stocks or bonds that will outperform all others) very rarely manage to beat the indexes. Over the course of a decade or more, the number is infinitesimally small, and even those chosen few fail to beat the indexes by very much.

In Chapter 16, I tell you where to find the best bond *index funds* — funds that try to capture the returns of the entire market rather than attempting in vain to beat the market.

3. Diversification is just about the only free lunch you'll ever get

So if you can't pick certain securities that will outperform, how can you become a better investor than the next guy? Not that hard, really. Keep your costs low. Keep your taxes minimal. Don't trade often. Most importantly, diversify your portfolio across several *asset classes* — different kinds of investments, such as bonds, stocks, and commodities — so that all the components can contribute to your returns. Because the components move up and down at different times, the volatility of your entire portfolio is kept to a minimum.

In Chapter 11, I discuss something called *Modern Portfolio Theory (MPT)*. The essence of MPT is this: You can add a highly volatile (high risk, high return) investment to a portfolio, and — if that investment tends to zig while other investments in your portfolio zag — you can actually lower the volatility (and risk) of the entire portfolio. So who says there's no such thing as a free lunch?

4. Reversion to the mean — it means something

Sometimes called *reversion to the mean,* sometimes called *regression to the mean,* what it means is that most things in this world — from batting averages to inches of rainfall to investment returns — tend over time to revert back to their historical averages.

Suppose, for example, that a certain kind of investment (say, intermediate-term Fannie Mae bonds) showed extraordinary returns for the last two to three years (say 18 percent a year). (That kind of return on a bond would be rare, but it does happen, and I explain how in Chapter 4.) We know from the past several decades that intermediate-term, high quality bonds such as Fannie Maes typically return about one-third as much. Would you be well advised to assume that Fannie Mae bonds will continue to earn 18 percent for the next two years?

In fact, most investors assume just that. They look at recent returns of a certain asset class and assume that those recent returns will continue. In other words, most fresh investment money pours into "hot" investment sectors. And this often spells tragedy for those who don't understand the concept of reversion to the mean. In reality, hot sectors often turn cold — and they are generally to be avoided.

In fact, if anything, you might expect an asset class that overperforms for several years to underperform in the upcoming years. Why? Because all investments (like batting averages and inches of rainfall) have a tendency to return to their historical average return.

To look at it another way, investments tend to move in and out of favor in cycles. It is hard, if not impossible, to imagine that any one investment that historically has yielded modest returns would suddenly, for any extended period of time, become a major moneymaker. That would be akin to the Oldsmobile minivan suddenly becoming the favored vehicle of pistol-packing mobsters.

5. Investment costs matter — and they matter a lot!

Oh, sure, 1 percent doesn't sound like a prodigious sum, but the difference between investing in a bond mutual fund that charges 1.50 percent annually in management fees and one that charges 0.50 percent is enormous. Over the course of the next ten years, assuming gross returns of 5 percent, compounded annually, a $20,000 investment in the more expensive fund would leave you, after paying the fund company, with $28,212. That same investment in the less expensive fund would leave you with $31,059 — a difference of $2,847.

Of course, fund companies that charge more tend to have a lot of money to spend on advertising, and they do a great job conning the public into thinking that their funds are somehow worth the extra money. That is rarely, rarely true. In Chapter 16, I include a sidebar on mutual bond-fund advertising, explaining how mediocre funds are often dolled up to look much better than they are.

Studies galore show that the investors who keep their costs to a minimum do best. That's especially true with bonds, where the returns tend to be more modest than with stocks. Whether you are buying bond funds or purchasing individual bonds, transaction costs and operating expenses need to be minimized. That's largely what Chapters 14 through 16 of this book are all about.

Chapter 3

The (Often, but Not Always) Heroic History of Bonds

*F*or some people, success in life means owning a Rolls Royce. For others, it means having someone to love. And for still others it could mean leaving a legacy. Winston Churchill once quipped that success in life is the ability to move from one mistake to the next without losing enthusiasm. Perhaps he was right.

You can't deny that "success in life" means different things to different people. But what about "success in investing"? That, too, is a somewhat subjective term. Consider investment returns over the past 80 years or so. By some counts, bonds, at least from the investor's vantage point, have been a lamentable failure — the veritable Edsel of investments. By other counts, bonds have been a reigning success — a Rolls Royce with a full tank and a fresh wax job.

In this chapter, I explain that puzzling contradiction. I take you back in time beyond 80 years . . . way back to the Middle Ages to explore the role of bonds before there was even a printing press. I give you some perspective on how bond markets evolved — and continue to evolve. And, as I escort you into the present era, I describe how the bond market has changed enormously for the better, making bonds both easier to invest in and potentially more profitable than ever before.

Reviewing the Triumphs and Failures of Fixed-Income Investing

Picture yourself in the year 1926. Calvin Coolidge occupies the White House. Ford's Model T can be bought for $200. Charles Lindbergh is gearing up to fly across the Atlantic. And you, having just arrived from your journey back in time, brush the time-travel dust off your shoulders and reach into your pocket. You figure that if you invest $100, you can then return to the present, cash in on your 80-year-old investment, and live like a corrupt king. So you plunk down the $100 into some long-term government bonds.

Fast-forward to the present, and you discover that your original investment of $100 is now worth $7,200. It grew at an average compound rate of return of 5.5 percent. (In fact, that's just what happened in the real world.) Even though you aren't rich, $7,200 doesn't sound too shabby. But you need to look at the whole picture.

Beating inflation, but not by very much

Yes, you enjoyed a return of 5.5 percent a year, but while your bonds were making money, inflation was eating it away . . . at a rate of about 3.0 percent a year. What that means is that your $7,200 is really worth only about $700 in 1926 dollars. Your investment, in *real* dollars (inflation-adjusted dollars), actually grew seven times.

To put that another way, your real (after-inflation) yearly rate of return for long-term government bonds was only 2.4 percent. In half of the 80 years, your bond investment either didn't grow at all in real dollar terms or actually lost money.

Compare that scenario to an investment in stocks. Had you invested the very same $100 in 1926 in the S&P 500 (500 of the largest U.S. company stocks), your investment would have grown to $2,385,000 in *nominal* (pre-inflation) dollars. In 1926 dollars, that would be $240,000. The average nominal return was 10.4 percent, and the average real annual rate of return for the bundle of stocks was 7.2 percent. (Those rates ignore income taxes.)

So? Which would you rather have invested in: stocks or bonds? Obviously, stocks were the way to go. In comparison, bonds seem to have failed to provide adequate return.

Saving the day when the day needed saving

But hold on! There's another side to the story! Yes, stocks clobbered bonds over the course of the last 80 years. But who makes an investment and leaves it untouched for 80 years? Rip Van Winkle, maybe. But outside of fairy tale characters, no one! Real people in the real world usually invest for much shorter periods. And there have been some shorter periods over the past 80 years when stocks have taken some stomach-wrenching falls.

The worst of all falls, of course, was during the Great Depression that began with the stock market crash of 1929. Any money that your grandparents may have had in the stock market in 1929 was worth not even half as much four years later. Over the next decade, stock prices would go up and down, but Grandma and Grandpa wouldn't see their $100 back until about 1943. Had they planned to retire in that period, well . . . they may have had to sell a few apples on the street just to make ends meet.

A bond portfolio, however, would have helped enormously. Had Grandma and Grandpa had a diversified portfolio of, say, 70 percent stocks and 30 percent long-term government bonds, they would have been pinched by the Great Depression but not destroyed. While $70 of stock in 1929 was worth only $33 four years later; $30 in long-term government bonds would have been worth $47. All told, instead of having a $100 all-stock portfolio fall to $46, their 70/30 diversified portfolio would have fallen only to $80. Big difference!

Closer to home, a $10,000 investment in the S&P 500 at the beginning of 2000 was worth only $5,800 after three years of a growly bear market. But during those same three years, long-term U.S. government bonds soared. A $10,000 70/30 (stock/bond) portfolio during those three years would have been worth $8,210 at the end. Another big difference!

Clearly, long-term government bonds can, and often do, rise to the challenge during times of economic turmoil. Why are bad times often good for many bonds? I explain the reasons for this phenomenon in Chapters 4 and 5. For now, know that bonds have historically been a best friend to investors at those times when investors have most needed a friend. Given that bonds have saved numerous stock investors from impoverishment, bond investing in the past eight decades may be seen not as a miserable failure but as a huge success.

Whatever happened to Grandpa's bearer bonds?

For years, bonds were issued as certificates — many of them genuine works of art — called *bearer bonds*. Quite simply, if you had the certificate in your hands, the bond was yours, and the attached coupons (generally good for six months' interest) could be turned in for cold cash. Your name appeared nowhere on the bond, nor in the company's records. If you earned any interest, the IRS expected you to voluntarily report it and pay the appropriate tax.

The 20-year bearer bond shown here was issued by the General Electric Company in 1956, carried a face value of $1,000, and bore coupons redeemable every six months for $17.50 each.

Photo courtesy of Scripophily.com

Needless to say, the IRS was not a big fan of bearer bonds, and in 1982, it became illegal for any corporation or municipality to issue them. With the sole exception of U.S. savings bonds, bonds have been issued electronically since that time, and anonymity is no longer possible.

You own the bond. The brokerage house has your name. You pay the tax.

On the up side, today's bonds, unlike bearer bonds, cannot be stolen or lost in a fire. Today, your ownership of a bond is registered in cyberspace and protected from thievery or flames.

Looking Back Over a Long and (Mostly) Distinguished Past

Whether or not we deem bonds a success in the 20th century, if we go back in time to the 19th century, the track record seems more clear. Not only were bonds a source of stability during most of the 1800s, but the difference in returns between stocks and bonds wasn't nearly so great as it became in later years.

Although the data from over 100 years ago isn't quite as solid as it is today, most economists believe that bonds in the United States returned to investors an average of about 5 percent a year throughout the 1800s, versus roughly 6.5 percent a year for stocks. Inflation was quite low prior to 1900, so nominal and real returns were largely one and the same.

If you consider the inherently large volatility of stocks (probably similar 100 years ago to today), it would seem that bonds were perhaps the better investment during the early industrial age.

In trying to predict future returns of bonds and stocks, most investors today look at data only from the 20th century and assume that the returns for stocks and bonds moving forward will be similar to what they've been. However, when making predictions, it may be helpful to note that financial markets were quite active prior to 1900 . . . even prior to 1800! In fact, bonds have been issued in Europe for hundreds of years (looking rather similar to the way they look today).

Yielding returns to generations of your ancestors

Notre Dame, the Leaning Tower of Pisa, the Palace at Versailles, the Tower of London . . . our medieval European ancestors knew how to create things with lasting power. When the Venetian government of the 13th century issued bonds, it didn't issue the 10- or 20-year bonds that are popular today. It didn't issue 50- or 100-year bonds that were popular in 1800s, either. No, the Venetian *prestiti* was a bond designed to pay interest *forever,* without ever paying off the principal.

The prestiti paid 5 percent interest a year, payable — like most bonds today — in two annual installments. Also like most bonds today, it was not issued in certificate form. Rather, the bondholders had their claims registered in a central location: the city's loan office. Prestiti could be bought and sold on the open market and, depending on prevailing interest rates of the day, might sell at a discount or a premium of the face value of the loan — just as bonds trade today.

Buy war bonds!

Even before the United States entered World War II, a massive effort was underway to raise money to build the military and support our allies in war-torn Europe and Asia. At the heart of the fundraising effort was the creation of war bonds. In April 1941, with great fanfare, President Franklin D. Roosevelt purchased the very first such bond from Secretary of the Treasury Henry Morgenthau, Jr. Posters (such as the ones shown here), radio commercials, newspaper advertisements, and newsreels in theaters spread the word that purchasing a bond was the patriotic thing to do. The government made it easy to invest by issuing cards with slots for quarters. When a person collected 75 quarters — $18.75 — he or she could bring the card into any post office and receive a $25 bond redeemable in ten years (with no actual interest payments in the interim). That worked out to 2.9 percent annual compound interest — considerably lower than prevailing rates at the time. More than six out of ten U.S. citizens bought war bonds, almost $200 billion was raised (which would be about 12 times as much in today's dollars), and Hitler and Hirohito got what was coming to them.

a

b

Confidence in the prestiti led to its use as a medium of exchange throughout Medieval Europe and helped Venice grow into the most prosperous city of the era. In later years, as England and France became dominant powers, they, too, issued bonds that never matured. The Brits called theirs *consols,* and the French (who, appropriately enough, backed their bonds with a tax on wine) called theirs *rentes.*

Venice continued to pay off the interest on its prestiti until the early 1500s and only stopped when Venice was pretty much destroyed in a series of wars with the Turks. Britain and France, although no longer issuing consols and rentes, still issue bonds today, as do most other nations. Governments generally sell more bonds when they need more cash to pay the bills. Historically, governments have needed the most cash in times of war. The United States became a major issuer of bonds during World War II, and the sale of war bonds, historians agree, helped to finance the Allied victory.

Gleaning some important lessons

Bonds have been a bulwark of portfolios throughout much of modern history, but that's not to say that money — some serious money — hasn't been lost.

Corporate bonds — generally considered the most risky kind of bonds — did not become popular in the United States until after the Civil War, when many railroads, experiencing a major building boom, found a sudden need for capital. During a depression in the early to mid 1890s, a good number of those railroads went bankrupt, taking many bondholders down with them. During the Great Depression of the 1930s, plenty of companies of all sorts went under, and many corporate bondholders again took it on the chin.

In more recent years, the global bond default rate has been less than 1 percent a year. But still, that equates to several dozen companies a year. In the past few years, a number of airlines (Delta, Northwest), energy companies (Enron), and one auto parts company (Delphi) have defaulted on their bonds. General Motors and Ford both saw big downgrades on their bonds (from *investment-grade* to *speculative-grade,* terms I explain in Chapter 4), costing bondholders (especially those who needed to cash out of their bondholdings) many millions.

Municipal bonds, although much safer overall than corporate bonds, have also seen a few defaults. In 1978, Cleveland became the first major U.S. city to default on its bonds since the Great Depression. Three years prior, New York City likely would have defaulted on its bonds had the federal government not come to the rescue.

The largest default in the history of the municipal bond market was that of the Washington Public Power Supply System (WPPSS, known informally as "Whoops"). In 1982, bond investors lost out on $2.25 billion following the municipal corporation's failed program to build five nuclear power plants in Washington to supply electricity to the Pacific Northwest. Only one of the five planned nuclear plants was ever completed. Investors got seriously nuked.

On the national level (government-issued bonds are often called *sovereign* bonds), perhaps the largest default of all time occurred in 1917 as revolution-aries in Russia were attempting to free the people by breaking the bonds of imperialist oppression. Bonds were broken, for sure; with the collapse of the czarist regime, billions and billions of rubles worth of Russian bonds were suddenly worth less than nonalcoholic vodka. Most had been sold to Western Europeans. In France, where the Parisian government urged people to buy Russian bonds to support the monarchy, it is estimated that about half of all households held at least some Russian debt.

Sometimes history repeats . . . or at least echoes. One of the largest bond defaults of the modern era was again born in Moscow. It was 1998, and the Russian government, facing a collapse of its currency, stopped payment on about $40 billion of bonds. In 2002, Argentina paid 25 cents on the dollar for its outstanding bond debt of $90 billion.

As I discuss in Chapter 9, bonds of *emerging-market* nations, such as Russia, Argentina, Mexico, and Turkmenistan, have been one of the hottest invest-ment sectors in the past several years. The returns of late have been phe-nomenal, but how quickly people forget the past! Those bonds can be very volatile, and investing in them means risking your principal.

Realizing How Crucial Bonds Are Today

I could talk about the importance of corporate debt to the growth of the economy, the way in which municipal bonds help to repair roads and build bridges, and how Ginnie Mae and Fannie Mae bonds help to provide housing to the masses, but I think I'll just let this one sentence suffice. This is, after all, not a book on macroeconomics and social policy but a book on personal investing. So allow me to address the crucial role that bonds play in the lives of individual investors — people like me and you.

With $15 trillion invested in bonds, U.S. households' economic welfare is closely tied to the fortunes of the bond market.

I would argue that with the demise of the traditional pension, bond investing is more important than ever. Back when you knew your company would take care of you in old age, you may have played footloose and fancy free with your portfolio without having to worry that a scrambled nest egg might mean you couldn't afford to buy eggs. Today, a well-tuned portfolio — that almost certainly includes a good helping of bonds — can make the difference between living on Easy Street and living on the street.

Keep in mind that most of the money in the bond market today is institutional money. Should you have a life insurance policy, chances are that your life insurance company has most of your future payoff invested in bonds. Should you have money in your state's prepaid college tuition program, chances are that your money is similarly indirectly invested in bonds. Should you be one of the fortunate persons whose company still offers a pension, chances are that your company has your future pension payout invested in bonds.

In total, more than $60 trillion is invested in bonds worldwide (see Figure 3-1), and the amount is growing year by year. Many economists speculate that as the Boomer generation retires, the demand for income-generating investments like bonds will only grow. If you live and work in a developed nation, your economic well-being is much more closely tied to the bond markets than you think!

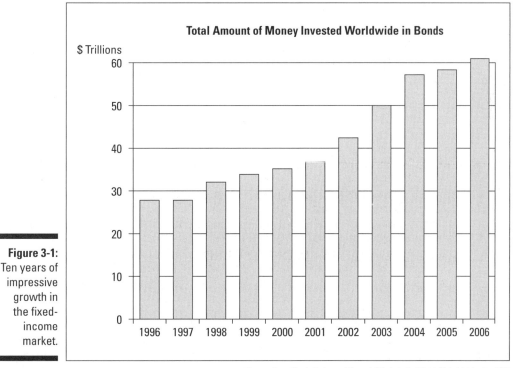

Total Amount of Money Invested Worldwide in Bonds

Figure 3-1:
Ten years of impressive growth in the fixed-income market.

Source: Securities Industry and Financial Markets Fact Book Global Addendum 2006

Need a hobby? Try scripophily

The term *scripophily* (pronounced *scrip awful lee*) derives from a contest held by the *Financial Times* newspaper in 1978 to come up with an appropriate name for collecting antique stocks and bonds. Bob Kerstein, CEO of Scripophily. com, estimates that the hobby boasts 20,000 to 30,000 enthusiasts in the United States alone.

Kerstein's Web site features more than 12,000 old certificates from various nations, industries, and eras. Many of them are works of art, some even featuring paintings from famous artists of their day. But the vast majority of the old stocks and bonds have one thing in common, says Kerstein: "They may be valuable as collector items, but they are worthless as securities." He says he has seen scams whereby con artists try to sell old, retired bonds at face value (typically $1,000) to unknowing investors. "Those old bonds may look like they're still redeemable, but they are not," he warns.

Photo courtesy of Scripophily.com

The bond shown here, issued by the Southern Life Insurance and Trust Company of Florida Territory in 1839, is one of the oldest corporate bond issues known. This $1,000 bond, paying 8 percent, was signed by the governor of the territory. It was payable in either U.S. dollars or British pounds.

Viewing Recent Developments, Largely for the Better

As the price of everything from groceries and gas to college tuition and medical care continues to climb, it's nice to know that at least two things on this planet have gotten cheaper in the past few years: computers and bond trades. And, as any seasoned bond investor will tell you, saving money on trades isn't the only exciting development of late. Here are some others worth noting:

✔ **New and better bond funds:** According to Morningstar, there are now roughly 5,000 bond funds in which to invest. Of these, 50 are bond *index funds* — funds that seek to capture the returns of an entire swatch of the bond market — which, from my vantage point, tend to be the best options for most bond investors. These funds carry an average yearly expense ratio of 40 basis points (40/100 of 1 percent), which is way, way less than most bond funds.

The newest kid on the block, *exchange-traded funds* (ETFs) — index funds similar to mutual funds, but in some ways better — are the greatest thing to happen to bond investing in a very long time. As of this printing, there are 30 bond ETFs in which to invest. Some of them, such as several Treasury-bond ETF offerings from Vanguard, carry expense ratios of a mere 11 basis points (11/100 of 1 percent). I discuss these Vanguard ETFs, and other top fund picks, in Chapter 16.

✔ **Greater access to information:** One of the advantages of exchange-traded funds over traditional mutual funds is their relative *transparency.* That means that when you invest in an ETF, you know exactly what you're buying. Traditional mutual funds are not required to reveal their specific investments; you may think you're buying one thing but you get another.

When it comes to buying and selling individual bonds, it's as if a muddy pond has been transformed into a glass aquarium. Not long ago, a bond broker would give you a price for a bond, and you'd have absolutely no idea how fair a deal you were getting. Nowadays, you can search online and usually get a very good idea of how fair a deal you're getting, how much the broker is making, and whether there are better deals to be had. I give you a complete tour of the aquarium in Chapter 15.

✔ **The expansion of Uncle Sam's treasury chest:** If you are going to invest in individual bonds, U.S. Treasury bonds may make the most sense. The Treasury now has a Web site where you can buy its bonds directly and not have to deal with any brokers whatsoever, nor fork over any kind of markup. I walk you through www.treasurydirect.gov in Chapter 5.

One special kind of Treasury bond — Treasury Inflation-Protected Securities, or TIPS — has been in existence since the mid-1990s. It is a very exciting development in the world of bonds. TIPS offer only very modest interest rates, but the principal is readjusted annually to keep up with inflation. TIPS represent an entirely new *asset class* (kind of investment), and I advocate that most of my clients hold at least one-third of their bond allocation in TIPS. They are wonderful portfolio diversifiers and are among the safest of all investments. Read all about them in Chapter 5.

✔ **Internationalization of the bond market:** The United States government isn't the only government to issue bonds. U.S. corporations aren't the only corporations to issue bonds, either. For added portfolio diversification, and possibly a higher yield, you may want to look abroad. Until recently, international diversification in fixed income was very difficult. Now, it's as easy as (but not as American as) apple pie. As with U.S. bonds, you have your pick of short-term or long-term bonds, safe-and-simple or risky-with-high-return potential. You can invest in the calm waters of England, Germany, and France, or travel to countries such as Thailand and Brazil where the bond markets are choppy and exciting. Join me on the voyage abroad in Chapter 9.

Chapter 4

Sweet Interest Is the Name of the Game

· ·

In This Chapter

▶ Calculating true return on bond investments

▶ Understanding the meaning of various yields

▶ Explaining what makes the bond markets move

▶ Discovering why tomorrow's interest rates matter today

▶ Figuring out your potential for profit

· ·

*I*n the city of Uruk, in the month of Ululu, on the 11th day of the 9th year of Nebuchadnezzar (that would be 595 B.C.), a man named Nabu-usabsi lent a half mina (about half a pound) of silver to Nabu-sar-ashesu. They signed an agreement witnessed by a holy priest and four countrymen. The agreement stated that within one year, Nabu-sar-ashesu would return to Nabu-usabsi his half mina of silver plus another ten shekels, each shekel equal to about 1⁄60 of a pound of silver. If you do the math, that equates to a yearly rate of interest of 16⅔ percent.

That story from an ancient Babylonian text was retold, nearly 2,600 years later, in *A History of Interest Rates,* a 700-page textbook by Sidney Homer and Richard Sylla, first published in 1963. (A fourth edition was published by Wiley in 2005.) The book is an amazing collection of research into credit and interest rates going back not only to the 9th year of Nebuchadnezzar, but even offering some speculation that interest payments of one sort or another existed in prehistoric times.

And why, pray tell, am I bringing this up in a book on bond investing in the computer age? Because most of today's credit is tied up in bonds, and the most salient feature of any bond is the interest rate paid. Interestingly (pardon the pun), many of the same forces that drove interest rates 2,600 years ago are *still* driving interest rates today, as you find out in this chapter.

On the following pages, I examine what forces affect interest rates and the demand for credit. I introduce the many (and often confusing, sometimes *purposely* confusing) ways in which bond returns are measured and reported. And I give you the tools you need to determine whether Mr. Nabu-usabsi was getting a fair return on his investment, as well as what you, as a thoroughly modern bond investor, should expect in return for *your* bond investments.

Calculating Rates of Return Can Be Like Deciphering Ancient Babylonian

Bond investing can be tricky business indeed — way trickier than stock investing. To help me explain why, I'm going to call upon our Babylonian friends, Nabu-usabsi and Nabu-sar-ashesu. And I'm going to introduce two new characters, Lila-Ir-lender and Kudur-Broker. The two Nabus are real characters from a bygone era. Lila-Ir-lender (said to be a distant cousin of Hammurabi) is fictional. Kudur-Broker is also fictional.

(Note to any Hollywood types reading this text: These are *my* characters; if you decide to turn *Bond Investing For Dummies* into a blockbuster movie, I demand a cut!)

Lila-Ir-lender, like Nabu-sar-ashesu, is a money lender. Kudur-Broker is, appropriately enough, a broker. Instead of dealing only in minas and shekels and agreements written on parchment or stone, let's now assume the existence of bonds. With lenders, borrowers, and a broker, we now have a complete bond market!

Figure 4-1 shows our four players in the fictional Babylonian bond market, illustrated by Addie Wild, my 11-year-old daughter, and polished for publication by the Wiley graphics team.

Figure 4-1:
Nabu-sar-ashesu, bond issuer; Nabu-usabi, bond buyer; Lila-Ir-lender, bond buyer; and Kudur-Broker, bond broker.

Okay, are you ready now to see why this bond business can be so tricky? Good. Let's return to ancient Babylonia!

Cutting deals

Instead of merely signing an agreement, suppose that Nabu-usabsi, in return for lending his half mina of silver to Nabu-sar-ashesu, gets a bond. Nabu-sar-ashesu's bond clearly states that Nabu-usabsi will get his investment back in one year, plus 16⅔ percent interest. In the parlance of the bond world, the bond is issued with a *face value* of a half mina of silver, a *coupon rate* (or interest rate) of 16⅔ percent, and a *maturity* (or expiration date) of one year. I talk about these terms in more detail later.

For now, I want to impress upon you that measuring bond returns is not always an easy matter. Why not? After all, the agreement calls for 16⅔ percent interest. Simple enough, eh? Not really.

Suppose that Nabu-usabsi wants to get his 16⅔ percent interest not as a lump sum at the end of the year but in two installments (as most bonds work): 8⅓ percent after six months, and another 8⅓ percent after another six months. That is obviously a better deal for Nabu-usabsi because he gets the 8⅓ percent sooner and can, if he wishes, reinvest that money for another six months. Let's suppose that, in fact, he is able to reinvest that money for a very high interest rate. By the end of the year, Nabu-usabsi will actually earn more than 16⅔ percent on his original investment. But how is his *real* rate of return calculated?

Changing hands

To complicate matters further, suppose that Nabu-sar-ashesu, our bond issuer, has agreed that his bond can be sold, and that he will continue to pay 16⅔ percent interest to whomever buys the bond. In walks Lila-Ir-lender, who wants to buy the bond from Nabu-usabsi but uses Kudur-Broker, the bond broker, to make the deal. Kudur-Broker pays Nabu-usabsi one-half pound of silver to obtain the bond. He turns around and sells it to Lila-Ir-lender for ⁹⁄₁₀ pound of silver and pockets the difference for himself.

Lila-Ir-lender is now the proud owner of a bond that is paying 16⅔ percent on the *original face value* (one-half pound of silver). She, however, paid more for the bond, thanks to the bond broker's markup. So even though she is holding a bond that is paying 16⅔ percent, she isn't really getting 16⅔ percent on her money; she's getting less.

Now how much is the true rate of return on the bond? Is it 16⅔ percent, or is it 13.88 percent, which is the actual percentage return that Lila-Ir-lender would be getting on the money she laid out?

Embracing the complications

You see why this bond business can be so confusing? (Yes, it would be just as confusing if the names were "Mike" and "Sue" instead of Nabu-usabsi and Nabu-sar-ashesu!)

I need to warn you in advance that this is the most technical chapter of this book. You are about to read some things that confuse even many financial professionals. I do my best to present the information as clearly as possible. And I promise that I'll even give you an intermission halfway through the chapter so you can catch your breath! But you are probably right now wondering the following: Do you really have to know all this? Can you skim this chapter, or should you really know how to calculate yield-to-maturity, yield-to-call, and things like that? It depends.

If you are okay investing in bond mutual funds, especially the bond index funds that I recommend later in this book (see Chapter 16), and you're going to buy and hold your investment, then a cursory knowledge of what makes bonds tick will probably be just fine. (Knowing how they fit into your portfolio, as outlined in Chapters 11 and 12, is probably more important.)

If you are intent, however, on dealing in individual bonds or trying to flip bonds to make a profit (good luck!), you'd better either know this stuff or find a bond broker you can really trust.

Understanding what follows will be easier than finding a bond broker you can really trust. Trust me!

Conducting Three Levels of Research to Measure the Desirability of a Bond

Determining the true value of a bond investment, and how much you're really going to get out of it in the end, requires three levels of research. I could compare it to buying a home. Shopping for a home, here are the three levels of research you conduct:

- **Level one:** You notice the curb appeal. You take note of the size of the home and whether or not you find it attractive. You also, of course, note the offering price.

- **Level two:** You look at the property taxes, the age of the plumbing, the cost of utilities, and the condition of the roof.

- **Level three:** You expand your view to look critically at the surroundings. How are the schools? Are area homes appreciating? Do the neighbors park their pick-up trucks on the front lawn?

With a bond, you go through similar levels of research:

- **Level one:** You notice the curb appeal of the bond: What is the face value, coupon rate, and sales price?

- **Level two:** You dig deeper into the qualities of the bond: What are its ratings and maturity, and is it callable?

- **Level three:** You look at broader economic factors (the bond's "neighborhood"), which can greatly influence the value of your bond investment: the prevailing interest rates, inflation rate, state of the economy, and forces of supply and demand in the fixed-income market.

I know that you may not be familiar with all the terms I'm using here — *ratings, callable,* and so on. You soon will be! I introduce them all in this chapter.

Level one: Getting basic, easily available information

Here are the first things you want to know about a bond:

- What is its face value?

- What is the coupon rate?

- How much are you being asked to pay for the bond?

These can all be ascertained quite readily, either by looking at the bond offer itself or by having a conversation with the broker.

Face value

Also known as *par value* or the *principal,* the *face value* is the amount the bond was issued for. This is the amount that the bond issuer promises to pay the bond buyer at maturity. The face value of the vast majority of bonds in today's market is $1,000. But note that a $1,000 par value bond doesn't necessarily have to sell for $1,000. After it is on the open market, it may sell for an amount well above par or below par. If it sells above par, it is known as a *premium* bond. If it sells below par, it is known as a *discount* bond.

Know this: Discount bonds are discounted for a reason (generally because the bond isn't paying a very high rate of interest compared to other similar bonds). Don't think you are necessarily getting a bargain by paying less than face value for a bond.

Coupon rate

The *coupon rate* is the interest rate the bond issuer (the debtor) has agreed to pay the bondholder (the creditor), given as a percent of the face value. It is called the coupon rate because bonds in the old days had actual coupons attached that you would rip off at regular intervals to redeem for cash. Bonds no longer have paper coupons to rip off, but the term remains.

The coupon rate never changes. That's the reason that bonds, like CDs, are called *fixed-income* investments, even though, as you will see shortly, it is a bit of a misnomer. A 5 percent bond will always pay 5 percent of the face value (which would usually be $50 a year, typically paid as $25 every six months). As I mention in the previous section, the bond doesn't have to be bought or sold at par. But whatever price a bond sells at doesn't affect the coupon rate.

Know this: The coupon rate, set in stone, tells you how much cash you'll get from your bond each year. Simply take the coupon rate and multiply it by the face value of the bond. Divide that amount in half. That's how much cash you'll typically receive twice a year. A $1,000 bond paying 8 percent will give you $40 cash twice a year.

Sale price

In general, a bond will sell at a *premium* (above face value) when prevailing interest rates have dropped since the time that bond was issued. If you think about it, that makes sense. Say your bond is paying 6 percent, and interest rates across the board have dropped to 4 percent. The bond in your hand, which is paying considerably more than new bonds being issued, becomes a valuable commodity. On the other hand, when general interest rates rise, existing bonds tend to move to *discount* status (selling below face value). Who wants them when new bonds are paying higher rates?

Don't ask why, but bond people quote the price of a bond on a scale of 100. If a bond is selling at *par* (face value), it will be quoted as selling at 100. But that doesn't mean that you can buy the bond for $100. It means you can buy it at par. On a $1,000 par bond, that means you can buy the bond for $1,000. If the same bond is selling at 95, that means you're looking at a discount bond, selling for $950. And if that bond is selling for 105, it's a premium bond; you'll need to fork over $1,050.

Know this: Most investors put too much weight on whether a bond is a discount bond or a premium bond. Although it matters somewhat, especially with regard to a bond's volatility (see the final section of this chapter), it doesn't necessarily affect a bond's total return. *Total return* refers to the sum of your principal and income, plus any capital gains on your original investment, *plus* any income or capital gains on money you've earned on your original investment and have been able to reinvest. Total return is, very simply, the entire amount of money you end up with after a certain investment period, minus what you began with. More on that later in this chapter.

Level two: Finding out intimate details of the bond

After you know the face value, coupon rate, and sale price (discount or premium), you are ready to start a little digging. Here's what you want to know next about the bond:

✔ Is the bond issuer capable of repaying you your money? Or is there a chance that the issuer may go belly-up and *default* on (fail to repay) all or part of your loan?

✔ When will you see your principal returned?

✔ Is there a chance that the bond will be called*?*

Ratings: Separating quality from junk

Not all bonds pay the same coupon rates. In fact, some bonds pay way more than others. One of the major determinants of a bond's coupon rate is the financial standing of the issuer.

The United States Treasury, a major issuer of bonds, pays modest rates of return on its bonds (generally a full percentage point less than similar bonds issued by corporations). The reason? Uncle Sam doesn't have to pay more. People know that the United States government isn't going to welsh on its debts, so they are willing to lend the government money without demanding a high return. Shakier entities, however, such as a new company, a city in financial trouble, or the Russian government (which has a history of defaulting) would have to offer higher rates of return in order to find any creditors. So they must, and so they do.

An entire industry of bond-rating companies, such as Moody's, Standard and Poor's (S&P), Fitch IBCA, and Duff & Phelps, exists to help bond investors figure their odds of getting paid back from a company or municipality to which they lend money. These firms dig into a bond issuer's financial books to see how solvent the entity is. The higher the rating, the safer your investment; the lower the rating, the more risk you take. Concurrently, there are other places you can turn that will tell you how much extra interest you should expect for taking on the added risk of lending to a shaky company. Much more on the ratings in Chapter 6.

Know this: Ratings are very helpful — it is hard to imagine markets working without them — but neither the ratings nor the raters are infallible. In the case of Enron, the major ratings firms — S&P and Moody's — had the company's bonds rated as *investment-grade* until four days prior to the company declaring bankruptcy! Investment-grade means that the risk of loss is very low and the odds of getting repaid very high. Weren't Enron bondholders surprised!

Insurance

Some bonds come insured and are advertised as such. This is especially prominent in the municipal bond market, famous for its largely tax-free bonds. Even though default rates are very low among municipalities, cities know that people buy their bonds expecting safety. So they sometimes insure. If a municipality goes to the trouble of having an insurance company back its bonds, you know that you are getting a safer investment, but you shouldn't expect an especially high rate of interest. (No, you can't decline the insurance on an insured bond. It doesn't work like auto-rental insurance.)

Know this: Some proponents of holding individual bonds say that you should delve not only into the financial health of the bond issuer but also, in the case of an insured bond, the financial health of the insurance company standing behind the issuer. That's a fair amount of work, which is one reason I tend to favor bond funds for most family portfolios.

Maturity

Generally, the longer the maturity of the bond, the higher the interest rate paid. The reason is simple enough: Borrowers generally want your money for longer periods of time and are willing to pay accordingly. Lenders generally don't want their money tied up for long periods and require extra incentive to make such a commitment. And finally, the longer you invest your money in a bond, the greater the risk you are taking.

Know this: I don't care who the issuer is, when you buy a 20-year bond, you are taking a risk. Anything can happen in 20 years. Who would have thought 20 years ago that General Motors might find itself on the verge of bankruptcy (as it is as I'm typing these words)?

Callability

A bond that is *callable* is a bond that can be retired by the company or municipality on a certain date prior to the bond's maturity. Because bonds tend to be retired when interest rates fall, you don't want your bond to be retired; you generally aren't going to be able to replace it with anything paying as much. Because of the added risk, callable bonds tend to carry higher coupon rates to compensate bond buyers.

Know this: Please be careful when buying any individual callable bond. Much of the real pain I've seen in the bond market has occurred over calls. I've seen cases where a bond buyer will pay a broker a hefty sum to buy a bond callable in, say, six months. The bond, sure enough, gets called, and the bondholder suddenly realizes that he paid the broker a fat fee and made nothing — perhaps got a *negative* return — on his investment. Of course, the broker never bothered to point out this potentially ugly scenario. (Reading this book, especially Chapter 15, will ensure that *you* never meet with a similar fate!)

Taxes

Back in the early days of the bond market in the United States, the federal government made a deal with the cities and states: You don't tax our bonds, and we won't tax yours. And, so far, all parties have kept their word. When you invest in Treasury bonds, you pay no state or local tax on the interest. And when you invest in municipal bonds, you pay no federal tax on the interest. Accordingly, muni bonds pay a lower rate of interest than equivalent corporate bonds. But you may still wind up ahead on an after-tax basis.

Know this: Whether or not the tax-free status of municipal bonds makes them appropriate for your portfolio is the subject of Chapter 8. I'll warn you in advance that the simple taxable versus tax-free calculators you find online will not always steer you in the best direction.

Okay, I promised earlier that I'd give you a break about halfway through this chapter. Now's the time: INTERMISSION! Feel free to step away, get a snack, and come back when the glaze has cleared from your eyes.

All right . . . Ready to move onto that third level now? Remember, this chapter is all about estimating the value of a bond investment. As I show next, getting that estimate requires the use of a broad-angle lens.

Level three: Examining the neighborhood

Your home, no matter how well you maintain it or whether or not you renovate the kitchen, will tend to rise or fall in value along with the value of all

other houses in your neighborhood. Many things outside of your control —
the quality of the schools, employment opportunities, crime rates, and earthquake tremors — can greatly influence the value of homes in your area,
including yours. Similarly, a bond, no matter its quality or maturity, will tend
to rise and fall in value with the general conditions of the markets and of the
economy.

Prevailing interest rates

Nothing affects the value of bonds (at least in the short to intermediate
run) like prevailing interest rates. When interest rates go up, bond prices go
down — usually in lockstep. When interest rates fall, bond prices climb. The
relationship is straightforward and logical enough. If you are holding a bond
paying yesterday's interest rate, and today's interest rate is lower, then you
are holding something that is going to be in hot demand, and people will pay
you dearly for it. If you are holding a bond paying yesterday's interest rate,
and today's rate is higher, then you are holding mud.

Okay, that part is simple. Interest rates drive bond prices. But what drives
interest rates?

Interest rates come in many different flavors. At any point in time, there will
be prevailing interest rates for home mortgages, credit card payments, bank
loans, short-term bonds, and long-term bonds, but to a great extent they all
move up and down together. The forces that drive interest rates are numerous, entwined, and largely unpredictable (even though many people claim
they can predict).

In the short run — from hour to hour, day to day — the Federal Reserve,
which controls monetary policy in the United States, has great power to
manipulate interest rates across the board. The Federal Reserve's job is to
help smooth the economy by tinkering with interest rates to help curb inflation and boost growth. Low interest rates make borrowing easy, both for
businesses and consumers. That helps to heat up the economy, but it can
also result in inflation. High interest rates discourage borrowing and so tend
to slow economic growth, but they also help to rein in inflation. So when
inflation is running too high, in the eyes of the Fed, it will move to raise interest rates. And when the economy is growing too slowly, the Fed will tend to
lower interest rates. Obviously, it's a balancing act, and perfect balance is
hard to achieve.

In the longer run — month to month, year to year — interest rates tend to
rise and fall with inflation and with the anticipated rate of future inflation.

Know this: Rising interest rates are, in the short run, a bondholder's worst
enemy. The possibility that interest rates will rise — and bond prices will
therefore fall — is what makes long-term bonds somewhat risky. If you wish
to avoid the risk of price volatility, go with short-term bonds, but be willing to
accept less cash flow from your bond holdings.

How exactly does the Federal Reserve move interest rates?

The U.S. Federal Reserve has three "magic" powers with which to expand or contract the money supply, or move interest rates: open market operations, the discount rate, and reserve requirements:

✔ **Open market operations:** This term means nothing more than the buying and selling of Treasury and federal agency bonds. When bonds are sold (and the public's money is funneled into government hands), the money supply is tightened, inflation tends to slow, and interest rates tend to rise. When bonds are purchased back (and the public's money is returned), the economy is given a boost, and interest rates tend to fall.

✔ **The discount rate:** This refers to the interest rate that commercial banks must pay for government loans. The more the banks have to pay, the more they tend to charge their customers, and interest rates tend to rise.

✔ **Reserve requirements:** The *reserve* is the amount of money that banks must hold on hand as a percentage of their outstanding loans. The higher the reserve requirements, the tougher it is for banks to lend money, and interest rates tend to rise as a result.

The rate of inflation

The *inflation rate* signals the degree to which you have to cough up more money to buy the same basket of goods; it indicates your loss of purchasing power. In the long run, the inflation rate has great bearing on returns enjoyed by bondholders. The ties between the inflation rate and the bond market are numerous.

In economic theory, bondholders are rational beings with rational desires and motivations. (In reality, individual investors often act irrationally, but as a group, the markets seem to work rather rationally.) A rational buyer of bonds demands a certain *inflation-risk premium.* That is, the higher the rate of inflation or the expected rate of inflation, the higher an interest rate bondholders demand. If inflation is running at 3 percent, bond buyers know that they need returns of at least 3 percent just to break even. If the inflation rate jumps to 6 percent, the inflation-risk premium doubles; bond buyers won't invest their money (or won't invest it happily) unless they get double what they were getting before.

Inflation is also a pretty good indicator of how hot the economy is. When prices are rising, it usually reflects full employment and companies expanding. When companies are expanding, they need capital. The need for capital raises the demand for borrowing. An increased demand for borrowing raises prevailing interest rates, which lowers the price of bonds.

Know this: As a bondholder, you can get stung by inflation. Badly. That's why I recommend that a certain proportion of your bonds (around one-third) be held in inflation-adjusted bonds, such as Treasury Inflation-Protected Securities (TIPS). It's also why a 100-percent bond portfolio rarely, if ever, makes sense. Stocks and commodities have a much better track record at keeping ahead of inflation.

Forces of supply and demand

The public is fickle, and that fickleness is perhaps nowhere better seen than in the stock market. Although the bond market tends to be less affected by the public's whims, it does happen. At times, the public feels pessimistic, and when the public feels pessimistic, it usually favors the stability of government bonds. When the public is feeling optimistic, it tends to favor the higher return potential of corporate bonds. When the public feels that taxes are going to rise, it tends to favor tax-free municipal bonds. As in any other market — shoes, automobiles, lettuce — high consumer demand can raise prices, and low demand tends to lower prices.

Understanding (and Misunderstanding) the Concept of Yield

Okay, time to hold onto your hat. Now that you know something about researching the particulars of a bond offering, and the climate of the bond market, it's time to talk *yield*. Yield is what you want in a bond. Yield is income. Yield contributes to return. Yield is confusion! People (and that includes overly eager bond salespeople) often misuse the term or use it inappropriately to gain an advantage in the bond market.

Don't be a yield sucker! Understand what kind of yield is being promised on a bond or bond fund, and know what it really means.

Coupon yield

This one is easy. The coupon yield, or the coupon rate, is part of the bond offering. A $1,000 bond with a coupon yield of 5 percent is going to pay $50 a year. A $1,000 bond with a coupon yield of 7 percent is going to pay $70 a year. Usually, the $50 or $70 or whatever will be paid out twice a year on an individual bond.

Bond funds don't really have coupon yields, although they have an average coupon yield for all the bonds in the pool. That average tells you something, for sure, but you need to remember that a bond fund may start the year and end the year with a completely different set of bonds — and a completely different average coupon yield.

Current yield

Like coupon yield, current yield is easy to understand, at least on a superficial level. But there's a deeper level. And because of that, it is the most often misused kind of yield. In short, *current yield* is derived by taking the bond's coupon yield and dividing it by the bond's price.

Suppose you had a $1,000 face value bond with a coupon rate of 5 percent, which would equate to $50 a year in your pocket. If the bond sells today for 98 (in other words, it is selling at a discount for $980), the current yield is $50 divided by $980 = 5.10 percent. If that same bond rises in price to a premium of 103 (selling for $1,030), the current yield is $50 divided by $1,030 = 4.85 percent.

The current yield is a sort of snapshot that gives you a very rough (and possibly entirely inaccurate) estimate of the return you can expect on that bond over the coming months. If you take today's current yield (translated into nickels and dimes) and multiply that amount by 30, you'd think that would give you a good estimate of how much income your bond will generate in the next month, but that's not the case. The current yield changes too quickly for that kind of prediction to hold true. The equivalent would be taking a measure of today's rainfall, multiplying it by 30, and using that number to estimate rainfall for the month. (Well, the current yield would be *a bit* more accurate, but you get my point.)

Yield-to-maturity

A much more accurate measure of return, although still far from perfect, is the *yield-to-maturity*. It's a considerably more complicated deal than figuring out current yield. Yield-to-maturity factors in not only the coupon rate and the price you paid for the bond, but also how far you have to go to get your principal back, and how much that principal will be.

Yield-to-maturity calculations make a big assumption that may or may not prove true: They assume that as you collect your interest payments every six months, you reinvest them at the same interest rate you're getting on the bond. With this (often faulty) assumption in mind, here's the formula for calculating yield-to-maturity:

Um, I don't know.

I can't remember it. Like most other financial planners, I would have to look it up. It's a terribly long formula with all kinds of horrible Greek symbols and lots of multiplication and division and I think there's a muffler and an ice tray thrown in. But (thank goodness) I don't need to know the formula!

Thanks to the miracle of modern technology, I can punch a few numbers in my financial calculator, or I can go to any number of online calculators. (Try putting "yield-to-maturity calculator" in your favorite search engine.) I like the calculator on MoneyChimp.com (a great financial Web site that features all sorts of cool calculators).

After you find a yield-to-maturity calculator, you'll be asked to put in the par (face) value of the bond (almost always $1,000), the price you are considering paying for the bond, the number of years to maturity, and the coupon rate. Then you simply punch the "calculate" icon. If, for example, I were to purchase a $1,000 par bond for $980, and that bond was paying 5 percent, and it matured in ten years, the yield-to-maturity would be 5.262 percent.

A few paragraphs ago, I calculated the current yield for such a bond to be 5.10 percent. The yield-to-maturity on a discounted bond (a bond selling for below par) will always be higher than the current yield. Why? Because when you eventually get your principal back at maturity, you'll be, in essence, making a profit. You paid only $980, but you'll see a check for $1,000. That extra $20 adds to your yield-to-maturity. The reverse is true of bonds purchased at a premium (a price higher than par value). In those cases, the yield-to-maturity will be lower than the current yield.

Unscrupulous bond brokers have been known to tout current yield, and only current yield, when selling especially premium-priced bonds. The current yield may look great, but you'll take a hit when the bond matures by collecting less in principal than you paid for the bond. Your yield-to-maturity, which matters more than current yield, may, in fact, stink.

Yield-to-call

If you buy a *callable* bond, the company or municipality that issues your bond can ask for it back, at a specific price, long before the bond matures. Premium bonds, because they carry higher-than-average coupon yields, are often called. What that means is that your yield-to-maturity is pretty much a moot point. What you're likely to see in the way of yield is yield-to-call. It's figured out the same way that you figure out yield-to-maturity (use MoneyChimp.com if you don't have a financial calculator), but the end result — your actual return — may be considerably lower.

Keep in mind that bonds are generally called when market interest rates have fallen. In that case, not only is your yield on the bond you're holding diminished, but your opportunity to invest your money in anything paying as high an interest rate has passed. From a bondholder's perspective, calls are not pretty, which is why callable bonds must pay higher rates of interest to find any buyers. (From the issuing company's or municipality's perspective, callable bonds are just peachy; after the call, the company or municipality can, if it wishes, issue a new bond that pays a lower interest rate.)

Certain hungry bond brokers may "forget" to mention yield-to-call and instead quote you only current yield or yield-to-maturity numbers. In such cases, you may pay the broker a big cut to get the bond, hold it for a short period, and then have to render it to the bond issuer, actually earning yourself a *negative* total return. Ouch.

Worst-case basis yield

Usually a callable bond will not have one possible call date, but several. *Worst-case basis yield* (or *yield-to-worst-call*) looks at all possible yields and tells you what your yield would be if the company or municipality decides to call your bond at the worst possible time.

Callable bonds involve considerably more risk than noncallable bonds. If interest rates drop, your bond will likely be called. Your yield on the existing bond just dropped from what you expected, and you won't be able to re-invest your money for a like rate of return. If interest rates have risen, the company probably won't call your bond, but you are stuck with an asset, if you should try to sell it, that has lost principal value. (Bond prices always drop when interest rates rise.)

The 30-day SEC yield

Because there are so many ways of measuring yield, and because bond mutual funds were once notorious for manipulating yield figures, the U.S. Securities and Exchange Commission (SEC) requires that all bond funds report yield in the same manner. The 30-day SEC yield, which attempts to consolidate the yield-to-maturity of all the bonds in the portfolio, exists so the mutual-fund bond shopper can have some measure with which to comparison shop. It isn't a perfect measure, in large part because the bonds in your bond fund today may not be the same bonds in your bond fund three weeks from now. Nonetheless, the 30-day SEC yield can be helpful in choosing the right funds. (More on fund shopping in Chapter 16.)

Recognizing Total Return (This Is What Matters Most!)

Even though bonds are called *fixed-income* investments, and even though bond returns are easier to predict than stock returns, ultimately you can't know the exact total return of any bond investment until after the investment period has come and gone. That's true for bond funds, and it's also true for most individual bonds (although many die-hard bond investors I've met refuse to admit it). *Total return* is the entire pot of money you wind up with after the investment period has come and gone. In the case of bonds or bond funds, that involves not only your original principal and your interest, but also any changes in the value of your original principal. Ignoring for the moment the risk of default (and losing all your principal), here are other ways in which your principal can shrink or grow.

Figuring in capital gains and losses

In the case of a bond fund, your principal is represented by a certain number of shares in the fund multiplied by the share price of the fund. As bond prices go up and down (usually in response to prevailing interest rates), so too will the share price of the bond fund go up and down. As I discuss in a couple of pages when I get to bond volatility, the share price of a bond fund may go up and down quite a bit, especially if the bond fund is holding long-term bonds, and doubly-especially if those long-term bonds are of questionable quality (junk bonds).

In the case of individual bonds, your principal will come back to you whole — but only if you hold the bond to maturity or if the bond is called. If, on the other hand, you choose to sell the bond before maturity, you'll wind up with whatever market price you can get for the bond at that point. If the market price has appreciated (the bond sells at a premium), you can count your capital gains as part of your total return. If the market price has fallen (the bond sells at a discount), the capital losses will offset any interest you've made on the bond.

Factoring in reinvestment rates of return

Total return of a bond can come from three sources:

- Interest on the bond
- Any possible capital gains (or losses)
- Whatever rate of return you get, if you get any, when you reinvest the money coming to you every six months

Believe it or not, on a very long-term bond, the last factor — your so-called *reinvestment rate* — will probably be the most important of the three! That's because of the amazing power of compound interest.

The only kind of bond where the reinvestment rate is not a factor is a *zero-coupon* bond, or a bond where your only interest payment comes at the very end when the bond matures. In the case of zero-coupon bonds, there is no compounding. The coupon rate of the bond is your actual rate of return, not accounting for inflation or taxes.

Example: Suppose you buy a 30-year, $1,000 bond that pays 6 percent on a semiannual basis. If you spend the $30 you collect twice a year, you'll get $1,000 back for your bond at the end of 30 years, and your total annual rate of return (ignoring taxes and inflation) would have been 6 percent simple interest. But now suppose that on each and every day that you collect those $30 checks, you immediately reinvest them at the same coupon rate. Over the course of 30 years, that pile of reinvested money will grow at an annual rate of 6 percent *compounded.*

In this scenario, at the end of six months, your investment will be worth $1,030. At the end of one year, your investment will be worth $1,060.90. (The extra 90 cents represents a half year's interest on the $30.) The following six months, you'll earn 6 percent on the new amount, and so on, for 30 more years. Instead of winding up with $1,000 after 30 years, as you would if you spent the semi-annual bond payments, you will instead wind up with $5,891.60 — almost six times as much!

Allowing for inflation adjustments

Of course, that $5,891.60 due to 6 percent compound interest probably won't be worth $5,891.60 in 30 years. Your truest total rate of return will need to account for inflation. If *inflation* — the rise in the general level of prices — were 3 percent a year for the next 30 years (roughly what it has been in the past decade), your $5,891.60 will be worth only $2,366.24 in today's dollars — a real compound return of 2.91 percent.

To account for inflation when determining the real rate of return on an investment, you can simply take the nominal rate of return (6 percent in our example) and subtract the annual rate of inflation (3 percent in our example). That will give you a very rough estimate of your total real return.

But if you want a more exact figure, here is the formula to use:

1 + nominal rate of return / 1 + inflation rate − 1 x 100 = Real rate of return

Assuming a 6 percent nominal rate of return and 3 percent inflation:

1.06 / 1.03 – 1 x 100 = 2.91

Why the more complicated calculation? You can't just subtract 3 from 6 because inflation is eating away at both your principal *and* your gains throughout the year.

Weighing pre-tax versus post-tax

Of course, we can't finish up this discussion without mentioning taxes. Taxes almost always eat into your bond returns. Here are two exceptions:

✔ Tax-free municipal bonds where there is neither a capital gain nor a capital loss, nor is the bondholder subject to any alternative minimum tax. (More on taxes and munis in Chapter 8.)

✔ Bonds held in a tax-advantaged account, such as an IRA or a 529 college savings plan.

For most bonds, the interest payments are taxed as regular income, and any rise in the value of the principal, if the bond is sold (and sometimes even if the bond is not sold), is taxed as capital gain.

For most people these days, long-term capital gains (more than one year) on bond principal are taxed at 15 percent. Any appreciated fixed-income asset bought and sold within a year is taxed at your normal income-tax rate, whatever that is. (Most middle-income Americans today are paying somewhere around 30 percent in income tax.)

Measuring the Volatility of Your Bond Holdings

When investment pros talk of *volatility,* they are talking about risk. When they talk about risk, they are talking about volatility. Volatility in an investment means that what is worth $1,000 today may be worth $900 . . . or $800 . . . tomorrow. Bonds are typically way less risky than stocks (that's why we love bonds so much), but bonds can fall in value. Some bonds are much more volatile than others, and before you invest in any bond, you should have a good idea what kind of volatility (risk) you are looking at.

Time frame matters most

The more time until the bond matures, the greater the bond's volatility. In other words, with long-term bonds, there's a greater chance that the principal value of the bond can rise or fall dramatically. Short-term bonds sway much less. On the other hand — and here's a somewhat funny contradiction — the further off your need to tap into the bond's principal, the less that volatility should matter to you.

As I explain earlier in this chapter, nothing affects the value of your bond holdings as much as prevailing interest rates. If you are holding a bond that pays 5 percent, and prevailing interest rates are 6 percent, your bond isn't worth nearly as much as it would be if prevailing interest rates were 5 percent (or, better yet, 4 percent). But just how sensitive is the price of a bond to the ups and downs of interest rates? It depends, mostly on the maturity of the bond.

Suppose you are holding a fresh 30-year bond with a coupon rate of 5 percent, and suddenly prevailing interest rates move from 5 percent to 6 percent. You are now looking at potentially 30 years of holding a bond that is paying less than the prevailing interest rate. So how attractive does that bond look to you, or anyone else? Answer: It looks like used oil dripping from the bottom of an old car.

But suppose you are holding either a very short-term bond or an old 30-year bond that matures next month. In either case, you will see your principal very soon. Does it matter much that prevailing interest rates have risen? No, not really. The price of your bond isn't going to be much affected.

Quality counts

High quality, investment-grade bonds, issued by solid governments or corporations, tend to be less volatile than junk bonds. This has nothing to do with interest rates but, rather, with the risk of default. When the economy is looking shaky and investor optimism fades, few people want to be holding the debt of entities that may fail. In times of recession and depression, high quality bonds may rise in value and junk bonds may fall, as people clamor for safety. Overall, the junk bonds will bounce in price much more than the investment-grade bonds.

The coupon rate matters, too

Returning to the effect of interest rates on bond prices, not all bonds of like maturity will have the same sensitivity to changes in prevailing rates. Aside from the maturity, you also need to consider the coupon rate. Bonds with the highest coupon rates on the market (bonds currently selling at a premium) tend to have the least volatility. Can you guess why that might be?

Imagine that you are considering the purchase of two $1,000 bonds: One matures in three years and is paying a 10 percent interest rate ($100 a year). The other also matures in three years and is paying a 5 percent rate of interest ($50 a year). Obviously, the market price of the 10 percent bond will be much higher. (It will sell at a premium vis-à-vis the 5 percent bond.) It will also be less sensitive to interest rates because you are, in effect, getting your money back sooner.

With the 5 percent bond, your investment won't pay off until the bond matures and you get your $1,000 face value (probably much more than you paid for the bond). And who knows where interest rates will be then? With the 10 percent bond, you get your investment paid back much sooner, and you are free to reinvest that money. There is much less *reinvestment* risk — the risk that you will be able to reinvest your money only at pitifully low rates.

The most volatile of bonds — those most sensitive to fluxes in interest rates — are zero-coupon bonds that pay all their interest at maturity.

Fortunately, a mathematical whiz named Frederick Macaulay gave us a formula back in the 1930s for calculating the sensitivity of a bond to prevailing interest rates. The formula works regardless of whether the bond is a zero-coupon bond or is paying regular coupons. The formula allows us to compare and contrast various bonds of various kinds to estimate their future volatility.

The wickedly complex formula measures something called *duration*. Duration tells you how much a bond will move in price if there is a 1 percent change in interest rates.

Figuring out the duration of a bond is pretty much impossible without either a Ph.D. in mathematics or a computer. If you don't have the Ph.D., use the computer (just search "bond duration calculator"), or ask the broker who wants to sell you the bond to do it for you. If you're considering purchasing a bond mutual fund, you'll find the fund's average duration (sometimes called *average effective duration*) in the prospectus or other fund literature. You'll also find it on www.morningstar.com, your brokerage firm's Web site, or any other number of sources where bond funds are contrasted and compared.

The duration formula takes into account a bond's or bonds' par value, coupon rate, yield-to-maturity, and the number of years until the bond or bonds mature. It then spits out a single number. Here is what that number means: The principal value of a bond or bond fund with a duration of, say, 6, can be expected to change 6 percent with every 1 percent change in interest rates. If prevailing interest rates go up 1 percent, the bond or bond fund should drop in value 6 percent. If interest rates fall by 1 percent, the bond or bond fund should rise 6 percent.

Of course, if you're holding an individual bond to maturity, or if you have no intention of selling off your bond fund any time in the near future, such fluctuations in price are less important than if you plan to collect your money and run any time soon.

Returning to the Bonds of Babylonia

Before moving along to Part II, I'd like to return for a moment to the beginning of this chapter and to ancient Babylonia. Here's my question: Was Mr. Nabu-usabsi's 16⅔ percent return a good or bad investment?

Part of the answer lies in the ability of Mr. Nabu-sar-ashesu (the guy who got the silver) to repay the loan. History doesn't tell us if he was a good credit risk or if, in fact, the loan was ever repaid. The other part of the answer is whether that interest rate was fair for the time. Was it in line with other similar loans? We don't quite know that, either.

Interest short run, interest long run

What we do know is that lending money at a certain fixed interest rate (such as you do when you buy a bond) is often a good idea if prevailing interest rates are falling and a bad idea if interest rates are rising. At least that's true in the short run, such as a one-year period. Mr. Nabu-usabsi was probably gleeful if interest rates fell throughout the 9th year of Nebuchadnezzar.

In the longer run, it isn't clear that falling interest rates are a bond buyer's best friend. Buying bonds at a time of rising interest rates is not necessarily a mistake. I explain in Part IV how to strategize your bond buys and sells to make money in just about any kind of economy, any interest-rate environment.

Interest rates as a barometer of society's strength

The History of Interest Rates, the tome I reference at the start of this chapter, tracks the great ups and downs of interest rates over the centuries, from ancient Babylonia to medieval Europe and from America's colonial days to today. The one conclusion that can be drawn, say the authors, is that interest rates generally show a progressive decline as each society develops and thrives, and then they rise sharply as each society declines and falls.

In Ancient Rome, for example, prevailing short-term interest rates were above 8 percent until about 250 B.C. They then fell and continued to fall until, at the height of the Roman Empire (100 B.C.–100 A.D.), loans could be had for about 4 percent. As the empire fell apart over the ensuing centuries, interest rates rose to over 12 percent by the fourth century. Similar patterns can be seen in Ancient Greece and Babylonia, and in most societies since.

The tie between interest rates and society's fortunes is easily explicable. When the times are uncertain, lenders demand more in compensation for tying up their money. After all, anything could happen in the interim. When the barbarians are knocking at the gate, you aren't going to buy any low-interest bonds in the hopes of a comfortable retirement watching gladiator games in the Coliseum.

Interest past, interest future

Historical records make it clear that interest rates have fluctuated all across the board over the millennia. But lending your money (again, as you do when you buy a bond), if done wisely, is a time-honored way of making your money work for you. Throughout the rest of this book, I show you exactly how to do that.

Part II
Numerous and Varied Ways to Make Money in Bonds

The 5th Wave   By Rich Tennant

"I'm not sure — I like the global bonds with rotating dollar signs, but the dancing municipal bonds look good too."

In this part . . .

In the next five chapters, you get a good picture of the major categories of bonds, including Treasuries (Chapter 5), corporate bonds (Chapter 6), agencies (Chapter 7), and municipal bonds (Chapter 8). Should none of the major categories suit you, I provide in Chapter 9 a thumbnail sketch of some of the more unusual, sometimes quirky kinds of bond offerings available, such as church bonds and catastrophe bonds.

In each chapter, you discover the nuances that make each bond category unique. I show you why certain kinds of bonds pay higher rates of interest than others and, at the same time, may carry more risk. You can start to zero in on the kinds of bonds that make the most sense for you — the kinds of bonds that will make your portfolio shine.

Chapter 5

"Risk-Free" Investing: U.S. Treasury Bonds

Although not from a terribly religious family, I did have a bar mitzvah. As Jewish boys have done for several millennia, I stood before the congregation and recited from the teachings of the Torah, whereupon the rabbi blessed me and told me that I had become a man.

Who was I to argue?

Soon following the rabbi's pronouncement, I found myself in a large, Long Island catering hall where I was smiled upon by the masses, told *mazel tov!* ("way to go!" in Hebrew), and handed many crisp white envelopes. Much later that memorable night, I went home, sat on my bed, and opened those many envelopes. Out poured U.S. savings bond after U.S. savings bond.

I was rich!

Or so I thought.

Little did I know at the time that a freshly minted U.S. savings bond with $100 emblazoned all over it isn't worth $100 at all. Adults like giving savings bonds as gifts to young people, because, well, I guess they figure that young people are gullible. Even smart 13-year-olds who read the Torah can get fooled. The ancient teachings may help us to know right from wrong, but, alas, they say nothing whatsoever about U.S. government debt securities.

There are some things, I suppose, that a young boy-turned-man just has to figure out for himself. And I eventually figured out that all those savings bonds strewn across my bed were worth only half as much as whatever denominations were printed on them. (I'm not complaining, mind you. I'm grateful for that money, but discovering that I had only half as much as I thought came as a bit of a blow.) Over the years, I've learned a number of other things about savings bonds and other Treasury debt securities, and in this chapter, I share that knowledge.

Please join me. You don't have to be Jewish.

Exploring the Many Ways of Investing with Uncle Sam

There are umpteen different kinds of debt securities issued by the U.S. Treasury. *Savings bonds,* which can be purchased for small amounts and come in certificate form (making for nice, if not slightly deceptive, bar mitzvah and birthday gifts), are but one kind. In fact, when investment people speak of *Treasuries,* they usually are not talking about savings bonds but, rather, about larger-denomination bonds known formerly as *Treasury bills, Treasury notes,* and *Treasury bonds* that are issued only in electronic (sometimes called *book-entry*) form. (I explain the differences between bills, notes, and bonds very shortly.)

All U.S. Treasury debt securities, whether a $50 savings bond or a $1,000 Treasury note, share four things in common:

✔ Every bond, an IOU of sorts from Uncle Sam, is backed by the "full faith and credit" of the United States government and, therefore, is considered by most investors to be the safest bet around.

✔ Because it is assumed that any principal you invest is absolutely safe, Treasury bonds, of whatever kind, tend to pay relatively modest rates of interest — lower than other comparable bonds, such as corporate bonds, that may put your principal at some risk.

✔ True, the United States government is very unlikely to go bankrupt anytime soon, but Treasury bonds are nonetheless still subject to other risks inherent in the bond market. Prices on Treasury bonds, especially those with long-term maturities, can swoop up and down like hungry hawks in response to such things as prevailing interest rates and investor confidence in the economy.

✔ All interest on U.S. government bonds is off-limits to state and local tax authorities (just as the interest on most municipal bonds is off-limits to the Internal Revenue Service). But you do pay federal tax.

Beyond these four similarities, the differences among U.S. government debt securities are many and, in some cases, like night and day. Only because I started this chapter talking about savings bonds, I address those first.

Savings bonds for beginning investors

U.S. savings bonds make for popular gifts, in part because they are, unlike other Treasury debt securities, available in pretty certificate form. You can buy them from just about any bank or directly from the Treasury at www. treasurydirect.gov. You don't have to buy them in certificate form; from the Web site, you can also buy an electronic savings bond, which is registered online (no paper involved).

Savings bonds are a natural for small investors because you can get started with as little as $25. With that money, you can buy a bond that has $50 printed on it but won't actually be worth $50 for some time to come. (Any kid who had a bar mitzvah could probably tell you that.) At the current interest rate that savings bonds are paying (3.60 percent), you would have to wait 20 years until the true value caught up with the face amount.

Aside from the (optional) certificates and the ability to invest a small amount, a third thing that makes savings bonds unique among Treasury debt securities is that that are strictly non-marketable. When you buy a U.S. savings bond, either direct from the government or from a bank, you either put your own name and Social Security number on the bond or the name and Social Security number of someone you're gifting it to. You or that person are then entitled to receive interest from that bond. The bond itself (just like an airline ticket, or your daughter) cannot be sold to another buyer. This is in stark contrast to Treasury bills and bonds that can, and often do, pass hands more often than poker chips.

Electronic savings bonds' small advantage

Savings bonds in certificate (paper) form can be purchased for $25, $50, $75, $100, $200, $500, $1,000, $5,000 and $10,000. If you go through www.treasurydirect.gov, you also have the option of buying your savings bonds — both Series EE and Series I — in electronic form. When you go that route, there's no need to pick a denomination. If you wish to invest, say, $43.45, go for it. If you want to invest $312.56, that's fine too. Any amount over $25 but under $60,000 (per individual, per year) will be accepted. Electronic bonds otherwise are just like their paper cousins: They pay the same rate of interest over the same period of time.

Note that these "denomination-free" bonds are available only through the Treasury Web site and available only with savings bonds. The marketable Treasury securities (bills, notes, or bonds) can also be purchased through the Web site but are available only in increments of $1,000.

Among savings bonds, there are various kinds. At present, the Treasury is producing only two varieties: EE Series bonds and I bonds. Some others you may have stored away in your dresser drawers may include E Series bonds and HH bonds. Each has its own characteristics.

EE (Patriot) bonds

EEs and Patriot bonds are one and the same. The word *Patriot* was added to some, but not all, EE bonds in 2001. According to the Treasury, "Patriot Bonds offer Americans one more way to express their support for our nation's anti-terrorism efforts."

Whatever you want to call them, however you wish to express your support, EE bonds are the most traditional kind of savings bond. They're the kind most people think of when they think savings bonds — the kind I got on my bar mitzvah (although they were called something different back then). Series EE bonds carry a face value of twice what you purchase them for. They are *accrual bonds,* which means that they accrue interest as the years roll on even though you aren't seeing any cash. You can pay taxes on that interest as it accrues, but in most cases it makes more sense to defer paying the taxes until you decide to redeem the bond. Uncle Sam allows you to do that.

Series EE bonds issued prior to May 2005 pay various rates of interest depending on the date of the bond. Most of these rates of interest are based on fairly complicated formulas and fluctuate over time. If you own a pre-May 2005 savings bond and you aren't sure what kind of interest the bond is paying, the best thing to do is to look it up on the Treasury Web site, www.treasurydirect.gov. EEs issued in May 2005 or afterwards pay a fixed interest rate. At the time I'm typing this paragraph, that rate is 3.60 percent. I don't know what it will be when you are reading this, but I can guarantee that it will be modest.

EE bonds are nonredeemable for the first year you own them, and if you hold them fewer than five years, you surrender three months of interest. EEs are available in eight different denominations, from $50 up to $10,000. Any individual can buy up to $30,000 in EE savings bonds a year (or a face amount of $60,000).

If you use your savings bonds to fund an education, the interest may be tax-free.

Russell's recommendation: Historically, savings bonds have paid a rate of interest that has barely kept up with inflation. Therefore, you do not want to make them a major part of your investment scheme. If you already have savings bonds, you may want to consider swapping them for a higher yielding investment. If you wish to keep them, consider opening an account at www.treasurydirect.gov and turning your paper bonds into electronic securities. That way, you won't need to worry about them getting lost or destroyed.

I bonds

These babies are built to buttress inflation. Issued in the very same denominations as EE bonds, the I Series bonds offer a fixed rate of return plus an adjustment for rising prices. Every May 1 and November 1, the Treasury announces both the fixed rate for all new I bonds and the inflation-adjustment for all new and existing I bonds. At the time I'm writing this, the fixed rate is 1.4 percent, and the inflation adjustment is a twice annual 1.55 percent. Adding them together, the I bonds are currently yielding 4.52 percent a year. (Yeah, I know that 1.55 + 1.55 + 1.4 = 4.50 percent, but the added .02 percent is due to interest on interest.)

After you buy an I bond, the fixed rate is yours for the life of the bond. The inflation rate adjusts every six months. You collect all your interest only after cashing in the bond. (That is called *accrual* interest.)

The rules and parameters for I bonds are pretty much the same as they are for EEs: You have to hold them a year, and if you sell within five years, you pay a penalty. There's a limit to how many I bonds you can invest in — $30,000 a year, per person. And in certain circumstances, the proceeds may become tax-free if used for education expenses.

Russell's recommendation: Because the rate of inflation can vary dramatically from six-month period to six-month period, there are times when I bonds make for fabulous short-term investments. In November 2005, for example, after a spike in the price of oil after Hurricane Katrina, the official inflation rate shot up, and I bonds were paying a very impressive 6.73 percent. At that point, I was recommending that anyone who had cash to invest might want to consider them very seriously. But by the following May, with inflation having cooled, the yield on I bonds dropped rather precipitously to 2.43 percent. They were no longer such a hot investment — you could have done much better with a bank CD.

Savings bonds for education

The interest on savings bonds — both EE and I bonds — may be tax-free if you use the proceeds to pay for higher education expenses. The guidelines are fairly complex, and you're eligible only if your income falls below a certain limit. Currently, for single taxpayers, the tax exclusion begins to be reduced with a $65,600 modified adjusted gross income and is eliminated for adjusted gross incomes of $80,600 and above. For married taxpayers filing jointly, the tax exclusion begins to be reduced with a $98,400 modified adjusted gross income and is eliminated at $128,400. If you're uncertain whether you qualify, speak to your tax adviser.

If you plan to hold I bonds as a long-term investment (longer than a year or two), you should be more concerned with the fixed rate, which will be in effect throughout the life of the bond, than the inflation adjustment, which will vary. Remember that if you cash out before five years, you'll pay a penalty of three months' interest. You can purchase I Bonds at your bank or by visiting www.treasurydirect.gov.

The dinosaurs

Other kinds of savings bonds pre-date today's EE and I bonds. Each series of the past has its own peculiarities, but since you won't be buying any of them, there's no need to get into detail. Suffice to say that some of the older bonds are still paying interest, and others are not. (See the sidebars "Check your savings bond stash for dead wood" and "Savings bonds don't pay interest forever!" for more info.) If you have any questions on the status of a savings bond you have tucked away in the back of your sock drawer, you can simply type the serial numbers into the Savings Bond Calculator at www.treasury direct.gov, or jot down the serial number and write a letter to

Bureau of the Public Debt
P.O. Box 7012
Parkersburg, WV 26106-7012

The Bureau of the Public Debt needs a written and signed request from the owner of the bond, at which point, it will tell you whether the bond is still earning interest, when it will stop paying interest, and how much you could redeem it for today.

Check your savings bond stash for dead wood

According to www.treasurydirect.gov, the following savings bonds no longer earn any interest. Cash them in! (As this book ages, of course, these dates will change.)

Series	Issue Date
E	May 1941–December 1976
H	June 1952– December 1976
HH	January 1980– December 1986
Freedom Shares	All
A, B, C, D, F, G, J, K	All issues

Savings bonds don't pay interest forever!

According to www.treasurydirect.gov, here's how long savings bonds earn interest based their series and issue date:

Series	Issue Date	Number of Years Bonds Earn Interest
E	May 1941–November 1965	40 years
	December 1965–June 1980	30 years
EE	All issues	30 years
H	June 1952–January 1957	29 years, 8 months
	February 1957–December 1979	30 years
HH	All issues	20 years
I	All issues	30 years
Savings Notes	All issues	30 years

Treasury bills, notes, and bonds for more serious investing

About 98 percent of the approximately $5 trillion in outstanding Treasury debt is made up not of savings bonds but of *marketable* (tradable) securities known as bills, notes, and bonds (see Figure 5-1). This "bills, notes, and bonds" stuff can be a little confusing because technically they are all bonds. They are all backed by the full faith and credit of the U.S. government. They are all issued electronically (you don't get a fancy piece of paper as you do with savings bonds). They can all be purchased either directly from the Treasury or through a broker. They can all trade like hotcakes. The major difference among them is the time you need to wait to collect your principal:

- Treasury bills have maturities of a year or less.

- Treasury notes are issued with maturities from two to ten years.

- Treasury bonds are long-term investments that have maturities of 10 to 30 years from their issue date.

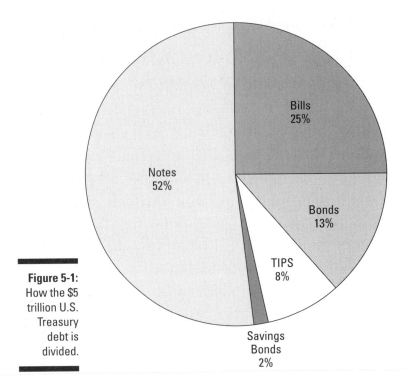

Bills
25%

Notes
52%

Bonds
13%

TIPS
8%

Savings
Bonds
2%

Figure 5-1:
How the $5
trillion U.S.
Treasury
debt is
divided.

The bills, like savings bonds, are sold at a discount from their face value. You get the full amount when the bill matures. The notes and bonds, on the other hand, are sold at their face value, have a fixed interest rate, and kick off interest payments once every six months. The minimum denomination for all three is $1,000, and you can buy them all in any increment of $1,000.

Russell's suggestion: The main difference among various Treasury offerings is the maturity. Generally, but not always, the longer the term, the higher the rate of interest. Therefore, the longer you can tie your money up, the greater your investment profits are likely to be. So one of the first questions you need to ask yourself before investing in Treasuries (or most other bonds, for that matter) is the following: *When might I need to cash this baby out?*

Keep in mind that you don't have to hold any of these securities (bills, notes, or bonds) till maturity. You can, in fact, cash out at any point. The longer until the maturity of the bond, however, the more its price can fluctuate and, therefore, the more you risk losing money. (It is because of this risk that I put the quotation marks around "Risk-Free" in the heading of this chapter — just in case you were wondering.)

U.S. Treasuries are the Mickey Mice of the international investment world

Never mind Mickey Mouse T-shirts and McDonald's hamburgers — the U.S. product that foreigners are hottest for these days is the U.S. Treasury bond. The percentage of all U.S. government bonds held by non-U.S. citizens increased from about 20 percent just a decade ago to something over 50 percent today. Some economists are very thankful for this foreign investment because it arguably fills a desperately needed role. The American people, both strapped by their medical and college bills and eager to live in homes the size of the Coliseum, aren't saving, and without saving, there can't be economic growth. But other pundits argue that all that U.S. debt in foreign hands is creating a potential debt bomb. They argue that the United States is becoming terribly vulnerable, its economy resting in the hands of foreigners who could at any moment turn evil (as foreigners often do in movies) and crush us by suddenly dumping all their Treasury bonds.

I'm not losing any sleep over this one. It's not as if all those bonds are in the hands of one rogue nation led by a crazed colonel in fatigues. They are in the hands of many nations that by and large embrace capitalism, and besides, they can't stand each other. Heck, if the Germans tried to dump U.S. Treasuries, the French would buy those bonds up, just to spite the Germans. If the Japanese were to start dumping, the Koreans would buy them up, just to anger the Japanese. And if the Canadians were to start dumping, eh? Canadians are way too polite and would never do such a thing. We should worry more about other economic issues, such as why those medical and college bills are so astronomical, than we should the exportation of our national debt.

Treasury Inflation-Protected Securities (TIPS)

Like the I bonds, Treasury Inflation-Protected Securities (TIPS), introduced in 1997, receive both interest and a twice-yearly kick up of principal for inflation. As with interest on other Treasury securities, interest on TIPS is free from state and local income taxes. Federal income tax, however, must be coughed up each year on both the interest payments and the growth in principal.

TIPS, unlike I bonds, are transferable. You can buy TIPS directly from the Treasury or through a broker. (More detailed purchasing instructions are coming later in this chapter.) They are currently being issued with terms of 5 and 10 years, although there are plenty of 20-year term TIPS in circulation. The minimum investment is $1,000.

One of the sweet things about TIPS is that if inflation goes on a rampage, your principal moves north right along with it. If *deflation,* a lowering of prices, occurs (which it hasn't since the 1930s), you won't get any inflation adjustment, but you won't get a deflation adjustment, either. You'll get back at least the face value of the bond.

TIPS sound great, and in many ways they are. But be aware that the coupon rate on TIPS varies with market conditions and tends to be minimal — perhaps a couple of percentage points. If inflation is calmer than expected moving into the future, you will almost certainly do better with traditional Treasuries. If inflation turns out to be higher than expected, your TIPS will be the stars of your fixed-income portfolio.

Russell's suggestion: Over the very long haul, I would fully expect the return on TIPS to be roughly the same as that on other similar-maturity Treasuries. But on a year-to-year basis, the two kinds of bonds will flip-flop. Flip-flopping — another word for diversification — is a good thing! I generally recommend to clients that about one-third of their bond portfolio be devoted to inflation-protected securities. I would recommend more, but most portfolios also have stocks (and some have commodities and real estate), and these have a good track record of keeping up with inflation.

Setting the Standard by Which All Other Bonds Are Measured

Because the market assumes that the U.S. government is not going under in our lifetimes (probably a fair assumption), there are no ratings on Treasury bonds as there are with corporate bonds and municipal bonds. (I cover corporates and munis in Chapters 6 and 8.) The markets for Treasuries are also extremely *efficient,* meaning that there are so many buyers and sellers, and any information worth having is way public, that any true "deal" will be very hard to find. So the only real questions you need to ask yourself about Treasuries are the following:

- Do I want Treasuries in my portfolio and, if so, how much?
- Do I want short-term, intermediate-term, or long-term Treasuries?
- Do I want inflation protection?
- How do I go about buying a Treasury?

Turning to Treasuries in times of turmoil

When you buy Treasury bonds, you get the full faith and credit of the U.S. government assuring you your money back. In addition, there's no chance of a costly downgrade, there's no chance of an early call should interest rates fall, and the liquidity is downright oceanic. These problems — downgrading, callability, and lack of liquidity — are alien to investors in Treasuries but all too common to investors in corporate bonds (see Chapter 6) and municipal bonds (see Chapter 8).

Perhaps the most succulent thing about Treasuries, however, is their delightfully low correlation to the stock market. When the world is in turmoil and the economy starts to quiver, stocks tend to tumble. But Treasuries — as money pours in from investors looking for a safe place to hide — start to shine. History has seen this over and over.

According to data from Ibbotson Associates, a Morningstar company, during the darkest economic days of September 1929 through June 1932, long-term Treasuries showed a total annualized return of 4.84 percent. Not bad for a time when the general price level was dropping. During the more recent bear market of September 2000 through September 2002, Treasuries returned an annual 12.81 percent, as people flocked to safety and prevailing interest rates fell.

The downside to Treasuries: Modest returns over the long run. Since 1926, the U.S. stock market has seen an average annual return of 10.4 percent. Long-term government bonds have seen an average annual return of 5.5 percent. These numbers are before inflation. After inflation, the numbers move quite far apart: 7.1 percent annual return for the stock market and 2.4 percent for Treasuries — a real-return advantage of almost 300 percent for stocks. (Inflation eats away at your investment every day of the year, while interest is paid semiannually, so the formula for figuring post-inflation returns is a bit complicated. Trust me, the numbers above are correct.)

Russell's suggestion: Yes, you want Treasuries in your portfolio. Given their modest returns, you don't want overkill, however. Some Treasuries, some higher-yielding corporate or other bonds, some stock, some commodities, and maybe some real estate make the most sense for most people. As for the fixed-income side of your portfolio, depending on your risk profile, you may want to put somewhere between one-third and two-thirds of your bond allocation into Treasuries (see Chapter 13).

Picking your own maturity

Just like the question of bonds versus stocks, and government bonds versus corporate bonds, the question of maturity is largely a question of how much risk you care to stomach. In general, the more years till a bond's maturity, the more volatile the price swings.

Not only are price swings an issue when buying a long-term bond (granted, less of an issue if you plan to hold the bond till maturity), but long-term bonds carry a much greater *reinvestment* risk. In other words, if you're holding a 20-year Treasury bond and the coupon rate is 6 percent, you have no guarantee that you'll be able to reinvest your twice-yearly interest payments at 6 percent. If prevailing interest rates drop to 5 percent or 4 percent, you stand to lose . . . a very considerable amount over the 20 years.

Of course, the longer the term of the bond, generally the higher the coupon rate. So choosing a maturity can be a tricky decision. Many financial professionals suggest a compromise and going primarily with intermediate-term Treasuries (seven- to ten-year maturities).

Russell's suggestion: It's hard to go wrong with an intermediate-term Treasury note. On the other hand, if you're investing for the long run, and especially if you are investing in a bond fund where the interest is automatically reinvested, getting the extra juice from longer-term Treasuries may be the way to go. Short-term Treasuries, for the individual investor, generally make sense only when the rate those bonds are paying is higher than that of money market funds and bank CDs. Sometimes that will be the case, other times not. Keep in mind that you will pay state and local tax on the interest from the CDs and from most money market funds, but not on the interest from the Treasuries.

The yield curve and what it means

Every amateur weathercaster knows that black clouds above mean a stormy day ahead. For economists, an *inverted yield curve* serves as a black cloud indicating stormy economic times ahead.

An inverted yield curve simply means that short-term Treasuries are paying higher yields than long-term Treasuries. In normal times, longer-term bonds pay higher interest rates than short-term bonds. That's because investors demand higher returns for agreeing to tie up their money for longer and to take the inherent risks that doing so involves.

Why might things occasionally turn on their head? The common belief is that inverted yield curves result when bond buyers collectively get nervous about the economic future. To alleviate their anxiety, they commit their money to long-term bonds. That way, they figure, when things tank and interest rates drop (as they often do in times of recession), their existing bonds will be worth more.

Are bond buyers right? Can they foretell a recession coming? Historically, the answer is sometimes yes and sometimes no. While an inverted yield curve has preceded a number of recessions, there have also been times, such as in 1995 and again in 1998, when yield-curve inversions were followed by a decidedly robust year. Like all other economic indicators, the bond yield curve, although better than tea leaves at predicting the future, is far, far from perfect.

Here is what a normal bond yield curve looks like and what an inverted one looks like. Note that what you're looking at, unlike a stock chart, does not show price movements over time. Rather, it shows the current interest being paid on short-term bonds versus long-term bonds.

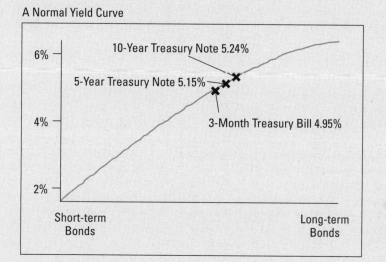

A Normal Yield Curve

10-Year Treasury Note 5.24%
5-Year Treasury Note 5.15%
3-Month Treasury Bill 4.95%

Short-term Bonds — Long-term Bonds

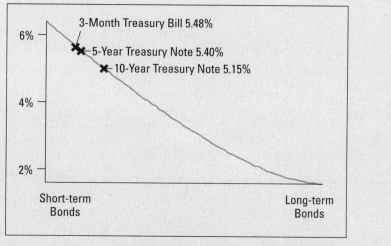

An Inverted Yield Curve

3-Month Treasury Bill 5.48%
5-Year Treasury Note 5.40%
10-Year Treasury Note 5.15%

Short-term Bonds — Long-term Bonds

Deciding whether you want inflation protection or not

As I'm writing this chapter, the current yield on a traditional ten-year Treasury is 4.70 percent. The yield on ten-year TIPS is 2.4 percent. I look at each. I compare. Inflation has been running at about 3 a year lately. I reckon the Feds will therefore adjust my TIPS by 3 percent a year. I add that 3 percent to the 2.4 percent, and I come up with 5.4 percent for the TIPS versus 4.7 percent for the traditional. If my calculations are correct and the TIPS do, in fact, adjust upward 3 percent, I wind up ahead.

My hunch is that most bond buyers and maybe the people at the Treasury are figuring on a lower inflation rate moving forward. If it winds up as 2 percent a year over the next ten years, I'll see only a 4.4 percent return on my TIPS, and I'll kick myself for not loading up on traditional Treasuries. But if inflation shoot ups, I'll be in the catbird seat.

Who the heck knows.

 Russell's suggestion: Unless you can tell the future and predict interest rates and inflation (um, you can't), you want both traditional bonds *and* inflation-protected bonds in your portfolio.

Entering the Treasury Marketplace

Buying a Treasury bill, note, bond, or inflation-protected security is a heck of a lot easier than buying most other bonds. With Treasuries, you needn't worry about such things as credit rating, callability, liquidity, and getting socked with high broker markups. (I talk about all these delightful aspects of bond-buying in the next several chapters.)

Uncle Sam's bonds can be purchased directly from, and sold to, the old man himself. Or not. It's your call.

Buying direct or through a broker?

Buying directly from, or selling to, the federal government is simply a matter of logging onto www.treasurydirect.gov. Or, if you prefer to do it the old fashioned way, by phone and mail, your can contact Legacy Treasury Direct at 1-800-722-2678. (For savings bonds, call 1-800-245-2804.) Buying and selling direct is certainly the most economical way to go. In fact, there is no charge for any transactions. You can keep all your Treasuries with Treasury Direct, and there is no fee. If you go with Legacy Treasury Direct, there is no fee until your account tops $100,000, at which point, you have to pay $25 a year.

Treasury strips

One kind of Treasury issue is available only through brokers, and that is called a *strip*. A Treasury strip is something of a strange duck. It is, in essence, a single interest payment of a bond that has been "stripped" from the rest of the bond.

For example, a $1,000, 20-year Treasury bond paying 5 percent offers 40 semiannual payments of $40 and one final principal payment of $1,000. If you want to invest in such a bond but have no need for immediate income, you may purchase a strip, which would offer you, say, only the final interest payment and the principal.

Strips are sold, like Treasury bills, at a deep discount. You collect no interest for the time you hold the strip and collect your cash only when you redeem it. You may, for example, pay $400 for a strip that will pay you back $1,000 in 20 years. That would represent an annual interest rate of 4.688 percent.

Debt securities that work this way are called *zero-coupon* securities. Zero-coupons can be very volatile. If you need to cash out early, you may not get nearly what you bargained for. They are also not very tax friendly. You're taxed on the interest as if you are paid annually, even though you get no cash. You may want to consider a strip only for your retirement account.

The only reason to go through a broker, really, would be if you have a compulsion to house all your assets under one roof. Most brokers charge a minimal amount for dealing in Treasuries. Fidelity, for example, charges $1 per bond if done by phone; 50 cents if done online.

The market for Treasuries is extremely *efficient,* which means that there are so many buyers and sellers and bonds that the chance of finding a "deal" (as you may — or may not — in the corporate bond market) is rather remote. What you pay for a ten-year Treasury is pretty much what the next guy is going to pay. Your yield is pretty much what the next guy is going to get.

Before you deal with any bond broker, whether for Treasuries or any other bond, please read Chapter 15. For Treasuries, I'd rather see you buy direct.

Appreciating the difference between new and used bonds

Does it make much difference whether you buy new (*on-the-run*) or old (*off-the-run*) Treasuries? In other words, if you want to make a 10-year investment in Treasuries, does it matter whether you buy a new 10-year note or an old 20-year bond that has 10 years till maturity? No, not much. The yields should be very, very similar. The only difference, really, is that when buying the old bond, you'll have to go through a broker, and the broker will likely charge you a nominal fee.

No repose for investors in repos

Repos, short for *repurchase agreements,* are contracts for the sale and future repurchase of a financial asset, most usually Treasury securities. The repo market is huge and complex, and most of the players are professional investment types. For the average person with a mortgage to pay and mouths to feed, plunking money into repos is potentially dangerous business. But if risk is your middle name, you can enter the repo market through most large brokerage houses.

In essence, you buy a barrelful of Treasuries for little money. That's known as *leveraging.* If you're familiar with buying stocks on margin, it's somewhat similar to that. But instead of banking on a company stock's rise or fall, you'll be banking on a rise or fall in interest rates, which, in turn affects the price of Treasuries. If interest rates fall and bond prices go up, you can make out like a bandit. If you're wrong, however, you pay the piper. The broker will be lending you money to finance this speculation; make sure you ask for the repo rate of interest, which is generally less than the interest on other kinds of borrowing (as it should be, because the broker has your leveraged bonds as collateral).

Tapping Treasuries through mutual funds and exchange-traded funds

According to Morningstar, U.S. investors have 660 federal government bond mutual funds and exchange-traded funds from which to choose. You could also buy your government bonds packed in something called a *unit investment trust.* Whichever of these three options you choose, you could, in a flash, own a bevy of Treasuries, either with similar or different maturities. If you choose your fund well, your instant diversification will come at very little cost.

Diversification of Treasury bonds isn't as important as it is with, say, corporate high-yield bonds, but still . . . for the minimal cost of some bond funds (as little as 15 *basis points* or 15/100 percent a year in operating expenses), they make a darned good option for most investors. I share my pick of favorite Treasury funds in Chapter 16.

Chapter 6

Industrial Returns: Corporate Bonds

*O*h sure, the strength of our economy and the vigor of our industry rely much on the progress of science, the foundations of democracy, and the labors of a motivated and educated workforce. I don't mean to belittle any of that, but what *really* moves our economy and bolsters our industry, the single most driving force in capitalism, without which we'd all be living in huts and eating cold gruel, is *OPM*: Other People's Money.

New businesses start every day, with the initial funding typically coming from the savings of an intrepid entrepreneur or the good graces of a supportive mom and dad. But to move a seedling of a business from the garage (where Bill Gates started) to the storefront on Main Street to the malls or industrial parks of America requires OPM. And OPM comes to a business mainly from two sources: selling shares of the business to stockholders, or borrowing money from bondholders.

In this chapter, I ask you to consider becoming a corporate bondholder. By so doing, you can help drive our economy and our society to new heights and spare the masses from having to eat gruel. Well, maybe. That's perhaps an overstatement. And possibly, it's beside the point. Let's forget about society and gruel for the moment and just talk about what corporate bonds can do for your personal wealth, shall we?

Why Invest in These Sometimes Pains-in-the-Butt?

To put it bluntly, corporate bonds can be something of a pain in the pants, especially when compared to Treasury bonds (see Chapter 5). Here's what you need to worry about when investing in corporate bonds:

- ✔ **The solidity of the company issuing the bond:** If the company goes down, you may lose some or all of your money. Even if the company doesn't go down but merely limps, you can lose some or all of your money.

- ✔ **Callability:** There's a chance that the issuing company may call in your bond and spit your money back in your face at some terribly inopportune moment (such as when prevailing interest rates have just taken a tumble).

- ✔ **Liquidity:** Will someone be there to offer you a fair price if and when you need to sell? Will selling the bond require paying some broker a big, fat mark-up?

- ✔ **Economic upheaval:** In tough economic times, when many companies are closing their doors (and the stocks in your portfolio are plummeting), your bonds may decide to join in the unhappy nosedive, *en masse*. There go your hopes for an easy, sleep-in-late retirement.

So why even mess with corporate bonds?

Ah . . . that is a question that some of the world's most prominent investment experts have also asked, and they don't all come up with the same answer. Some argue that corporate bonds are indeed worth all the hassle and doubt because the higher rates of interest they pay make them preferable to Treasuries. Others argue that the difference in interest rates between corporate bonds and Treasuries (known as *the spread*) isn't worth the potential trouble of holding corporates.

Comparing corporate bonds to Treasuries

You may ask yourself why I start a chapter on corporate bonds by comparing them to Treasuries. There are, of course, other kinds of bonds. Municipals (which I cover in Chapter 8) are often appropriate for people in higher income brackets, but they are never a good choice for tax-advantaged accounts such as IRAs and 401(k) plans, where the vast majority of Americans have most of their savings. Agency bonds (Chapter 7) can sometimes substitute for Treasuries, but their inordinate complexities make them inappropriate for many individual investors. High-yield bonds, otherwise known as *junk bonds* (which I discuss later in this chapter), don't add much stability to a portfolio. And international bonds (Chapter 9) are good for added diversification but, because of currency flux, should probably play a limited role in your investment strategies.

No, when it comes to adding stability to a portfolio — the number one reason that bonds belong in your portfolio, if you ask me — Treasuries and investment-grade (high quality) corporate bonds are your two best choices. They may have saved your grandparents from destitution during the Great Depression. They may have spared your 401(k) when most stocks hit the skids in 2000–2002.

But which is preferable: government-issue bonds or bonds issued by the for-profit sector of our economy?

Hearing it from the naysayers

Some people, including David Swensen, chief investment officer of Yale University, see little virtue in corporate debt. Swenson argues in *Unconventional Success: A Fundamental Approach to Personal Investment* (Free Press) that corporations have a primary duty to their shareholders to make as much money as possible for the company — and that means the financial officers have a duty to make sure that their bondholders never get a fair shake. He writes:

> Many investors purchase corporate bonds, hoping to get something for nothing by earning an incremental yield over that available from U.S. Treasury bonds. . . . At the end of the day, excess returns prove illusory as credit risk, illiquidity, and optionality work against the holder of corporate obligations, providing less than nothing to the corporate bond investor.

"In general, I'd say that Swensen is right, and the modestly excess yield you're going to get in corporates is not worth it," says Don Taylor, Ph.D., CFP, associate professor of finance with The American College in Bryn Mawr, Pennsylvania. (Many U.S. financial planners get their education at The American College.) "With Treasuries, you're getting the full faith and credit of the U.S. government, and you're buying an asset class that is not correlated to the stock market," he says. "You're going to get better diversification — and you're especially going to get better protection in a worst-case market scenario."

But then there's the other side of the argument.

Taking a cue from the other side

"Those people who make unequivocal statements about never buying corporate bonds because the excess return over Treasuries is so paltry are generally not the same people who have to live on a limited fixed income," says Marilyn Cohen, president of Envision Capital Management, an investment advisory firm in southern California specializing in fixed income. "The experts are generally pretty well-heeled people, and it's hard for them to relate to the small investor, especially the retired small investor, who is seeing his grocery prices go up every week and desperately needs a few extra *basis points* just to pay the bills." (One basis point equals 1/100 of a percentage point.)

Dan Fuss, vice chairman of Loomis, Sayles & Company, a highly regarded bond mutual fund company, says there's nothing wrong with Treasuries, for sure, but despite the credit risk and the frequent callability features, corporate bonds often offer real economic opportunity — "especially for those willing to do some work, and uncover value in the marketplace." The veteran fund manager isn't just blowing smoke. His flagship Loomis Sayles Bond Fund (LSBRX), which taps mostly intermediate- and long-term good quality corporate bonds, has a 15-year annualized return of roughly 11 percent. (I talk more about Loomis Sayles and other bond funds in Chapter 16. In Chapter 21, I feature a Q&A with Dan Fuss.)

So there you have it. What, you may wonder, do I expect you to do with this contradictory advice?

Well, not to cop a line from old King Solomon or anything, but you could split the baby and include both Treasuries *and* corporate bonds in your portfolio. That's what I do with my own money and for most of my clients. That way, you can get the best of both worlds.

Considering historical returns

It's hard to argue with Professor Don Taylor's logic: During worst-case scenarios, people do flock to safety. However, if we look at some of the worst economic times in our nation's history, corporate investment-grade (high quality) bonds have held up remarkably well. According to data from Ibbotson Associates, a Morningstar company, during the gloomiest economic days of September 1929 through June 1932, long-term corporate bonds showed a total annualized return of 2.99 a year, versus 4.84 for long-term Treasuries. During the more recent bear market of September 2000 through September 2002, long-term corporates surprisingly outperformed Treasuries, 15.08 percent versus 12.81 percent.

Generally, corporate bonds tend to outperform Treasuries when the economy is good and underperform when the economy lags.

Over the long run, corporate bonds outdistance Treasuries by a solid margin. According to Lehman Brothers data, corporate investment-grade bonds of all maturities and durations have collectively outperformed their counterpart Treasury issues in 17 of the past 26 years, averaging about 90 basis points (90/100 of one percent) more a year (see Figure 6-1).

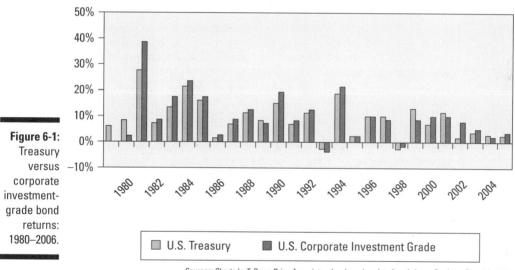

Figure 6-1: Treasury versus corporate investment-grade bond returns: 1980–2006.

Sources: Charts by T. Rowe Price Associates, Inc. based on data from Lehman Brothers. Copyright 2007. Used with permission. Lehman Brothers Global Family of Indices. Copyright 2007. Used with permission.

Since 1980, the overall annualized real return on Treasuries, give or take a few basis points, has been about 3 percent. The overall annualized return on corporate investment-grade bonds has been roughly 4 percent. That's a difference in return (if you're looking up from down below, and talking ratios) of one-third. A basket of corporate bonds invested over the past 26 years would now be worth nearly15 percent more than a basket of Treasury bonds (see Figure 6-2).

Most years, but not all, corporate bonds show greater returns than Treasury bonds of similar maturity. Over time, the incremental difference grows, as you can see in the squiggly line over the top of the bar chart.

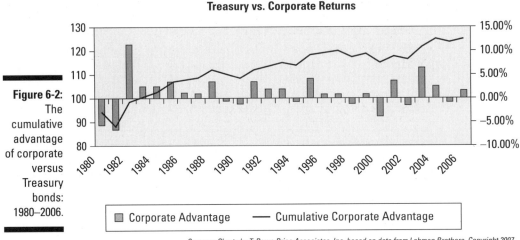

Figure 6-2:
The cumulative advantage of corporate versus Treasury bonds: 1980–2006.

Getting Moody: The Crucial Credit Ratings

Appropriately weighing potential risk and return is what good investing is all about, really. As for the risk and return on corporate bonds, the potential return (always something of a guessing game) is quoted in terms of yield, and there are many kinds of yield. If you haven't yet read Chapter 4, now may be a good time to do so; I detail the various kinds of yield there. The most oft-quoted kind of yield, used for example by *The Wall Street Journal* and most other business papers, is the *yield-to-maturity*.

The spread between corporate bonds and government bonds is quoted in most newspapers and financial Web sites in terms of basis points (1/100 of a percentage) and given as a range. For example, on the day I'm writing this, the range for corporate investment-grade bonds is 84–98. That means investment-grade corporate bonds, as a whole, are offering a yield-to-maturity that is between 84/100 and 98/100 of 1 percentage point higher than that of Treasury bonds of similar maturity. So, for example, if a 20-year Treasury bond were currently yielding 5 percent to maturity, you would expect 20-year corporate bonds to be paying somewhere between 5.84 and 5.98 percent.

Is that extra .84 to .98 percent worth the added risk of owning a corporate bond? That depends largely on your individual risk tolerance, something I help you determine throughout this book, especially in Chapter 10.

But just as risk–return tradeoff exists between corporate bonds and Treasuries, there is also a big risk–return tradeoff among corporate bonds. The largest determinant of the risk and return you take on a bond is the fiscal muscle of the company behind the bond. That fiscal muscle is measured by a company's credit ratings.

Revisiting your ABCs

There's an entire industry devoted to rating companies by their financial strength. The most common ratings come from Moody's and Standard & Poor's, but there are other rating services, such as Fitch Ratings, Dominion, and A.M. Best. (See the nearby sidebar "Growing discomfort with the credit-rating business.")

Your broker, I assure you, subscribes to at least two of these services and will be happy to share the ratings with you.

The highest ratings — Moody's Aaa and Standard & Poor's AAA — are the safest of the safe among corporate bonds, and those ratings are given to few corporations. If you lend money to one of these stellar companies, you should expect in return a rate of interest only modestly higher than Treasuries. As you progress from these five-star companies down the ladder, you can expect higher rates of interest to compensate you for your added risk.

Table 6-1 shows how Moody's, Standard and Poor's, and Fitch define corporate bond credit quality ratings.

Table 6-1	Corporate Bond Credit Quality Ratings		
Credit Risk	*Moody's*	*Standard & Poor's*	*Fitch*
Investment grade			
Tip-top quality	Aaa	AAA	AAA
Premium quality	Aa	AA	AA
Near-premium quality	A	A	A
Take-home-to-Mom quality	Baa	BBB	BBB
Not investment grade			
Borderline ugly	Ba	BB	BB
Ugly	B	B	B

(continued)

Table 6-1 *(continued)*

Credit Risk	Moody's	Standard & Poor's	Fitch
Definitely don't-take-home-to-Mom quality	Caa	CCC	CCC
You'll be extremely lucky to get your money back	Ca	CC	CC
Interest payments have halted or bankruptcy is in process	C	D	C
Already in default	C	D	D

If you are going to invest in individual bonds, diversification through owning multiple bonds becomes more important as you go lower on the quality ladder. There's a much greater risk of default down there, so you'd be awfully foolish to have all your eggs in a basket rated Caa or CCC. (*Default* in bond-talk means that you bid adieu to your principal.)

Keep in mind that one risk inherent to corporate bonds is that they may be downgraded, even if they never default. Say a bond is rated A by Moody's. If Moody's gets moody and later rates that bond a Baa, the market will respond unfavorably. Chances are, in such a case, that the value of your bond will drop. Of course, the opposite is true, as well. If you buy a Baa bond and it suddenly becomes an A bond, you'll be sitting pretty. If you wish to hold your bond to maturity, such downgrades and upgrades are not going to much matter. But should you decide to sell your bond, they can matter very much.

It's a very good idea to diversify your bonds not only by company but also by industry. If there is a major upheaval in, say, the utility industry, the rate of both downgrades and defaults is sure to rise. In such a case, you would be better off not having all utility bonds.

Gauging the risk of default

How often do defaults occur?

According to a study by the folks at Moody's covering the years 1970 to 2005, the odds of a corporate bond rated Aaa defaulting were rather miniscule: 0.36 percent within 10 years and 0.64 percent within 20 years. Of all corporate bonds, only about 2 percent are given that gloriously high rating.

Growing discomfort with the credit-rating business

Two of the bond-rating service companies, Moody's and Standard & Poor's, together control some 80 percent of the reportedly very lucrative credit-rating market. The U.S. government was willing to look the other way until both companies failed to notice some rather serious problems at both Enron and WorldCom shortly before they went bankrupt.

After years of investigation, a law was signed in September 2006 called The Credit Agency Reform Act. The act gave birth to a designation — NRSRO (Nationally Recognized Statistical Rating Organization) — that the government now awards to rating-service companies. The new designation, currently held by both Moody's and Standard & Poor's and a handful of others, gives the Securities and Exchange Commission some oversight over these companies. Industry insiders seem to agree that the oversight, while a good thing in theory, hasn't quite shaken the industry yet. Most industry insiders also seem to agree that the major bond-rating services generally do a good job and that the Enron and WorldCom disasters were rare occurrences. Of course, if you were one of those people who lost a bundle . . .

As you move down the ladder, as you would expect, the default numbers jump. Bonds rated A can be expected to default at a rate of 0.87 percent over 10 years and 1.55 percent over 20 years. Among Baa bonds, 11.40 percent can be expected to go belly up within a decade, and 13.84 percent within two decades.

By the time you get down to Caa bonds, the rate of default is generally expected to be about 40 times that of Aaa bonds — approximately 14 percent within one decade and 26 percent within two decades. (Of course, these rates can vary greatly with economic conditions.)

Special Considerations for Investing in Corporate Debt

Just as maturity is a major consideration when choosing a Treasury (see Chapter 5), it should also be tops on your shopping list when picking a corporate bond. In general (but certainly not always), the longer the bond's maturity, the higher its interest rate will be because your money will potentially be tied up longer. And the longer the maturity, the greater the volatility of the price of the bond should you wish to cash out at any point.

One consideration that pertains to corporate bonds but not to Treasuries is the nasty issue of callability. Treasuries aren't called. (Once upon a time they were, but no longer.) Corporate bonds (as well as municipal bonds and agency bonds) often are. And that can make a huge difference in the profitability of your investment.

Calculating callability

Few things in life are as frustrating as a computer crashing. It seems to catch all of us at the least opportune moment, such as right smack in the middle of a huge work project. If you own a callable bond, chances are that it will be called at the worst moment — just as interest rates are falling and the value of your bond is on the rise. At that moment, the company that issued the bond, if it has the right to issue a call, no doubt will. And why not? Interest rates have fallen. The firm can pay you off and find someone else to borrow money from at a lower rate.

Because calls aren't fun, callable bonds must pay higher rates of interest.

If you're inclined to go for that extra juice that comes with a callable bond, I say fine. *But,* you should always do so with the assumption that your callable bond will be called. With that in mind, ask the broker to tell you how much (*after* taking his markup into consideration) your yield will be between today and the call date. Consider that a worst-case-yield. (It is often referred to as *yield-to-worst-call,* sometimes abbreviated YTW.) Consider it the yield you'll get. And compare that to the yield you'll be getting on other comparable bonds. If you choose the callable bond and it winds up not being called, hey, that's gravy.

I speak more of comparing yields in Chapter 15 where I discuss the mechanics of buying and selling individual bonds. For now, I'll just say that some squirrelly bond brokers, to encourage you to place your order to buy, will assure you that a certain callable bond is unlikely to be called. They may be right in some cases, but you should never bank on such promises.

Coveting convertibility

The flip side of a callable bond is a *convertible* bond. Some corporate bond issuers sell bonds that can be converted into a fixed number of shares of common stock. With a convertible bond, a lender (bondholder) can become a part owner (stockholder) of the company by converting the bond into company stock. Having this option is a desirable thing (options are always desirable, no?), and so convertible bonds generally pay lower interest rates than do similar bonds that are not convertible.

If the stock performs poorly, then there is no conversion. You are stuck with your bond's lower return (lower than what a nonconvertible corporate bond would get). If the stock performs well, there is a conversion. So you win, so to speak.

Know this: Convertible bonds, which are fairly common among corporate bonds, introduce a certain measure of unpredictability into a portfolio. As I explain in Chapter 12, perhaps the most important investment decision you can make is how to divide your portfolio between stocks and bonds. With convertibles, whatever careful allotment you come up with can be changed overnight. Your bonds suddenly become stocks. You are rewarded for making a good investment. But just as soon as you receive that reward, your portfolio becomes riskier. It's the old trade-off in action.

While I'm not saying that convertible bonds are horrible investments, I'm not sure they deserve a very sizeable allotment in most individuals' portfolios.

Reversing convertibility . . . imagine that

One relative newcomer to the world of corporate bonds is the *reverse convertible* security, sometimes referred to as *a revertible* or *a revertible note*. I've gotten a lot of calls lately from hungry and pushy salespeople trying to get me to buy one, but I'm really not too thrilled with this product.

A reverse convertible converts to a stock automatically if a certain company stock tumbles below a certain point by a certain date. Why would anyone want such a thing? You guessed it: The bond pays a thrillingly high interest rate (perhaps 2 or 3 percentage points above and beyond even the high rates paid on junk bonds), but only for a year or so. That's the hook. The catch is that the company paying the high interest rate is often in dire trouble. If it goes under, you could lose a bundle. Is that really the kind of risk you want to take with a fixed-income investment?

Appreciating High-Yield for What It Is

There is no fine line between investment-grade and high-yield bonds, sometimes known as *junk* bonds. But generally, if a bond receives a rating less than a Baa from Moody's or a BBB from Standard & Poor's, the market considers it high-yield.

High-yield bonds offer greater excitement for the masses. The old adage that risk equals return is clear as day in the world of bonds. High-yield bonds offer greater yield than investment-grade bonds, and they are more volatile. But they are also one other thing: much more correlated to the stock market. In fact, Treasuries and investment-grade corporate bonds aren't correlated to the stock market at all. So if bonds are going to serve as ballast for our portfolios, which is what they do best, why would anyone want high-yield bonds?

Um . . . I'm not entirely sure. I think that many people misunderstand them, and if they understood them better, they probably wouldn't invest.

Anticipating good times ahead

If the economy is strong, then companies are making money, the public is optimistic, and stocks are going to sail. So may high-yield bonds, but stocks historically return much more than high-yield bonds.

In general, a basket of high-yield bonds may return a percentage point or two or three more than high quality bonds, but very rarely more than that. Stocks have a century-old track record of returning about five percentage points more than high quality bonds. And, unless you have those bonds in a retirement account, you're going to pay income tax on the interest. Most of the gain in your stocks, however, won't be taxed at all until you sell the stock. Even then, it will most likely be taxed as capital gains — 15 percent — which is probably lower than your income tax.

If there are good times coming, stocks are very likely going to do better than any kind of fixed income.

Preparing for the bad times

If the economy starts to sour and companies start closing their doors, then stocks will fall and high-yield bonds very likely will too. In 2000, for example, when the stock market started to crumble, a basket of high-yield bonds would have lost between 3 and 4 percent. That's not a tragedy, but the last thing you want is for your bonds to turn south right along with your stocks.

Investing in high-yields judiciously

You can see that I'm not a big fan of high-yield bonds. For most people, I don't suggest a very large allocation, if any at all.

For people who really want junk bonds in their portfolios, I often suggest a serious look at foreign high-yield bonds, especially the bonds of emerging-market nations, which can make a lot of sense. That's because they don't have much, if any, correlation to the ups and downs on Wall Street. I discuss emerging-market bonds in Chapter 9.

In some cases, I may add domestic high-yield bonds to a portfolio as a means of reducing risk. But rather than substituting high-yield bonds for investment-grade bonds, I substitute the high-yield bonds for stocks. Less potential return. Less potential loss. High-yield bonds are a sort of hybrid equity/fixed income. But I generally suggest this strategy only if you can place the high-yields in a tax-advantaged account, such as an IRA.

Whenever you invest in riskier securities, the importance of diversification becomes magnified. Investing in individual junk bonds, unless you're very wealthy and can spread the risk among many junk bonds, is not something I would ever recommend. There are some very good high-yield bond funds available, and I would suggest you choose one of those. I list some of my favorites in Chapter 16.

If you're wealthy (or not-so-wealthy but you choose to ignore my advice and invest in individual high-yields anyway), know that the broker markups can sometimes kill you. I discuss how to buy individual corporate bonds and not get killed in Chapter 15.

Chapter 7

Lots of Protection (and Just a Touch of Confusion): Agency Bonds

*Y*ou've no doubt heard the story of the three blind, er, sight-impaired men and the elephant . . . how the first man touches the tail and assumes the elephant is like a snake; the second touches the tusk and assumes the elephant is like a spear; and the third touches the side of the animal and assumes the elephant is like a wall. Welcome to the touch-me, feel-me, open to wide interpretation world of agency bonds!

Don't get me wrong. There are some good investments to be had here. All you have to do is figure out the tusk from the tail.

Some agency bonds are, like Treasury bonds (see Chapter 5), backed by the so-called full faith and credit of the United States government. You're going to get your principal back even if Congress has to do the unthinkable and tax the rich.

Most agency bonds, however, are not backed by full faith and credit, but perhaps half the faith and credit of the United States government. The language used is that the federal government has assumed a "moral obligation" or "an implied guarantee" to stand behind these bonds. We investment experts nod when we hear this, try to look smart, and say that we know what that means. Truth be told, we're all a bit cloudy on the concept. No one I've ever met seems to know what "an implied guarantee" really means.

I can tell you, however, that no one ever lost his principal investing in agency bonds due to a default.

Some agency bonds are traditional in the sense that they pay a steady rate of interest and usually, like most bonds, issue payments twice a year. Others are more free-floating. And yet others are entirely different animals — not big elephants with tusks and tails, but maybe odd ducks with oily wings. These odd ducks are called *mortgage-backed securities*; they pay interest *and* principal, usually monthly, with the amount potentially varying greatly from payment to payment.

It would be impossible in one chapter, perhaps even in an entire book, to cover all the ins and outs, whys and wherefores of agency bonds. I do my best on the following pages to give you a good overview.

Slurping Up Your Alphabet Soup

Who or what issues agency bonds? Following are just some of the many agencies that issue bonds:

- Federal Farm Credit Banks (FFCB)
- Federal Home Loan Bank (FHLB)
- Federal Home Loan Mortgage Corporation (FHLMC)
- Federal National Mortgage Association (FNMA)
- Financial Assistance Corporation (FAC)
- Financing Corporation (FICO)
- General Services Administration (GSA)
- Government National Mortgage Association (GNMA)
- Government Trust Certificates (GTC)
- Private Export Funding Corporation (PEFCO)
- Resolution Funding Corporation (REFCORP)
- Small Business Administration (SBA)
- Tennessee Valley Authority (TVA)
- U.S. Agency for International Development (USAID)

Don't get lost in this alphabetical muck!

The first thing to know about these various government agencies is that they fit under two large umbrellas. Some of them really are United States federal agencies; they are an actual part of the government just as are Congress, the jet engines on Air Force One, and the fancy silverware at the White House. Such official agencies include the General Services Administration, the Government National Mortgage Association, and the Small Business Administration. The U.S. Post Office also once issued bonds but has not done so lately.

Most of the so-called agencies, however, aren't quite parts of the government. They are, technically speaking, *government-sponsored enterprises* (GSEs): corporations created by Congress to work for the common good but then set out more or less on their own. Many of these faux agencies are publicly held, issuing stock on the major exchanges. Such pseudo-agencies include the Federal Home Loan Mortgage Corporation and the Federal National Mortgage Association. You notice, of course, that these nongovernmental enterprises start with the word "Federal." Confusing, isn't it?!

What's the difference between the two groups, especially with regard to their bonds? The first group (the official-government group) issues bonds that carry the full faith and credit of the U.S. government. The second group, well, their bonds carry that mysterious implicit guarantee or moral obligation. Because this second group is much larger than the first — both in terms of the number of agencies and the value of the bonds they issue — when investment experts speak of "agency bonds," they are almost always talking about the bonds of the GSEs.

There are many GSEs, but the three represented in Figure 7-1 issue the vast majority of bonds.

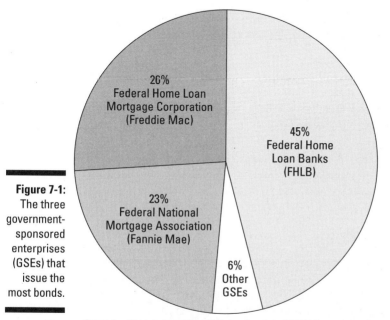

Figure 7-1: The three government-sponsored enterprises (GSEs) that issue the most bonds.

20% Federal Home Loan Mortgage Corporation (Freddie Mac)

45% Federal Home Loan Banks (FHLB)

23% Federal National Mortgage Association (Fannie Mae)

6% Other GSEs

Source: Securities Industry and Financial Markets Association (SIFMA). Figures are for 2005.

Sizing up the government's actual commitment

No GSE has yet to default on its bonds. The closest we've ever seen was the Federal Farm Credit Banks (FFCB) during the 1980s when banks were foreclosing on small farms faster than a swarm of locusts can chew up a crop. No FFCB bonds were defaulted, but nervousness in the markets caused their prices to plunge. Would the Treasury have stepped in to save the day if the crisis continued? In theory, yes. But because the theory has never really been put to the test, investors got sweaty palms.

Those who sold their FFCB bonds prior to maturity lost a bundle. Of course, those intrepid investors who scooped up the bonds at bargain prices made a mint.

Because of the very small risk of default inherent in agency bonds and the greater risk of price volatility due to public sentiment, agency bonds tend to pay higher rates of interest than Treasury bonds, although not a heck of a lot more. The spread between Treasuries and the faux-agency bonds is typically within half a percentage point, if even that much. As for the real government agencies, such as the Small Business Administration, which issue bonds backed by the full faith and credit of the U.S. government, the difference in yield between their bonds and Treasuries would be so small as to be almost immeasurable.

Introducing the agency biggies

To give you an idea of what GSEs are and what they do, I describe here the three largest (and most popular with retail investors) issuers of agency bonds: the Federal National Mortgage Association (known colloquially as *Fannie Mae*), the Federal Home Loan Mortgage Corporation (*Freddie Mac*), and the Federal Home Loan Banks.

Federal National Mortgage Association (Fannie Mae)

Fannie Mae, which dates back to 1968, raises money by selling bonds. It then turns some of that money over to banks. The banks use the money to make loans, mostly to homebuyers (believe it or not, 63 million homebuyers and counting).

Most Fannie Mae bonds (generally available in increments of $1,000) are purchased by institutions: insurance companies, other nation's central banks (especially China's), university endowments, and so on. But individual investors are certainly welcome to join in the fun, too. The agency issues bonds of varying maturities; and, naturally, there's a large secondary market where you can find any maturity from several months to many years down the pike. Fannie Mae sounds like a public agency, but it is really a private corporation with government oversight. For more information, see www.fannie mae.com.

If you believe that agency debt belongs in your portfolio (it certainly isn't a necessity, but it's a good option for many investors), Fannie Mae bonds may be an okay choice. It all depends on the price your broker offers you. Note that Fannie Mae bonds may be traditional interest-bearing bonds, or they may be mortgage-backed bonds. If you are considering the mortgage-backed variety, please make sure to read what I write about them later in this chapter. They are not for everyone!

Federal Home Loan Mortgage Corporation (Freddie Mac)

This agency (which is also, technically, a private corporation tied to the government) was formed in 1970 and is very similar to Fannie Mae. So are its multitude of bond issues with their many maturities, denominations of $1,000, and choice of traditional or mortgage-backed.

Freddie Mac buys one residential mortgage every seven seconds and, by so doing, helps to finance one in six homes in the United States. Most of the mortgages are purchased from primary lenders (such as your neighborhood bank). With the money those lenders get from Freddie Mac, they can go out and make more loans.

Like Fannie Maes, most Freddie Macs are bought by institutions. For more information, see www.freddiemac.com.

Federal Home Loan Banks

This is not a single agency but a coalition of 12 regional banks formed in 1932. Its mission is to fund low-income housing and housing projects. The money used for the funding comes from — you guessed it — selling bonds. *Lots of* bonds.

This coalition is far and away the largest issuer of so-called agency bonds. These bonds are a bit more popular with individual investors than Freddies and Fannies — as well they should be, at least for those in higher tax brackets: The interest earned is exempt from state and local taxes. For more information, see www.fhlbanks.com.

Like Fannies and Freddies, the FHLB bonds come in many different flavors as far as denominations and maturities.

An agency that broke its ties: Student Loan Marketing Association (Sallie Mae)

The Student Loan Marketing Association, otherwise known as Sallie Mae, owns and manages student loans for 10 million Americans. It used to be a government-sponsored enterprise (GSE) like Fannie Mae and Freddie Mac. But in 2004, after some years in transition, Sallie Mae became a private corporation with no government ties whatsoever. However, the millions and millions of dollars in bonds issued by Sallie Mae under its status as a GSE are currently grandfathered as agency debt, and will be until their maturity. If anything happens to Sallie Mae, the U.S. government has taken on a moral obligation to pay back the principal on Sallie Mae bonds — at least those issued prior to 2004.

If you buy a Sallie Mae issued prior to 2004, expect a price and yield comparable to other agency bonds. If you buy a Sallie Mae issued post-2004, expect a price and yield comparable to corporate bonds of similar quality. In either case, ask yourself if agency bonds or corporate bonds truly belong in your portfolio, and do your research (as outlined in Chapter 15) to compare and contrast these with other bonds to make sure you are getting the best investment possible.

Comparing and Contrasting Agency Bonds

All agency bonds are considered high quality with very little risk of default. The honest-and-true federal agencies, such as the Small Business Administration (SBA), are said to have no risk of default; therefore, their bonds pay more or less what Treasuries do (see Chapter 5). You may get a smidgen more interest (maybe 5 basis points, or 5/100 of 1 percent) to compensate you for the lesser *liquidity* of such agency bonds (the lesser ability to sell them in a flash).

The majority of agency bonds are issued by government-sponsored enterprises (GSEs), and the risk of default, although real, is probably next to nothing. You get a higher rate of interest on these bonds than you do with Treasuries to compensate you for the fact that the risk of default does exist.

With all agency bonds, you pay a markup when you buy and sell, which you don't with Treasuries if you buy them directly from the government. (I discuss buying and selling Treasuries in Chapter 5.) If you're not careful, that markup could easily eat up your first several months of earnings. It also could make the difference between agency bonds and Treasury bonds a wash.

Most agency bonds pay a fixed rate of interest twice a year. About 25 percent of them are *callable,* meaning that the agencies issuing the bonds have the right to cancel the bond and give you back your principal. The other 75 percent are non-callable bonds (sometimes referred to as *bullet* bonds). Callable bonds tend to pay somewhat higher rates of interest, but your investment takes on a certain degree of uncertainty. (See Chapter 6 for more on callability.)

Investing in individual agency bonds, or individual bonds of any kind, for that matter, is not an activity for poor people. Although you may be able to get into the game for as little as $1,000, bond brokers typically mark up such small transactions to the point that they simply don't make sense. I wouldn't suggest even looking at individual agency bonds unless you've got at least $50,000 to invest in a pop. Otherwise, you should be looking at bond funds, or individual Treasuries that you can buy without paying any markup whatsoever.

When choosing among different agencies, you want to carefully compare yields-to-maturity (see Chapter 4) and make sure that you know full well whether you are buying a traditional bond or a mortgage-backed security. They are totally different animals.

Weighing taxation matters

The taxes you pay on agency bonds vary. Interest from bonds issued by Freddie Mac and Fannie Mae is fully taxable. The interest on most other agency bonds — including the king of agency bonds, the Federal Home Loan Banks — is exempt from state and local tax.

Treasury bonds, which most resemble agency bonds, are always exempt from state and local tax. Municipal bonds are almost always free from federal tax. Needless to say, your personal tax bracket will make some bonds look better than others. I help you to better measure the effect of taxation on your bond selections in Chapter 8.

Making like John Travolta

Some agencies, in addition to issuing traditional bonds that pay semiannual interest, also issue *no-coupon discount notes,* known among bond traders as *discos.* Discos are similar to Treasury bills. They usually carry short-term maturities (up to one year), sell at a discount, and pay all interest along with principal at maturity. They are used more by institutions than by individuals, and it is probably better that way: Most individuals who buy bonds tend to enjoy the more regular income. I mention discos here mostly to appease your curiosity, should you come across the interesting term. They have nothing to do with dancing.

Another type of agency bond is called a *floater.* The coupon rate of a floater is based on some benchmark, such as the three-month T-bill (Treasury bill) rate, and can change from month to month. These are complicated beasts, and I suggest steering clear. Fixed-income investments should be fixed.

Not quite as unpredictable as the floater, yet another kind of agency bond is known as a *step-up.* With a step-up, you get a coupon rate that "steps up" according to a pre-set calendar. As time rolls on, you may collect more interest. Step-ups can be good investments in that they shield you from having to eat crow with a low-interest investment when interest rates are on the rise. The problem with them is that they are typically *callable,* which means the agency can toss your principal back to you at any time, and you're left holding cold cash with perhaps nowhere to go.

Banking Your Money on Other People's Mortgages

Far more complicated even than floaters are the mortgage-backed securities issued by federal agencies such as the Government National Mortgage Association (GNMA), otherwise known as *Ginnie Mae,* and some government-sponsored enterprises, such as Fannie Mae and Freddie Mac (see "Introducing the agency biggies" earlier in the chapter).

Mortgage-backed securities are very different from most other bonds. They do not offer as consistent and predictable a stream of interest income as do most bonds.

Bathing in the mortgage pool

When you purchase a mortgage-backed security from, say, Ginnie Mae (minimum investment $25,000), your money goes into a pool of mortgages. Whereas most bonds pay you a set rate of interest, usually twice a year, mortgage-backed securities pay you a certain rate of interest plus the steady or not-so-steady return of your principal. (You don't get a big lump sum when the bond matures.) Most mortgage-backed securities issue monthly payments.

The amount of principal you get back on a monthly basis is determined largely by the rate at which mortgage-holders pay off their debt. If interest rates drop and thousands of the mortgage-holders decide to suddenly prepay their existing mortgages (in order to refinance), you may get back your principal much faster than you had anticipated. In a sense, a mortgage-backed security has the same *back-at-ya* risk as a callable bond.

Deciding whether to invest in the housing market

You don't need to invest the $25,000 minimum required by Ginnie Mae to invest in mortgage-back securities. You can get a Freddie Mac for as little as $1,000. But should you?

No, I don't think so.

Neither does David Lambert, a financial planning colleague of mine who is currently with Valley National Financial Advisers in Bethlehem, Pennsylvania, and formerly the head trader at the agency-bond desk for a major Wall Street firm. This guy knows *a lot* about agency bonds. "If I were a retail investor, unless I had a really huge amount of money and felt that I really knew what I was doing, I wouldn't invest directly in mortgage-backed securities," Lambert says. "The complexity of them makes them inappropriate for the average investor."

Instead, says Lambert, if you want to invest in mortgage-backed securities, do so by investing in, say, a good Ginnie Mae mutual fund. "There are plenty of competent mortgage-backed fund managers out there. I'd look to a mutual-fund company like Vanguard or Fidelity," he says. I discuss bond funds, and mutual-fund companies such as Vanguard and Fidelity (both of which I also like), in depth in Chapter 16.

Considering Agencies for Your Portfolio

You don't *need* agency bonds. Their overall characteristics are similar enough to Treasuries that the substitution of one for the other isn't likely to make any huge difference in either the risk profile or the potential return of your overall portfolio. If, however, you are a smart bond buyer (which you certainly can be after reading this book!), substituting agency bonds for Treasuries may garner you a few extra bucks.

Mortgage-backed bonds, perhaps best purchased in mutual-fund form, add a smidgen of added diversification to a portfolio and potentially a touch more interest than do most other agency bonds. Again, there's no urgency to add mortgage-backed bonds to a portfolio, but if you have a large fixed-income allocation, a position in mortgage-backed bonds may make sense. Generally, you do better with mortgage-backed securities than traditional bonds when prevailing interest rates are stable. They tend to chug along or droop when interest rates begin to bounce.

Given their overall safety, agency bonds tend to be conservative investments and produce modest rates of return. Therefore, you *must* make sure that the return isn't eaten up in transaction costs or management fees.

If you plan to invest in an agency bond fund or funds, make sure you comb through Chapter 16 to find one with reasonable expenses. And if you think you may want to invest in individual agency bonds, read Chapter 15 so you don't get clipped with a high broker markup. Can't decide which is right for you, fund or individual bond? Chapter 13 is here to help!

Chapter 8

(Almost) Tax-Free Havens: Municipal Bonds

> *"I'm proud to be paying taxes in the United States. The only thing is — I could be just as proud for half the money."*
>
> — Arthur Godfrey

*W*ould you believe that this quote from the famous dead guy actually appeared on the home page of the official Internal Revenue Service Web site? No kidding. Who says these guys don't have a sense of humor?

No one, probably not even the Webmaster for the IRS Web site, likes paying taxes. That's why municipal bonds (commonly called *munis*), with their juicy exempt-from-federal-tax status, are such a darling investment, especially for those Camembert- and Evian-gulping folks in the northern tax brackets.

Perhaps you're an anti-government zealot who stockpiles guns in your linen closet for the upcoming revolution, and you'd rather die than pay taxes to Uncle Sam. In that case, munis should be your bond of choice. If you'd describe yourself in slightly more rational terms, what matters most is not the taxes you pay or don't pay, but what you take home at the end of the day.

That means that munis may make sense for you, or they may not. Munis, you see, typically pay considerably lower rates of interest than do taxable bonds. If you're a rational person, a municipal bond paying 4 percent, for example, would outshine a taxable bond paying 8 percent only if your tax bracket were way north of Norway.

In this chapter, I reveal the formula to figure out whether a tax-free muni will likely mean greater take-home than a comparable taxable bond. (It's a simple formula, really; no Ph.D. in mathematics necessary.) But I also point out that the formula should be used merely as a starting point. Munis may or may not belong in your portfolio for other reasons, as well, regardless of what you keep in your linen closet.

Appreciating the Purpose and Power of Munis

If not for the fact that municipal bonds are exempt from federal income tax, they would likely be about as popular as buttermilk at a college keg party. On the day I'm writing this chapter, for example, high quality munis with maturities of five years out are yielding an average of 3.75 percent. Five-year Treasuries, meanwhile, are currently yielding 4.75 percent — about one-quarter more the return. (Keep in mind that Treasuries aren't exactly world-famous for their high returns.) And while the munis carry some (limited) risk, the Treasuries do not.

But of course, munis *are* tax-exempt.

Why is that? Because in 1895, the Supremes (nine guys in black robes, not the lady singers) decided on a case involving "intergovernmental tax immunity." In essence, they ruled that the federal government had no right to mess with any local government's efforts to raise money. And the Supremes determined that taxing local bonds would, in fact, be a form of messing. From that point on, interest on municipal bonds has been largely untouched by those fun-loving Arthur Godfrey fans at the IRS.

When anyone in Washington is ever inclined to challenge that 1895 ruling (oh, yes, it does happen from time to time), he or she never gets very far. That's because the tax-exempt status of munis allows local governments, such as your township, to issue bonds that carry very modest interest rates. If local governments across the United States couldn't issue those bonds — couldn't get those relatively cheap loans — we'd probably start seeing potholes in the street as big as Rhode Island. A drying up of cheap loans might mean a drying up of ports; bridges and tunnels might not get built; and construction of new schools and low-income housing projects might come to a crawl.

Sizing up the muni market

About $2.3 trillion in municipal bonds is held primarily by U.S. households. That's roughly 15 percent of all household bond holdings. That's also about half of the entire market for U.S. government debt. Munis, undoubtedly because of their tantalizing tax advantage, are the only major kind of bond more popular with individual investors than with institutions. About two-thirds of all munis find themselves either in some normal Joe's portfolio or in a mutual or exchange-traded fund.

So who or what exactly issues these tax-exempt wonders, and what other qualities distinguish them from all other bonds? I'm so glad you asked!

The issuers of municipal bonds include, of course, municipalities (duh), such as cities and towns. But they also include counties, public universities, certain private universities, airports, not-for-profit hospitals, public power plants, water and sewer administrations, various and sundry nonprofit organizations, bridge and tunnel authorities, housing authorities, and an occasional research foundation.

Any government, local agency, nonprofit, or what-have-you that is deemed to serve the public good, with a blessing from the Securities and Exchange Commission and the IRS (and sometimes voters), may have the honor of issuing a municipal bond.

Comparing and contrasting with other bonds

The tax-exempt status of munis is unquestionably their most notable and easily recognizable characteristic — the equivalent of Kojak's cue ball or Groucho Marx's mustache.

Like most bonds, munis come with differing maturities. Some mature in a year or less, others in 20 or 30 years. Unlike most bonds, munis tend to be issued in minimal denominations of $5,000 and multiples of $5,000 (not a minimum of $1,000 and multiples of $1,000, like corporate bonds and Treasuries).

Like many corporate bonds, but unlike Treasuries, many municipal bonds are *callable,* meaning the issuer can kick back your money and sever your relationship before the bond matures. Like other bonds, the interest rate on munis is generally fixed, but the price of the bond can go up and down; unless you hold your bond to maturity, you may or may not get your principal returned whole. If the maturity is many years off, the price of the bond can go up and down considerably.

Delighting in the diversification of municipals

The tax-exempt status of munis isn't the only reason they may belong in your portfolio. Municipal bonds also offer a fair degree of diversification, even from other bonds.

Because they are the only kind of bond more popular with households than with institutions, the muni market is swayed more by public demand than the markets for other bonds. For example, when the stock market tanks and individual investors get butterflies in their stomachs, they tend to sell out of their stock holdings (often a mistake) and load up on what they see as less risky investments, such as munis.

When the demand for munis goes up, just as when the demand for, say, gold or oil goes up, it tends to drive prices higher. Popular demand or lack of demand for munis typically affects their prices more than it does the price of corporate bonds and Treasuries. Those taxable bonds, in contrast, tend to be more interest-rate sensitive than munis. As I discuss in Chapter 3, when interest rates rise, bond prices generally fall; when interest rates drop, bond prices tend to move up.

As an example of the kind of diversification I'm talking about, consider that in 2005, investment-grade (high quality) corporate bonds returned a measly 1.35 percent. (Interest rates were rising, so even though the bonds were paying fair coupon rates, the price of the bonds fell considerably.) Meanwhile munis overall returned an impressive tax-free 3.51 percent in 2005. But in other years, say 2003, for example (when interest rates were falling and bond prices were moving in the opposite direction), investment-grade corporate bonds returned an unusually delightful 11.81 percent, and municipal bonds returned a comparatively weak 5.31 percent.

Knowing That All Cities (Bridges or Ports) Are Not Created Equal

Like the corporations that issue corporate bonds, the entities (cities, hospitals, universities, and so on) that issue municipal bonds are of varying economic strength — although the degree of variance isn't nearly as large as it is in the corporate world.

One study looked at bond defaults between the years 1970 and 2000. Of all the muni bonds rated by credit-rating agency Moody's during that 30-year period (about 80 percent of the dollar volume of all municipal offerings), only 18 defaults occurred. That compares to 819 corporate-bond defaults during the same period.

Of those 18 municipal defaults reported in the study, 10 were healthcare facilities. All the defaulted bonds were revenue bonds; none were general obligation bonds. *General obligation bonds* are secured by the full faith and credit of the issuer and are typically supported by that issuer's power to tax the hell out of the citizenry, if necessary. *Revenue bonds'* interest and principal are secured only by the revenue derived from a specific project. If the project goes bust, so does the bond.

Enjoying low risk

The same study from Moody's also found a huge difference in recovery rates of munis as compared to other bonds. The *recovery rate* is the amount of money bondholders get back after the dust of a default settles. On defaulted munis from 1970 to 2000, the recovery rate was 66 percent of the face value of the bonds. In contrast, the poor corporate bondholders got back only 42 percent of the face value on their defaulted bonds.

So by and large, municipal bonds are very safe animals — at least those rated by the major rating agencies (such as Moody's), which are the vast majority of munis. If the mild nature of the beast weren't enough to put your investing soul at ease, know that roughly two-thirds of municipal bonds issued today come insured; you can't lose your principal unless the issuer *and* its insurance company go under. That is very unlikely to happen! And even if the insurance company were to fail, the general feeling among industry insiders is that most states would be very, very reluctant to allow one of their cities to default on a general obligation bond.

Municipal bonds, like corporate bonds, are rated by the major bond-rating agencies. But they have their very own rating system. (If municipalities were rated using the corporate ratings, almost all would hug the very top of the scale.) In Table 8-1, I show the ratings used by three major bond-rating agencies: Moody's, Standard & Poor's, and Fitch.

Table 8-1	Municipal Bond Credit Quality Ratings		
Credit Risk	*Moody's*	*Standard & Poor's*	*Fitch*
Prime	Aaa	AAA	AAA
Excellent	Aa	AA	AA
Upper medium	A	A	A
Lower medium	Baa	BBB	BBB
Speculative	Ba	BB	BB
Very speculative	B	B	B
Very, very speculative	Caa	CCC	CCC
In default	Ca, C	CC, C, D	CC, CCC, D

Choosing from a vast array of possibilities

You definitely want munis that are rated. Some municipal offerings are not rated, and these can be risky investments or very *illiquid* (you may not be able to sell them when you want, if at all). I suggest going with the top-rated munis: Moody's Aaa or Aa. The lower rated munis may give you a wee bit extra yield but probably are not worth the added risk.

Keep in mind that a lower rated bond can be more volatile than a high rated bond. Default isn't the only risk.

A good number of munis come insured, offering almost absolute safety. You lose a little bit in interest by opting for the insurance guarantee. As long as a muni is rated high and is a general obligation muni (not a revenue muni), consider going without the insurance for the drop of extra juice. General obligation bonds generally don't default. That's not to say it can't ever happen, but I'd say the odds are greater that my dog, Norman, will run for public office.

Of course, you also want to choose a municipal bond that carries a maturity you can live with. If the bond is callable, well, is that something you can live with and be happy with? Callable bonds pay slightly higher coupon rates but are less predictable than noncallable bonds. (See Chapter 6 for further discussion of callability.)

But perhaps most importantly, because the tax-free status of the muni is undoubtedly a prime motivation for buying a muni in the first place, you want to consider whether you want to buy a national muni or a state muni, and if you buy a state muni, do you want double- or triple-tax-free? Here's the scoop:

REMEMBER

✔ *National munis* are exempt from federal tax but are not necessarily exempt from state income tax. (Some states tax bond coupon payments and others do not.)

✔ *State munis,* if purchased by residents of the same state, are typically exempt from state tax, if there is one. Some, but not all, state munis are also exempt from all local taxes.

✔ Munis that are exempt from both federal and state tax are called *double-tax-free* bonds. Those exempt from federal, state, and local tax are often referred to as *triple-tax-free* bonds.

You need to do a bit of math to determine which kind is better for you: national or state, double- or triple-tax-free. If math doesn't frighten you too much, read on! Keep in mind, however, that the formulas I'm about to give you should be used only as rough guides. Consult your tax adviser before laying out any big money on munis. The tax rules are complicated and forever changing. Some states impose taxes on you if you invest in other states' munis; others do not. Some states even tax you if you invest in munis in your own state. Certain bonds issued in Puerto Rico and other U.S. territories are free from almost all taxation regardless of where you live. It's a jungle out there!

Consulting the Taxman

Your personal federal tax bracket, as well as the income taxes you pay in your particular state and perhaps to your local government, has a great bearing on whether munis make sense for you and, if so, what kind of munis.

"If you're in the highest tax brackets, especially if you live in a high-tax state like California or New York, you'd have to have your head examined if you buy any kind of bond except for an in-state muni," says Marilyn Cohen, a bond-manager buddy of mine who has helped build more bond portfolios than Henry Ford built cars.

On the other hand, says Cohen, some people choose to invest in munis only because they have such a revulsion to taxes. "Those people need to have their heads examined, too!" she says. For many of them, especially those in the lower tax brackets in states that tax little or none, munis clearly make no economic sense.

Bringing your bracket to bear

So let's determine whether you and I need to have our heads examined, shall we?

When looking at a national muni — a bond that is exempt from federal tax only — it isn't very hard to determine whether your after-tax take-home will be greater with that bond or with a fully taxable bond. For illustration purposes, let's suppose we are comparing two bonds: a $5,000 Metropolis muni paying 5 percent, and a $5,000 taxable bond from the International Dummies Consolidated Corporation (IDCC) paying 6.5 percent.

First, determine your tax bracket. Take a look at Table 8-2, which is based on IRS rules for 2007. It shows the likely percent of tax you'll pay on any interest from a taxable bond.

Table 8-2	2007 Federal Tax Brackets	
Status	**Taxable Income**	**Rate**
Married filing jointly	$0–$15,650	10.0%
	$15,651–$63,700	15.0%
	$63,701–$128,500	25.0%
	$128,501–$195,850	28.0%
	$195,851–$349,700	33.0%
	$349,701 & over	35.0%
Single	$0–$7,825	10.0%
	$7,826–$31,850	15.0%
	$31,851–$77,100	25.0%
	$77,101–$160,850	28.0%
	$160,851–$349,700	33.0%
	$349,701 & over	35.0%

Status	Taxable Income	Rate
Head of household	$0–$11,200	10.0%
	$11,201–$42,650	15.0%
	$42,651–$110,100	25.0%
	$110,101–$178,350	28.0%
	$178,351–$349,700	33.0%
	$349,701 & over	35.0%
Married filing separately	$0–$7,825	10.0%
	$7,826–$31,850	15.0%
	$31,851–$64,250	25.0%
	$64,251–$99,925	28.0%
	$99,926–$174,850	33.0%
	$174,851 & over	35.0%

Okay, got your tax bracket? Good. Now you can compare the take-home from the IDCC taxable bond to the federally tax-exempt Metropolis municipal 20-year bond paying 5 percent a year.

Start with 100 . . . a good round number. Subtract your tax bracket. Let's suppose you are in the 28 percent bracket. 100 – 28 = 72. That number — 72 — we'll call the *reciprocal* of your tax bracket. When you have the reciprocal, all you need is to divide the municipal yield by the reciprocal and it will tell you, Just like magic, what you would have to earn on the taxable bond to equal the amount you would get on the tax-exempt muni.

So, in this particular case, Metropolis muni is paying 5 percent. Divide 5 by 72 (the reciprocal of your tax bracket), and you get 6.94 percent.

That number, 6.94, represents your *tax-equivalent yield,* or your break-even between taxable and tax-exempt bond investing. If you can get 5 percent on a muni versus 6.94 percent on a taxable bond, go flip a coin. It won't matter which you choose, as far as take-home pay. (Of course, other factors may matter, such as the quality or the maturity of the bond.) If the taxable bond is paying more than 6.94 percent, the taxable bond will likely be your best bet. If the taxable bond is paying less than 6.94 percent, you're better off with the muni.

Back to our example, if the IDCC taxable bond is paying only 6.5 percent, you are better off, most likely, with the Metropolis tax-free bond paying 5 percent.

So far, so good?

Singling our your home state

Life in these United States is rarely simple. Chances are that you live in a state with income tax. Most people do.

In that case, figuring out your tax-equivalent yield is no longer a simple matter. State taxes, you see, are deductible from your federal taxes. So to figure out your tax-equivalent yield requires more math than any normal person with an Internet connection should ever have to suffer.

So instead of walking you through the long and painful formula, I'm simply going to suggest that you log onto one of the 50,000 tax-equivalent yield calculators on the Internet. One of my favorites is to be found on www.dinky-town.com. Click Investments in the column on the left side of your screen. Then click on Municipal Bond Tax Equivalent Yield. You can plug in your state income tax, and the calculator will show you the tax-equivalent yields, in colorful chart form, for federally exempt munis as well as munis exempt from state and local taxes.

Don't know your state tax? See Table 8-3.

Table 8-3	State Income Tax
State	*Rate*
Alabama	2.0–5.0
Alaska	No state income tax
Arizona	2.59–4.57
Arkansas	1.0–7.0
California	1.0–9.3
Colorado	4.63
Connecticut	3.0–5.0
Delaware	2.2–5.95

State	Rate
Florida	No state income tax
Georgia	1.0–6.0
Hawaii	1.4–8.25
Idaho	1.6–7.8
Illinois	3.0
Indiana	3.4
Iowa	0.36–8.98
Kansas	3.5–6.45
Kentucky	2.0–6.0
Louisiana	2.0–6.0
Maine	2.0–8.5
Maryland	2.0–4.75
Massachusetts	5.3
Michigan	3.9
Minnesota	5.35–7.85
Mississippi	3.0–5.0
Missouri	1.5–6.0
Montana	1.0–6.9
Nebraska	2.56–6.84
Nevada	No state income tax
New Hampshire	State income tax is limited to dividends and interest income only.
New Jersey	1.4–8.97
New Mexico	1.7–5.3
New York	4.0–6.85
North Carolina	6.0–8.0
North Dakota	2.1–5.54

(continued)

Table 8-3 *(continued)*

State	Rate
Ohio	0.649–6.555
Oklahoma	0.5–5.65
Oregon	5.0–9.0
Pennsylvania	3.07
Rhode Island	25% of federal tax liability
South Carolina	2.5–7.0
South Dakota	No state income tax
Tennessee	State income tax is limited to dividends and interest income only.
Texas	No state income tax
Utah	2.30–6.98%
Vermont	3.6–9.5%
Virginia	2.0–5.75%
Washington	No state income tax
West Virginia	3.0–6.5%
Wisconsin	4.6–6.75%
Wyoming	No state income tax
District of Columbia	4.5–8.7%

Matching munis to the appropriate accounts

Municipal bonds, like any tax-free investment, make most sense in a taxable account. In fact, I'd say that putting a muni into any kind of tax-advantaged account, such as an IRA or Roth IRA, makes about as much sense as putting a kidney pie on a vegetarian buffet.

If you're looking to fill your IRA with fixed-income investments (which may or may not make sense; see Chapter 13), don't be looking at munis. Taxable bonds provide greater return, and if the taxes can be postponed (as in an

IRA) or avoided (as in a Roth IRA), then taxable bonds are almost always the way to go.

Recognizing Why This Chapter is Titled "(Almost) Tax-Free Havens"

Will you *never* pay federal tax on a tax-exempt muni? Never say never. There are instances, rare as they may be, where the tax can grab you from behind and make you not want to wake up on the morning of April 15.

Reckoning with the AMT tax

The alternative minimum tax (AMT) is complicated enough to make Albert Einstein pull at his already pulled-looking hair. The AMT is a federal tax that exists in a parallel universe (Albert proved that they exist), which you enter unwillingly when you make a fair chunk of change, claim too many exemptions, or take too many deductions. Ask your tax guru if you are likely to be smacked by AMT at any point in the near future. If so, you may want to hand-pick your munis (and muni funds) to include only those that are exempt from the AMT.

In general, the interest on municipal bonds sold by state and local governments to finance very specific projects, as well as bonds issued by not-for-profit organizations and other "private activity" issuers such as airports and universities, is going to be included in the AMT. So if you are liable to pay the AMT, the tax-exempt status of these bonds will no longer be so exempt.

If you're not liable to pay the AMT, buying up these AMT bonds may make good sense because they tend to provide a slightly higher yield than do non-AMT bonds.

Capping your capital gains

If you buy a security at a certain price and then sell it at a higher price, that's a good thing! But you may be subject to pay capital gains tax to the IRS . . . even if the security you sold is a tax-exempt municipal bond. If you pay $1,000 to pick up a muni selling at par, and you later sell it for $1,100, you very likely owe the government capital gains tax on your $100. If the buy and sell both occur within a one-year period, the tax hit will likely be 28 percent,

33 percent, or whatever your normal marginal income tax rate happens to be. If your buy and sell span a period of more than one year, you need to pay long-term capital gains, which for most folks amounts to 15 percent.

(The tax rules governing municipal zero-coupon bonds bought at a discount and then sold at a lesser discount or a premium can be complicated; talk to your tax advisor.)

What pertains to individual bonds also pertains to municipal bond mutual funds. Sell your shares for more than you purchased them, and you'll have to pay capital gains. Of course, if you sell at a loss, whether a bond or a bond fund, you may then declare a capital-gains tax loss, which is usually used to write off capital gains.

Introducing the fully taxable muni. Huh? Say whaa?

At first glance, a taxable muni seems about as sensible as a race horse running in a yoke, but in fact, taxable munis offer potential return comparable to investment-grade corporate bonds or agency bonds, and sometimes they may make for an excellent bond choice. Taxable municipal bonds exist on the market because the federal government will not give a break to the financing of certain activities that it perceives do not offer a significant benefit to the public. The funding of a new hockey stadium or the refunding of a municipality's ailing pension plan are two examples of muni bond issues that would be federally taxable. They barely existed a decade or two ago but are becoming more and more popular.

Buying Munis Made Easier

Perhaps because the muni bond market is made up mostly of individuals rather than institutional buyers, the number of sharks in fancy suits out to rip the hide off unwary investors is highest in the muni bond market. Buyer beware! I've seen examples of people paying markups on individual bonds in some cases exceeding a full year's interest.

If you're interested (and can stomach it!), there's a Web site called www.municipalbonds.com, run by Kevin Olson, a former muni bond trader turned independent investor advocate. Olson delights in updating his Web site every day with municipal bond trades that should never have happened: trades with ridiculously high spreads between buys and sells, trades where individual investors got hurt. (Click on the red flag icon at the bottom of the home page.)

If you're buying individual munis on your own, you want to take full advantage of all the latest consumer tools that allow you, in many cases, to get a pretty good idea what kind of markup the bond broker is shooting to make. You don't want one of your trades to appear on Olson's Web site! If you go to a Web site such as www.investinginbonds.com or www.finra.org, you can research individual bonds to see the prices paid for past transactions. If the bond was traded recently, that should give you some idea whether a broker is offering you a fair price. The easiest way to research an individual bond is to ask the broker for its CUSIP number, and then plug that number into the Web site's search function.

Bond funds may make better sense altogether. By buying in bulk and using their professional prowess, fund managers can often get better deals than you can get buying bonds on your own. But, of course, funds charge you a yearly management fee, and given the low yields of munis, you don't want to pay too much for a fund. In fact, you want to pay as little as you can.

Whichever way you decide to go — individual bonds or municipal bond funds — Chapters 15 and 16 give you all the practical advice you need to build your muni bond portfolio wisely.

Chapter 9

Le Bond du Jour: Global Bonds and Other Seemingly Exotic Offerings

I once saw a cartoon showing an American-looking couple standing in a street in what looks like Mexico, watching a group of small children at play. The cartoon husband turns to the cartoon wife and cartoonishly says, "Isn't it amazing how these kids can conjugate all those verbs?"

What's amazing is how something that appears exotic to one person in one part of the world can be so run-of-the-mill to another. Consider that more than 60 percent of all fixed-income offerings exist outside the borders of the United States. To the hordes of well-heeled Europeans and Asians who invest in them, these bonds are about as exciting as bread and rice. Yet to the average Yank, an investment in a foreign bond may be considered as exotic as sautéed sea urchin in black truffle sauce.

In this chapter, I talk not only about foreign bonds but also about some rather unusual and, in some cases, even somewhat quirky bond offerings to be found closer to U.S. shores. None of the bonds discussed in this chapter are a must for your portfolio (some I would consider almost must-nots), but sprinkled throughout are a few bond options possibly worth your consideration.

Traveling Abroad for Fixed Income

The ratio between what we Americans invest in domestic bonds and what we invest in foreign bonds is somewhere in the ballpark (cricketfield) of *34 to 1.* Given the gargantuan size of the foreign bond market, you may find that a bit surprising — especially because foreign bonds sometimes make very sensible investments, even to people in Kansas.

When most investments professionals look at the world of global fixed income, they see two large categories of bonds. First, there are *developed-world* bonds. Second, for those who like to wash down their sautéed sea urchin with baby-bamboo-and-guava juice, there are *emerging-market* bonds.

Dipping into developed-world bonds

Just as the U.S. government and corporations issue bonds, so too do the governments and corporations of Canada, England, France, Italy, Germany, Sweden, Japan, Switzerland, and many other countries, large and small, hot and cold, rich and not-so-rich. True, it may be difficult to find a decent sirloin in some of these distant lands, but that doesn't mean their fixed-income offerings are all chopped meat. As you can see in Table 9-1, in any particular year, any developed nation's offerings may top the list of the world's highest yielding bonds.

Table 9-1	Highest Performing Bond Markets, 1996–2006	
Year	*Best Market*	*U.S. Ranking Out of the 13 Major Markets*
1996	Italy	9
1997	United Kingdom	2
1998	France	11
1999	Japan	4
2000	United States	1
2001	United States	1
2002	Sweden	12
2003	Australia	13
2004	Sweden	13

Year	Best Market	U.S. Ranking Out of the 13 Major Markets
2005	Canada	2
2006	Sweden	12

Sources: Table by T. Rowe Price Associates, Inc. based on data from JPMorgan. Copyright 2007. Used with permission. Information has been obtained from sources believed to be reliable, but JPMorgan does not warrant its completeness or accuracy. The JPMorgan Index Charts are used with permission. The JPMorgan Index Charts may not be copied, used, or distributed without JPMorgan's prior written approval. Copyright 2007, JPMorgan Chase & Co.

What are they?

Whether they are issued by corporations or by governments, foreign bonds, like U.S. bonds, come in all sorts of varying maturities and credit qualities. Some are dollar-denominated; these are often called *Yankee bonds.* But most are denominated in the currency of their home countries, be it Euros, pounds, yen, or Krona.

Over the long run, you can expect that bonds of similar credit quality and duration, bearing similar risk, should yield roughly equal returns, no matter in which country they are issued or sold. After all, if, say, British bonds consistently paid higher rates of interest than U.S. bonds, investment money would start to float eastward across the big pond. U.S. bond issuers, such as the Treasury, the State of California, and Exxon Mobil, would eventually either have to up their coupon rates or raise capital another way, such as bake sales or bingo games.

In the short run, however, interest rates can vary among bond markets, and more importantly, exchange rates can fluctuate wildly. For that reason, U.S. investors putting their money into foreign fixed income are generally looking at a fairly volatile investment with modest returns. (All fixed-income investments generally see modest returns.) On the flip side, foreign bonds, especially non-dollar-denominated bonds, tend to have limited correlation to U.S. bonds (meaning their value is independent of U.S. bonds), so owning some foreign fixed income in developed countries can be a sensible diversifier. Figure 9-1 offers a nice snapshot of the performance of U.S. versus foreign fixed-income securities from 1986 through March 2007.

Should you invest?

Investing in individual bonds is tricky. Investing in individual foreign bonds is trickier — kinda like buying a villa in Venice as opposed to a condo in Connecticut. To tap into the foreign fixed-income market, you're better off looking at investing through a mutual fund. Most foreign-bond mutual funds are fairly pricey, charging at least a percentage point a year in management fees. Is the diversifying power of foreign bonds worth that added expense? Just as importantly, is the added volatility that accompanies most foreign fixed-income investments worth the ride?

The answer (I apologize; please don't hate me): It depends.

Figure 9-1:
The rolling
12-month
returns of
developed-
nation
versus
U.S.-issued
bonds.

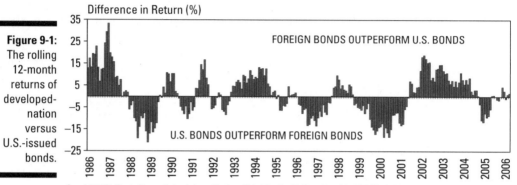

If you are still going to work every morning, still in the accumulation phase of your investing career, and already have a good percentage of your portfolio in foreign currency–based investments, such as foreign stock mutual funds or exchange-traded funds, then holding foreign bonds won't serve all that much purpose. If, however, you have a large bond portfolio (say $200,000 or more), and especially if you are living off those bonds, then putting a certain amount of your bond portfolio into foreign bonds — maybe a fifth or a quarter — may make a lot of sense. The diversification effect could help smooth out your total portfolio returns and possibly boost performance.

Please don't make the assumption that you can predict currency fluctuations and start loading up on foreign bond (or stock) funds as a way to speculate on a falling dollar. Currency exchange is as unpredictable as Britney Spears's behavior. Don't try it. You'll likely lose. If you buy into a foreign bond fund, do it only for the diversification benefit, and keep the allocation modest.

In Chapter 16, I provide the names of various mutual funds that offer exposure to foreign developed-world bonds at a relatively reasonable price. Most of these funds offer pure unhedged exposure. A few are dollar-hedged. When a fund is *dollar-hedged,* that means the manager is using sophisticated financial tools (usually currency futures) to offset any currency flux. These hedged funds (not to be confused with hedge funds) are less volatile than the currency unhedged funds. But you will lose a lot of the diversification power.

Embracing the bonds of emerging-market nations

Emerging markets is something of a euphemism for "poor countries." Those who invest in them *hope* that these nations are emerging, but no one can say with any certainty. In any case, if you want to buy bonds issued in Brazil, Turkey, Russia, Venezuela, Mexico, or Argentina, the opportunities are out there. The interest rates can be nose-bleed high; the volatility can be enough to make your stomach contents start emerging.

What are they?

The majority of emerging-market bonds are so-called *sovereign* bonds. That title sounds like it may have something to do with kings and queens, but all *sovereign* means is that these bonds are issued by federal governments. U.S. Treasury bonds are sovereign bonds.

Unlike the bonds issued by developed nations, most emerging-market bonds are dollar-denominated. Still, given the poverty, tsetse flies, and other problems of these nations, the governments can be shaky. To get enough people to lend them money, they must pay high rates of interest. Very high. At the time I'm writing this chapter, the Fidelity New Markets Income Fund has enjoyed a five-year annualized return of just about 16 percent and a ten-year annualized return of slightly over 12 percent. Woooahhh. Find *that* anywhere else in a fixed-income investment.

Of course, with the high return, as always, comes high volatility. In 1998, when Russian government bonds went into defaultski, investors in the Fidelity New Markets Income Fund, like investors in most emerging-market funds, quickly saw about a quarter of their investments disappear overnightski.

The following year, 1999, most emerging-market bond funds sprung back rather nicely, even though Ecuador defaulted on its bonds that year. By the way, certain dollar-denominated bonds issued by Latin American countries are often referred to as *Brady* bonds, named after former U.S. Treasury Secretary Nicholas Brady. The bonds were part of a scheme developed in the late 1980s to figure out a way for Latin American countries to deal with their giant-sombrero-sized debt burdens.

Should you invest?

I like emerging-market bonds, and I think they belong, in modest amounts, in most portfolios larger than $100,000 or so. If you're going to have high-yield bonds in your portfolio, then emerging-market bonds make sense. When recession hits the United States and the Dow and S&P have a rough year, U.S.

high-yield (junk) bonds usually tank. That makes sense. As companies hit hard times, marginal companies are most likely to default. Emerging-market bonds, however, have little correlation to the U.S. stock market. That's why I advocate a small allocation — perhaps 2 to 3 percent — of a well-diversified portfolio in emerging-market bonds.

But, given the volatility of these bonds and the potentially high returns, I look at them more like stock investments than bond investments; in fashioning portfolios, I put emerging-market bonds on the equity side of the pie. There's only one practical way to invest in emerging-market bonds, and that is through a mutual fund. I suggest some good fund options in Chapter 16.

Bond Investing with a Conscience

Whatever your religion, whatever your political leanings, there may be a bond or bond fund out there waiting for you to express your beliefs. No one ever said that making money has to be all about making money.

Having faith in church bonds

Talk about good deeds. Churches in the United States have issued bonds for more than a century now. The bonds are most often secured by a deed of trust on church real estate or other property. Traditionally, most of these bonds have been sold as private offerings to bona fide members of the church congregation only. But fairly recently, a market has been growing for church bonds offered to the general public — believer and heathen alike.

What are they?

Church bonds look and feel something like corporate bonds, but they have a certain advantage in that they are almost always backed by the issuer's real property. A leading broker for church bonds, Strongtower Financial of Fresno, California, reports not a single default among the church bonds it has sold since 1994. Not only that, but its church bonds have averaged slightly more than a full percentage point higher yield during that time than investment-grade (high quality) corporate bonds: about 8.5 percent versus 7.4 percent. And if you care where your money is going, you'll know that you're helping to fund the growth of a church, perhaps something that gives you emotional comfort.

There are a few downsides to church bonds. First, church bonds tend to be rather *illiquid;* you could have a hard time selling a church bond that you don't plan to hold to maturity. Second, all church bonds are *callable,* meaning that the church may give you your money back and retire the bond before it matures. Third, church bonds are generally too small to be rated by the major rating agencies, so you've really got to trust your broker to do due diligence (that means homework in financial-speak) and make you an honest deal.

Should you invest?

Church bonds are viable alternatives to high-quality corporate bonds. But the offerings are limited, and most are restricted to residents of certain states. There is one church-bond mutual fund — Capstone Church Bond Fund (XCBFX) — available to any investor in any state. Unfortunately, the yearly management fee is too high for me to recommend this fund. Nonetheless, for more information on this fund, contact Strongtower Financial at www.strong towerfinancial.com or 1-888-378-6683. The Strongtower folks can also talk to you about their individual church bond offerings, as well as church loan funds (CLFs), which are pools of church bonds in which certain residents of certain states may invest.

You may also try two other outfits devoted to the offering of church bonds:

- ✔ The American Church Mortgage Company at www.church-loans.net or 1-800-815-1175
- ✔ The Great Nation Investment Corporation at www.churchbonds.net or 1-800-468-3007

If you shop for church bonds, don't do it on a prayer; shop as you would for any other bond. Get competitive bids, and make sure that you are not paying an unreasonable markup to the broker. Know that church bonds are unrated by the major rating agencies, so you'll be depending more on your broker for solid research and impartial advice than you would be when buying most other bonds. Chapter 15 provides a list of commandments for dealing in individual bonds of any faith.

Adhering to Islamic law: Introducing the sukuk

According to the classical laws of Islam, paying or charging interest is a definite no-no. You'd think, therefore, that bond investing would be as sinful as slugging Jack Daniels while eating pork rinds and watching a swimsuit contest.

Well, it depends on the bond. Some very special bonds, called *sukuk* (pronounced *soo-cook*), actually allow for virtuous investing . . . at least according to some followers of Islam. Other followers see the sukuk as smoke and mirrors. But while the controversy continues, $17 billion in sukuk have been issued in a recent nine-month period. Most are being issued in Islamic countries and sold to Middle Eastern and European investors. But sukuk sales in the United States are now just beginning. In June 2006, Houston-based East Cameron Partners, an oil development company, issued $166 million in sukuk. Most of the buyers were U.S.-based hedge funds. They didn't buy the sukuk for religious reasons. These particular sukuk were paying 11.25 percent.

What are they?

Traditional bonds pay you a fixed interest amount over the life of the bond, and then you get your principal back upon maturity. Sukuk also pay you a fixed rate, but it isn't called interest, and the money is said to come not from the lending itself but rather from the sale or leasing of certain tangible assets, such as property, equipment, or (in the case of East Cameron) oil profits.

In Islamic law, money is seen as having no real value in and of itself, explains Yusuf DeLorenzo, a partner with Shariah Capital, a Connecticut-based financial product development firm specializing in Islamic offerings. "Income from an investment has to have something real and substantial backing it up," he says. Hence the sukuk. Like a traditional bond, a sukuk has a maturity date and a certain rate of return, but that rate of return may be either fixed or floating and is always backed by some hard asset.

Should you invest?

There is as yet not much of a market for sukuk in the United States. But keep your eyes and ears open. They may be coming. I (perhaps obviously) have no direct experience with sukuk, so all I can say is to do a lot of research before investing. If you are Islamic, you may want to check with your mullah to ascertain whether a particular offering meets your religious needs. The Web site of Shariah Capital, www.shariahcap.com, should bring regular updates on the development of sukuk in this country, as well as abroad.

Investing for the common good: Socially responsible bonds

Socially responsible investing (SRI) can mean different things to different people, but for most, the goal of SRI is to shun companies that produce tobacco and alcohol, engage in gambling activities, produce lethal weapons, pollute the environment, discriminate in employment, or violate human rights. Instead of investing in such companies, SRI investors go to sleep at night knowing that their money is instead helping to fund companies working, more or less, to create a better world with healthy products and practices.

Most SRI investing is done through stock mutual funds. Steve Schueth, president of First Affirmative Financial Network, a Colorado-based independent advisory firm specializing in SRI, finds that somewhat ironic. "Doing social action from the debt (bond), as opposed to the equity (stock) side of the portfolio is potentially much more powerful," he says.

Schueth points out that most stock transactions occur on the secondary market. After the initial public offering of stock by a company, people generally don't buy stock directly from the firm but rather from a third party through an impersonal exchange. Not so with bonds. Bonds are much more often purchased directly from the issuer. "As a lender of money, you actually have considerable power to affect a company's actions," says Schueth. Of course, he admits, only really big lenders have really big power. For the rest of us, however, there are a handful of SRI bond mutual funds where we may exert our influence in communal fashion.

What are they?

These mutual funds put companies through a social screen. Only those companies that act in accordance with the social guidelines of the fund managers get to sell their bonds to the fund. Examples of SRI bond funds include the following:

- ✔ **Calvert Social Investment Fund (CSIBX):** www.calvertgroup.com or 1-800-368-2748
- ✔ **Domini Social Bond Fund (DSBFX):** www.domini.com or 1-800-582-6757
- ✔ **PAX World High Yield Fund (PAXHX):** www.paxworld.com or 1-800-372-7827

All three of these funds use somewhat similar social criteria. From the people at PAX World:

> Pax World offers mutual funds dedicated to promoting peace, protecting the environment, advancing equality, and fostering sustainable development. We seek to invest in companies that meet positive standards of corporate responsibility and that provide products or services that improve the quality of life. We avoid investing in companies that we determine are significantly involved in the manufacture of weapons or weapons-related products, that manufacture tobacco products, that are involved in gambling as a main line of business, or that engage in unethical business practices.

The somewhat similar Calvert and Domini funds consist of mostly higher quality, intermediate-term bonds. The PAX fund, as the name implies, includes bonds of lesser quality but potentially fatter returns.

Should you invest?

None of these funds is terrible; none (from a strictly financial viewpoint) would likely make it to the top of my buy list. But there are things that matter in life more than money, more than even some of the things that money can buy, such as chocolate. If your values jive with those of the managers of these funds, I would recommend that you consider these funds, carefully, for the fixed-income side your portfolio. You could do a lot worse.

Playing with Bond Fire: Potentially Risky Bond Offerings

When rock star David Bowie decided in 1997 to produce his own bonds using his considerable talent (and future song royalties) as collateral, it struck some as a rocking good idea. Bowie got $5.5 million out of the deal, but some investors haven't fared as well as they thought they would. In this section, I introduce a few types of bonds that fall a few notes shy of being totally safe investments but nonetheless may make a reasonable addition to some people's portfolios.

Rocking with Bowie Bonds

David Bowie was the first artist to issue bonds using his future royalties as collateral. The bonds, issued in 1997, carried a coupon rate of 7.9 percent. Not too shabby. But in 2004, given some changes in the music industry, including the advent of file sharing on the Internet, Moody's downgraded the bonds to junk status. The price of Ziggy Stardust's bonds fell to earth. Those who needed to sell lost a good deal. But the concept of Bowie bonds — raising cash with talent — caught on nonetheless, and other artists soon followed.

What are they?

Since the original Bowie Bonds (sometimes called *Pullman Bonds* after David Pullman, the financier who pulled the Bowie deal together), other artists have followed suit. James Brown, The Isley Brothers, Iron Maiden, Ashford & Simpson, and Rod Stewart have all closed similar deals, raising cash with bonds backed by future song royalties. The music-makers get their money up front, and bondholders get to collect interest, they hope. Similarly, a few small bond issues have been backed by future revenues of Hollywood film sales and a handful of sporting events.

Should you invest?

These are all very modest bond issues, rather *illiquid* (meaning that should you wish to sell your bond, you may not be able to), and backed by assets of wavering value. I wouldn't go out of my way to purchase Bowie Bonds. Bond manager Marilyn Cohen, a California-based colleague of mine who knows the bond world inside and out, wisely suggests that if you do buy a Bowie-type bond, at least try to find a rocker in the grave! That way you know he or she is beyond scandal. Just imagine, says Cohen, what would likely have happened to the value of your investment if Michael Jackson had issued bonds just prior to being accused of child molesting.

Cashing in on catastrophe bonds

Call it strange (I think it is), but in the past year about $10 billion has poured into bonds that pay higher-than-market rates of interest, but only if the weather cooperates.

What are they?

Known as *catastrophe bonds,* they are issued mostly by insurers, pay juicy rates of return, and are backed by revenues from true moneymakers. That may sound great, but here's the catch: The issuer reserves the right to use the cash behind the bonds if a hurricane or tsunami or tornado or earthquake results in many people suddenly making claims against the insurance company. If the catastrophe results in massive claims, bondholders can wind up seeing their principal cast into the wind.

Should you invest?

Are you kidding? A few extra dollars in possible interest in exchange for risking your principal? No way. That's not what bonds are all about — or should be about. These bonds may possibly make sense for institutional buyers with huge resources but not for mere mortals like you and me, who hope to retire someday and live on more than peanut butter sandwiches.

Dealing in death

If catastrophe bonds weren't morbid enough, some of the world's biggest insurance companies have begun to issue *death bonds.* You stand to gain higher-than-market rates of interest, but only if a certain number of people don't die.

You read that right.

What are they?

These bonds are somewhat similar to catastrophe bonds. The bonds are issued by insurers and pay raucous rates of interest, but the insurer reserves the right to tap the money behind the bonds if more people than expected die. Some of these bonds directly tie your return to the death rates of a pool of the insured. If the insurance company's customers eat their vegetables, wear their seatbelts, and don't play with guns, you win. If an epidemic strikes or a volcano erupts, you lose, and your investment may turn to ash.

Should you invest?

Yuck. This investment is both risky and morbid. As with the catastrophe bonds, there may be a reason for institutional investors to take a risk on such an investment. For living, breathing individuals, these bonds make little to no sense.

Banzai Bonds: Hold on Tight

Whoooeeee! If you think of debt securities as safe and boring, cast a gander on some of these investments. You could double or triple your money overnight . . . or see it shrink and fade faster than the bankroll of a drunken gambler in Vegas on a not-so-hot night.

Daring to delve into derivatives

In general, a *derivative* is a financial something-or-other whose value is based on the price of some other financial something-or-other. (I apologize for the highly technical definition.)

Examples of derivatives include *futures* and *options*. Entire fun books are written on futures and options (such as *Futures & Options For Dummies* by Joe Duarte, M.D., published by Wiley). Suffice to say that they allow you to leverage your money and make big play on just about anything, including the price of pork bellies, orange juice, most stocks, and — yes — even "conservative-investment" bonds, too. Another kind of derivative, specific to bonds, is called the *collateralized mortgage obligation* (CMO).

What are they?

A CMO is a complicated beast created by a brokerage house. It is a certificate that represents partial ownership of a huge pool of mortgage bonds, such as Ginnie Maes, Fannie Maes, and Freddie Macs (see Chapter 7). Different owners in the pool get paid at different times, and the payments are contingent on the performance of the pool and the payoff of other partial owners. CMOs have a history of making fantastical profits for their creators but often limited and frequently unpredictable returns for investors.

Futures and options allow investors to purchase a contract that says on such-and-such a date, you're going to buy (in the case of a future) or you have the option of buying (in the case of an option) such-and-such a bond. The price is set today, not knowing what the price of the bond will be at that date in the future (the *expiry date*). If, on that day, the price of the bond is 110 and you have a contract to buy it at 100, BINGO — you win! If, however, the price of the bond has dropped to 95, ZINGO — you lose! Futures and options allow you to put up relatively little money (the price of the contract) and possibly profit a lot . . . or lose every penny.

Should you invest?

All derivatives are risky investments. In my mind, that's not the purpose that bonds serve in this universe. I wouldn't suggest dabbling in either CMOs or bond futures. Professional traders, who live-breathe-and-die this stuff, will very likely clean your clock.

Banking on losses with defaulted bond issues

In Chapter 6, I talk about junk bonds: bonds that offer high yields but carry high risk. Some bonds — bonds *in default* — are even junkier than junk.

What are they?

Bonds in default are almost always corporate bonds (very, very rarely municipal bonds). *In default* usually means that the company is bankrupt or very close to being bankrupt, coupon payments on the bonds have stopped, and there is an extremely high likelihood that investors' principal — or a good portion of principal — will never be returned.

But miracles do happen. Companies that seem to be going under or are forced into reorganization sometimes make surprising comebacks. And when they do, or even if it looks like they might, big profits can ensue. Defaulted bonds sell, as you would imagine, at very deep discounts. Those who purchased the defaulted bonds of Delphi, the bankrupt auto parts producer, saw their investments double in price within several months. The defaulted bonds of Calpine, the bankrupt energy company, quadrupled in value in a three-month period. Many other (most) defaulted bonds, however, fade into oblivion, and investors looking to make a quick buck are left with little to nothing to show.

Should you invest?

Hmmm. I spoke with Martin Fridson, CEO of FridsonVision LLC (an independent investment research firm in New York City) and something of an expert on defaulted bonds. Here is what he says:

> Buying a bond in default is the polar opposite of ordinary bond investing. You get no income. No security. You're purely speculating that the price will shoot up and you'll have a capital gain. Most people who buy these never see any gain.

> They [people who buy defaulted bonds] may have been talked into buying the defaulted bond by a fast-talking broker, and that *broker* will make a nice gain. But the person who bought the bond will generally see nothing.

I'm inclined to agree. Play the horses . . . Roll some dice . . . Go to Spain and bet on the bull to kill the matador . . . Buy defaulted bonds. Have fun, but don't call any of them investing. They are gambling.

Ah, but what if you are *already holding* a bond that goes into default? Should you keep it or sell it? That depends, says Richard Lehmann, publisher of the *Forbes/Lehmann Income Securities Investor* newsletter (`www.income securities.com`). If you're holding a municipal bond, keep it, he says. The recovery rate on munis is very high, in part because bondholders are usually the only creditors.

If you're holding a corporate bond that goes into default, that's another story. Banks and other creditors will tend to get their money before you do. Defaults usually begin with an announcement from a company that it will cease coupon payments on its bonds. Most often, such announcements come in November or December for tax reasons, says Lehmann. As soon as the announcement is made, the price of the bond will tumble as the market starts to panic.

After the initial panic, prices on defaulted corporate bonds usually, but not always, creep up. If you can get your hands on a corporate balance sheet, note what percentage of the company's assets are intangibles, such as goodwill and brand names, says Lehmann. "The higher the percentage of intangible assets versus hard assets, the lesser your chance of recovery (getting back any of your principal), and the more incentive you have to sell the bond as soon as possible," he says. "The greater the percentage of hard assets, such as land and property, the greater your odds of recovery, and the more incentive you have to hold onto the bond."

Evaluating exchange-traded notes

They sound like *exchange-traded funds* (investments similar to indexed mutual funds that trade like stocks), but exchange-traded notes (ETNs) are as different from ETFs as jellyfish are different from fish. ETNs are, in fact, debt instruments, bonds of sorts, but the income they produce is far from fixed. In fact, unlike most other debt securities, there is no coupon rate, and the maturity date, although it exists, is rather inconsequential.

What are they?

ETNs were first issued in 2006 by Barclays, the same firm that issues many ETFs. ETNs trade on the major exchanges, just like ETFs. You can buy as little as one share (under $100), or many shares. But instead of buying a basket of stocks or bonds, as you do when you buy a mutual fund or ETF, the purchase of an ETN represents a direct loan to Barclays. If Barclays were ever to go under, you could lose your money, just as you might if you were holding a Barclays bond.

Instead of promising you a steady rate of interest on your loan, as you'd get with a traditional bond, Barclays promises to pay you in accordance with the performance of a particular index. So, for example, if you were to purchase shares in the iPath Goldman Sachs Crude Oil Total Return Index (the ticker is OIL), your return would be commensurate with any rise (or fall) in the price of crude oil. If you were to purchase shares in the iPath Dow Jones-AIG Commodity Index Total Return ETN (DJP), your returns would be commensurate with the rise (or fall) in the value of an index that tracks a variety of commodities, from silver and gold to cotton futures and natural gas.

Barclays issues two general commodity index ETNs (DJP and GSP), the oil ETN, and an ETN that tracks stocks on the Indian stock market (which has the ticker INP). I believe that we'll be seeing many more ETNs in the next few years. At present, the IRS is taxing them very gingerly, asking only for capital gains tax if profits result from a sale of shares. But the IRS is known to be looking at ETNs with a magnifying glass, and the current favorable tax status may not last forever.

Should you invest?

If you're going to invest in commodities, including oil or Indian stocks, Barclays ETNs make enormous sense. They are low-cost, tax-efficient (for the moment) securities. They also are going to be highly volatile investments, so be sure you know what you're getting in to. These are not your father's debt instruments! Although Barclays is a very stable company with very little risk of default, that is still a remote possibility. I suspect that other companies, perhaps of lesser stability, will be issuing ETNs before long. Buyer beware.

To learn more about ETNs, visit the Barclays Web site, www.ipathetn.com.

Part III

Customizing and Optimizing Your Bond Portfolio

The 5th Wave   By Rich Tennant

"It's surprising considering his portfolio is so conservative."

In this part . . .

*I*f portfolio construction were done in the kitchen, Part II would be our list of ingredients, and Part III is where I begin to divulge the secret family recipes. In the four chapters that follow, I ask you to join me in mixing together various investments to build a delicious savings buffet. I focus, of course, on the bond side of the portfolio. But I don't want you to look at bonds in a vacuum, so I discuss other kinds of investments as well.

Before you step into the kitchen to begin the actual portfolio-cooking process, your first step is to look at investment risk and potential return: the yin and yang of wealth-building. I introduce you to something called Modern Portfolio Theory that explains how to balance your yin and yang for maximum yield and minimal insomnia. I explain the concept of correlation and how you want to incorporate into your portfolio some investments that zig while others zag (and preferably a few that zog).

Finally, I serve as official matchmaker, matching you with particular kinds of bonds that make sense for you — the kinds of bonds with which you can live happily ever after.

Chapter 10

Risk, Return, and Realistic Expectations

. . . .

. . . .

> *Dear Russell: I am 8 years old. Some of my little friends say there is no tradeoff between risk and return. Papa says, "If you see it in* Bond Investing For Dummies, *it's so." Please tell me the truth: Is there a tradeoff between risk and return?*
>
> VIRGINIA O'HANLON
> 115 WEST NINETY-FIFTH STREET

Yes, Virginia, there is a tradeoff between risk and return.

Your little friends are wrong. They have undoubtedly been thumbing through too many paperback books in airport kiosks that say you can get rich quick with absolutely no risk to your principal by following some crazy scheme or another.

That is all fantasy, Virginia. In this great capitalist system of ours the individual investor is a mere insect, an ant, whose hope to get rich quick is fed by the mass media and the greed of Wall Street and then squashed under the heel of financial reality.

Alas! How dreary would be the world if there were no tradeoff between risk and return. It would be as dreary as if there were no Virginias. You and your

Papa and all your little friends would simply invest in Treasury bonds and retire rich tomorrow. Variable-annuity salesmen would be out on the street. CNBC, instead of hyperventilating 24 hours a day over the stock market, would be airing reruns of *My Mother the Car*.

Not believe in the tradeoff between risk and return?! You may as well not believe in compound interest, or the miracle of modern orthodontics.

No tradeoff between risk and return?! A thousand years from now, Virginia, nay, ten times ten thousand years from now, there will STILL be a tradeoff between risk and return. This chapter explains why that is so, why understanding that tradeoff is integral to building a successful portfolio, and why trying to do so without bonds is as silly as . . . well, questioning the existence of Santa Claus.

Searching, Searching, Searching for the Elusive Free Lunch

Just in case you want to know the explanation, Virginia (Virgil, Vinny, Vicky. . . whoever is reading this page), there is a tradeoff between risk and return for roughly the same reason that a shiny new Lexus costs more than a 1993 Honda Civic. If both vehicles cost the same, everyone except maybe Ralph Nader would buy a new Lexus. Similarly, if you thought you could earn as much investing in Treasury bonds, backed by the U.S. government, as you could earn investing in shiny tech stocks, backed only by the capriciousness of the market, would you invest in the tech stocks? No, I don't think so.

A risk-free investment that paid high returns would be the equivalent of a free lunch. Sorry Charlie, but free lunches are very hard to find. No stable investment should be expected to pay a high rate of return. No luxury car should be expected to sell for the same amount as an old jalopy. The capitalist market, as Adam Smith once said (and even Ralph Nader can't deny), has an invisible hand.

Making a killing in Treasuries . . . yeah, right

What I'm saying, and what professor Smith was saying (sort of), is that risky investments — or at least investments perceived as risky — tend to return more than less risky investments for the very same reason that old jalopies sell for less than new luxury cars: at least over the long run, they *must*.

Look: If you could invest in the stock market, commodities, real estate, or Treasuries, all returns being equal, you'd invest in Treasuries, right? Everyone would invest in Treasuries. There'd be no market for more volatile investments. Similarly, if luxury cars and old jalopies were available at the same price, there'd be no market for old jalopies.

Only because of differing rewards (higher return potential or greater price bargain), there is a market for both. Honk honk. Ka-ching ka-ching.

Defining risk and return

In just a moment, I talk of the particular risk and return characteristics of bonds. But first, I want to make clear what risk and return really are. (No, it isn't obvious to everyone.)

Risk is the potential of losing money. Although you can lose (or gain) money a lot more easily in certain investments than others, there is some risk in all investments . . . including bonds. When most people think of risk, they think of wild market swings such as those that often occur in the market for, say, cocoa bean futures. They think of how much money they could potentially lose in a week, a month, or a year. But there are other ways to lose money in an investment, which I address in the next section.

Return is the potential of making money. Most of the money made in bonds is made in the form of interest payments. Sometimes, bonds also appreciate (or, alas, depreciate) in value. Overall, the return potential of bonds is modest compared to certain other investments, like an investment in the S&P 500 or a dry-cleaning franchise in the local strip mall. As I make clear, I hope, throughout this book, the benefit of bonds is more to temper risk and provide steady, predictable income than to capture huge gains.

Appreciating Bonds' Risk Characteristics

In Chapter 9, I talk about bond derivatives, defaulted bonds, and a few other bond investments that most people would consider wild and crazy by fixed-income standards. But the vast majority of bond offerings are rather staid investments. You give your money to a government or corporation. You receive a steady flow of income, usually twice a year, for a certain number of years. Then you get your original money back. Sometimes you pay taxes. A broker usually takes a cut. Beginning and end of story.

Investing with confidence

The reason for bonds' staid status is not only that they provide steady and predictable streams of income, but also that as a bondholder you have first dibs on the issuer's money. A corporation is legally bound to pay you your interest before it doles out any dividends to people who own company stock. If a company starts to go through hard times, any proceeds from the business or (in the case of an actual bankruptcy) from the sale of assets go to you before they go to shareholders.

Realizing, however, that bonds offer no ironclad guarantees

First dibs on the money aside, bonds are not FDIC-insured savings accounts. They are not without some risk. For that matter, even an FDIC-insured savings account — even stuffing your money under the proverbial mattress! — also carries some risk.

Following are seven risks inherent in bond investing. As a potential bond-holder, you need to know each of them.

Interest-rate risk

Interest rates go up, and interest rates go down. And whenever they do, bond prices move, almost in synch, in the opposite direction. Why? Because if you're holding a bond that is paying 5 percent, and interest rates move up so that most new bonds are paying 7 percent, your old bond becomes about as desirable to hold as a pet scorpion. Any rational buyer of bonds would, all things being equal, choose a new bond paying 7 percent rather than your relic, still paying only 5 percent. Should you try to sell the bond, unless you can find a real sucker, the price you are likely to get will be deeply discounted.

The longer off the maturity of the bond, the more its price will drop with rising interest rates. Thus long-term bonds tend to be the most volatile of all bonds. Think it through: If you have a bond paying 5 percent that matures in a year, and the prevailing interest rate move up to 7 percent, you're looking at relatively inferior coupon payments for the next 12 months. If you're holding a 5 percent bond that matures in ten years, you're looking at potentially ten years of inferior coupon payments.

No one will want to buy a bond offering ten years of inferior coupon payments unless she can get that bond for a steal.

That is why if you try to sell a bond after a period of rising interest rates, you take a loss. If you hold the bond to maturity, you can avoid that loss, but you pay an opportunity cost because your money is tied up earning less than the prevailing rate of interest. Either way, you lose.

Of course, interest-rate risk has its flip side: If interest rates fall, your existing bonds, paying the older, higher interest rates, suddenly start looking awfully good to potential buyers. They aren't pet scorpions anymore — more like Cocker Spaniel puppies. If you decide to sell, you'll get a handsome price. (I discuss the formulation of bond prices in Chapter 4.)

Inflation risk

If you are holding a bond that is paying 4 percent, and the inflation rate is 4 percent, you aren't making anything. You are treading water. If your bond is paying 4 percent, and inflation moves up to 5 percent, you are actually losing money. Inflation risk is perhaps the most insidious kind of bond risk because you can't really see it. The coupon payments are coming in. Your principal is seemingly intact. And yet, when all is said and done, it really isn't intact. You are slowly bleeding purchasing power.

Although inflation rarely hits you as fast and hard as rapidly rising interest rates, it is the fixed-income investor's greatest enemy over the long run. Interest rates, after all, go up and down, up and down. But inflation moves in only one direction. (Well, we could have *deflation,* where prices fall, but that hasn't happened since the Great Depression, and I don't believe it is likely to happen again anytime soon.) Inflation takes its toll slowly and steadily, and many bondholders don't even realize that they are losing ground.

Some bonds — Treasury Inflation-Protected Securities — are immune from the risk of inflation. Most bonds (and bondholders), however, suffer when inflation surges.

Reinvestment risk

When you invest $1,000 in, say, a 20-year bond paying 6 percent, you may be counting on your money compounding every year. If that is the case — if your money does compound, and you reinvest all your interest payments at 6 percent — after 20 years you'll have $3,262.

But suppose you invest $1,000 in a 20-year bond paying 6 percent and, after four years, the bond is *called.* The bond issuer unceremoniously gives back your principal, and you no longer hold the bond. Interest rates have dropped in the past four years, and now the best you can do is to buy another bond that pays 4 percent. Let's suppose that you do just that, and you hold that new bond for the remainder of the 20 years. Instead of $3,262, you are left with $2,387 — about 27 percent less money.

The risk I describe here is called *reinvestment* risk, and it is a very real risk of bond investing, especially when you buy callable or shorter-term individual bonds. Of course, you can buy non-callable bonds and earn less interest, or you can buy longer-term bonds and risk that interest rates will rise. Trade-offs! Trade-offs! This is what investing is all about.

Note that one way of dealing with reinvestment risk is to treat periods of declining interest rates as only temporary investment setbacks. What goes down usually goes back up. As long as they don't urgently need the cash, long-term bondholders considering selling their bonds may wait for interest rates to climb back up before going to market.

Default risk

This is the kind of risk that most people think of when they think of bond risk. In fact, most bond investors worry so much about default risk that it often blinds them to the more common and more insidious risks of bond investing, such as those I mention in the previous sections.

What is default risk? Simple: The issuer of your bond starts to go under; there's no money left to pay creditors; and not only do your interest payments stop coming in the mail every six months, but you start to wonder if you'll ever get your principal back. If there's actually a bankruptcy, your mailbox, instead of offering you interest payments, will be flooded with letters from lawyers explaining (in explicit Latin) that you are a sucker and a fool.

With Treasuries and agency bonds, this has never happened. Very, very rarely do municipal bonds or investment-grade corporate bonds default. Default risk is mostly an issue when you invest in high-yield (junk) bonds. When the economy is humming along, defaults are rare. When the economy slides and even companies that make hotcakes can't sell their wares, default rates jump. It's an especially nasty time to be losing money on your bonds because chances are good that your other investments are doing poorly, as well.

There is also a relatively high risk of default in buying certain foreign bonds, especially emerging-market bonds. But emerging-market bonds (bonds issued mostly by the governments of poor countries), unlike U.S. junk corporate bonds, have limited correlation to the U.S. stock market. For that reason, although emerging-market bonds have somewhat higher volatility than U.S. junk bonds, I often recommend them first for a portfolio (see Chapter 9).

Downgrade risk

Even if a bond doesn't go into default, rumors of a potential default can send a bond's price into a spiral.

When a major rating agency, such as Moody's, Standard & Poor's, or Fitch, changes the rating on a bond (moving it from, say, investment-grade to below investment-grade), fewer investors want that bond. It is the equivalent of *Consumer Reports* magazine pointing out that a particular brand of toaster oven is prone to explode. Not good.

In 2005, for example, the major rating agencies downgraded both Ford and General Motors bonds from investment-grade to junk. Investors fled. Bondholders saw their investment values drop by 20 to 30 percent. Many cashed out, making the loss permanent. As it happens, Ford and GM bonds both recouped somewhat, and, at least at the time of this writing, neither has actually defaulted. Honk honk.

Bonds that are downgraded may be downgraded a notch, or two notches, or three. The price of the bond drops accordingly. Sometimes, downgraded bonds are upgraded again. If and when that happens (it usually doesn't), prices can zoom right back up again. Holding tight, therefore, can sometimes make good sense.

Tax risk

When comparing taxable bonds to other investments, such as stocks, some investors forget to factor in the potentially high cost of taxation. Except for municipal bonds and bonds kept in tax-advantaged accounts, such as an IRA, the interest payments on bonds are generally taxable at your income-tax rate, which for most people will be in the 25 to 28 percent range but could be as high as 35 percent.

In contrast, stocks may pay dividends, most of which (thanks to favorable tax treatment enacted into law just a few years back) are taxable at 15 percent. If the price of the stock appreciates, that appreciation isn't taxable at all unless the stock is actually sold, at which point, it is usually taxed at 15 percent. So would you rather have a stock that returns 5 percent a year or a bond that returns 5 percent a year? From strictly a tax vantage point, bonds lose. Paying even 25 percent tax represents a 67 percent bigger tax bite than paying 15 percent.

Tax risk on bonds is most pronounced during times of high interest rates and high inflation. If, for example, the inflation rate is 3 percent, and your bonds are paying 3 percent, you are just about breaking even on your investment. You have to pay taxes on the 3 percent interest, so you actually fall a bit behind. But suppose that the inflation rate were 6 percent and your bonds were paying 6 percent. You have to pay twice as much tax as if your interest rate were 3 percent (and possibly even more than twice the tax, if your interest payments bump you into a higher tax bracket), which means you fall even further behind.

I don't believe that inflation will go to 6 percent. But if it does, holders of conventional (non-inflation-adjusted) bonds may not be happy campers, especially after April 15 rolls around.

Keeping-up-with-the-Joneses risk

Despite all the other risks I mention, bonds usually make good, safe investments. But the return on bonds generally isn't going to be anything to write home about. From a strictly financial point of view, that may not be so bad. Some people who live within their means and already have good nest eggs don't need, and really should not take, much risk with their investments. But if you're not taking that risk and your neighbors are, and the markets are good, and the economy is humming, your pesky neighbors may be making much more on their investments than you are. Ouch.

Studies show that *relative* wealth (making more than your neighbors) is more important to many people than *absolute* wealth (how much you actually have in the bank). Can you handle dinner with your neighbors and friends as between bites they boast about their major gains in the markets?

Regarding all these risks . . .

Please don't think that I'm trying to convince you not to buy bonds! Despite all the risks I mention, bonds still belong in your portfolio. Stay tuned for the numerous reasons why.

And in the meantime, check out Figure 10-1. To the left, see where bonds tend to fit into the investment-risk spectrum as compared to other kinds of investments. To the right and the far right, see where different kinds of bonds rank in order of relative risk.

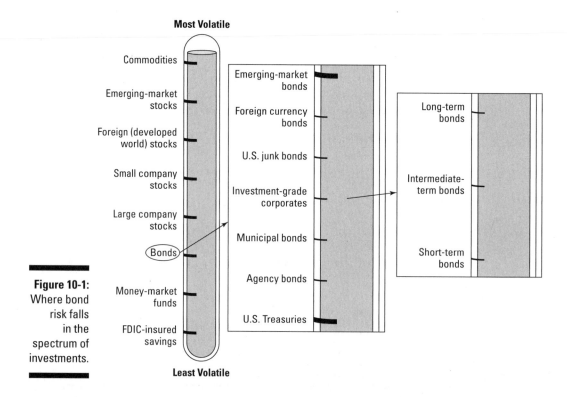

Figure 10-1:
Where bond risk falls in the spectrum of investments.

TECHNICAL STUFF

Understanding standard deviation

When comparing different kinds of bonds — or any investments, for that matter — it helps to know the *standard deviation*. It is the most oft-used measure of risk when comparing investments.

What does it mean? An investment with a standard deviation of, say, 3 will give you a return that is within one standard deviation (in this case, 3 percentage points) of the mean about two-thirds of the time. So suppose you have a bond fund that has an historical average annual return of 6 percent, and you know that the standard deviation is 3. What that means is that two-thirds of the time, the return from this bond fund will fall somewhere between 9 percent (6 percent average return + 3 percent standard deviation) and 3 percent (6 percent average return − 3 percent standard deviation). If that same bond fund had a standard deviation of 5, the returns you could expect would generally fall between 11 percent and 1 percent.

Is a high standard deviation good or bad? That depends on how much volatility you can stomach and how much return you need to get.

Thanks to Morningstar Principia software, I can readily find the ten-year standard deviation for any bond fund (which means how volatile the funds have been for the past ten years). Following are a few examples. The higher the number, the greater the price swings in years past and the greater the price swings, most likely, in years to come. In the world of bonds, the greatest factors affecting volatility are the maturity of the bonds and the stability of interest rates. The price of long-term bonds tends to be much more volatile than the price of short-term bonds. But the quality of the bonds matters, too. High-yield (junk) bonds tend to be more volatile. And foreign bonds, denominated in other currencies, also tend to be more volatile due to currency flux.

To help put things in perspective, the ten-year standard deviation for the stocks of the S&P 500, an index of the 500 largest companies in the United States, stands at 15.36. As you can see, only the most volatile of the volatile bonds are as volatile as that. And the S&P 500 is considerably less volatile than certain other investments, such as tech stocks, small-company stocks, and commodities.

Name of Fund	*Type of Bonds in Fund*	*Ten-Year Standard Deviation*
Fidelity New Markets Income	Emerging-market bonds, dollar denominated	16.52
Vanguard Long-Term U.S. Treasury	Government bonds with average maturity of 17 years	8.20
T. Rowe Price International Bond Fund	International bonds with average maturity of 8 years	8.03
Vanguard High-Yield Tax-Exempt	Municipal bonds of various grades with average maturity of 7 years	3.68
Vanguard GNMA	Government-backed bonds with average maturity of 7 years	2.88
Vanguard Short-Term Bond Index	Investment-grade corporate bonds with average maturity of 3 years	2.14

Measuring risk a simpler way

An outfit called RiskMetrics offers a new, easier way of comparing investment risk. Instead of using standard deviation (the most common way of measuring risk, as I explain in another sidebar in this chapter), the folks at RiskMetrics have come up with a scale that allows for much simpler understanding of risk.

I recommend that you check out the free Web site www.riskgrades.com. You plug in any investment you wish — single bond, bond fund, individual stock, stock fund — and voilà, you are given a number. The higher the number, the greater the risk. The lower the number, the lesser the risk. Unlike standard deviation numbers, RiskGrade numbers are logical and to scale (just like the metric system of measuring distance or weight). In other words, an investment with a RiskGrade of 20 is twice as volatile as an

investment with a RiskGrade of 10 and half as volatile as an investment with a RiskGrade of 40.

RiskGrades take into consideration various kinds of risk, including interest-rate risk, currency fluctuation, and default risk. Theoretically, at least, the RiskGrades methodology could prove to be a truer measure of future risk than the always backwards-looking standard deviation. Check with me in about 25 years, and I'll have the definitive answer! In the meantime, you may wish to compare and contrast the two measures, and take them both into consideration when choosing a bond category.

Following are the same bond funds that I give standard deviations for in the "Understanding standard deviation" sidebar. As a point of comparison, the RiskGrade for the S&P 500 is 65.

Name of Fund	Type of Bonds in Fund	RiskGrade
Vanguard Long-Term U.S. Treasury	Government bonds with average maturity of 17 years	32
T. Rowe Price International Bond Fund	International bonds with average maturity of 8 years	26
Fidelity New Markets Income	Emerging-market bonds, dollar denominated	16
Vanguard GNMA	Government-backed bonds with average maturity of 7 years	11
Vanguard High-Yield Tax-Exempt	Municipal bonds of various grades with average maturity of 7 years	8
Vanguard Short-Term Bond Index	Investment-grade corporate bonds with average maturity of 3 years	7

The RiskGrades Web site not only allows you to ascertain the relative risk of various investments; it also pumps out a risk rating for your entire portfolio. The cumulative risk rating of all your investments will be lower than the average of all the individual RiskGrades, illustrating the risk-reducing power of diversification.

Reckoning on the Return You'll Most Likely See

If all bonds were the same, this would be a very short book indeed. Bonds differ greatly as far as risk, expected return, taxability, sensitivity to various economic conditions, and other factors. Up until now, this chapter has focused more on risk than on expected return. (Yes, Virginia, I do believe that I already mentioned there's something of a connection between the two!) I now discuss expected returns.

I can hear you say with confidence, "But a bond yielding 5 percent can be expected to return 5 percent over the life of the bond, and a bond yielding 6 percent can be expected to yield 6 percent. How hard can this be?"

HA! Ha ha ha ha!

Calculating fixed-income returns is much easier said than done

So you invest in a $1,000 bond that yields 6 percent and matures in 20 years. What do you do with the $30 coupon payments that you receive every six months? Do you reinvest them or spend them on Chinese dinners? Do you keep the bond for the entire 20 years or cash it out beforehand? (If the bond is callable, of course, you may have no choice but to take back your principal before maturity.) And if you do cash out before maturity, what kind of price will you be able to get for the bond?

And what about *real* (after-inflation) rate of return — the return that really matters? If inflation runs at 2 percent, your real return will be a lot greater than if inflation runs at 8 percent. But how can future inflation be predicted?

And what if you invest in a bond fund? Just because the fund yielded, say, 5 percent annually over the past seven years, does that mean it will yield that much moving forward?

And (sorry, just a couple more questions here . . . I'm almost done) what about *after-tax* real return (return after both inflation *and* taxes)? Ultimately, that's the return that matters the most of all. That's the return that moves you ahead financially or sets you back. Do you know what your tax bracket will be in ten years? Do you know what *anyone's* tax bracket will be in ten years?

These are just some of the questions that make bond investing — or any kind of investing — so much fun! I now pull out my crystal ball.

Looking back at history is an imperfect guide, but . . .

Not to beat a dead horse or anything, but I said something earlier about the markets pretty much assuring that in the long term investors are appropriately rewarded for the risks they take. And so it stands to reason that if we know what kind of returns a certain kind of bond has seen in the past, oh, 30 years, it may give us a pretty good indication of the kind of returns that kind of bond is likely to provide in the next 30 or so years. Granted, history is only a guide. (Repeat: *History is only a guide.*) But aside from tea leaves and Tarot cards (which I don't put a whole lot of faith in), history is one of the only guides we have.

I've nabbed a few charts from Vanguard that show *nominal* (before inflation) bond returns over the past 30 years. You'll note that the past 30 years have been particularly good ones for government bonds, which, despite their lesser risk, have returned almost as much as corporate bonds.

Figure 10-2 shows the nominal returns of $1 invested in short-term government bonds from 1977 through 2006.

Figure 10-2:
The 30-year nominal returns of short-term (1- to 5-year) government bonds.

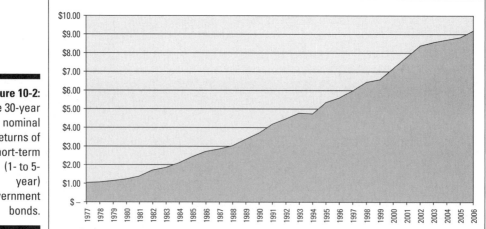

Source: Vanguard, with permission

Figure 10-3 shows the nominal returns of $1 invested in short-term corporate bonds from 1977 through 2006.

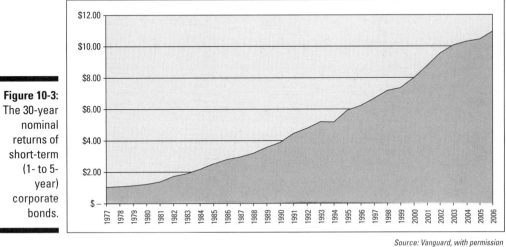

Figure 10-3:
The 30-year nominal returns of short-term (1- to 5-year) corporate bonds.

Source: Vanguard, with permission

Figure 10-4 shows the nominal returns of $1 invested in long-term government bonds from 1977 through 2006.

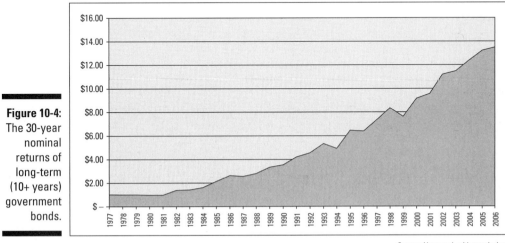

Figure 10-4:
The 30-year nominal returns of long-term (10+ years) government bonds.

Source: Vanguard, with permission

Figure 10-5 shows the nominal returns of long-term corporate bonds from 1977 to 2006.

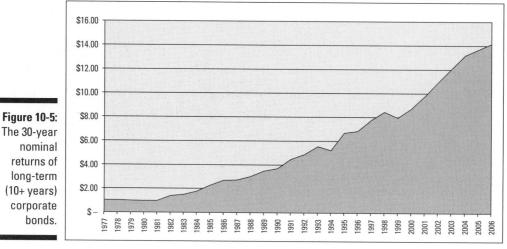

Figure 10-5:
The 30-year nominal returns of long-term (10+ years) corporate bonds.

Source: Vanguard, with permission

And now for a couple big-picture visuals. Figure 10-6 shows the nominal returns of $1 invested in the Lehman U.S. Aggregate Bond Index, which reflects the total U.S. bond market, during those same 30 years. Figure 10-7 represents the real (after inflation) returns of that same $1.

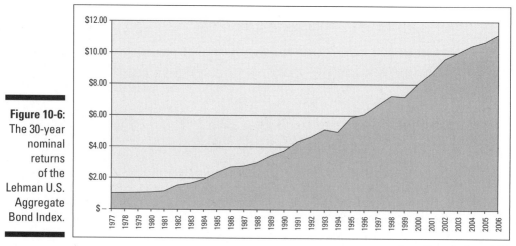

Figure 10-6:
The 30-year nominal returns of the Lehman U.S. Aggregate Bond Index.

Source: Vanguard, with permission

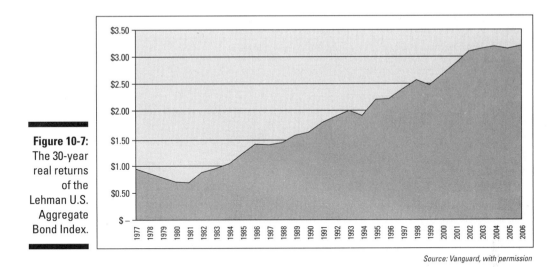

Figure 10-7:
The 30-year
real returns
of the
Lehman U.S.
Aggregate
Bond Index.

Okay, so much for the past 30 years. Now I invite you to look at bond returns over an even longer period.

As it happens, we have pretty good data about bond returns over the past 80 years, largely thanks to Ibbotson Associates, a Morningstar company. Here are the figures for the average annual *nominal* (before inflation) return of three categories of bonds for the period 1926 to 2006:

- ✔ One-month Treasury bills: **3.7 percent**
- ✔ Long-term government bonds: **5.5 percent**
- ✔ Long-term corporate bonds: **5.9 percent**

And here are those same figures translated into *real* (after inflation) returns for the same time period:

- ✔ One-month Treasury bills: **0.6 percent**
- ✔ Long-term government bonds: **2.4 percent**
- ✔ Long-term corporate bonds: **2.8 percent**

Um, I suppose as the author of *Bond Investing For Dummies* I'm not supposed to point this out, but quite honestly, the numbers aren't too awe-inspiring, are they? Keep in mind that they don't even factor in taxes, and you are taxed on the nominal (pre-inflation) returns of your bonds, not the real (post-inflation) rate of return.

Investing in bonds despite their lackluster returns

So what would you have earned, after taxes, investing in long-term government bonds over the past 80 years? Well, compared to stocks, which have returned about 10 percent a year before inflation and 7 percent after inflation, you would have earned squat. With corporate bonds, you would have earned slightly more than squat. And with short-term government bonds, you would have earned less than squat.

Keep in mind that all squat figures are rough approximations only. If you force me to get technical, the long-term return on all bonds, judging by the past 80 years, is about half that of all stocks. The real return on bonds (after inflation but before taxes) is about one-third that of stocks. For the average taxpayer, the after-tax, long-term return on bonds is very roughly one-quarter that of stocks. (I *told* you this wasn't a book on getting rich quick!)

So why even bother to invest in bonds? There are still several *very* good reasons:

✔ Even squat adds up when compounded year after year. Start with $10,000. Give yourself a mere 2 percent annual return, and — voilà — within a century, you'll have $72,450. Granted, you're not going to live another century unless you're from extremely good stock and you're reading this in diapers, but you get the point, right?

✔ In the last 80 years, stocks clearly clobbered bonds, but the next 80 years could be entirely different. Data from the 1800s show that the returns of stocks and bonds weren't all that different way back when.

✔ Investment-quality bonds have little — practically no — correlation to stocks, so they provide excellent balance to a portfolio. If you want to make sure that you're holding investments that don't all crash at once, stocks and bonds are a sweet mix to have.

✔ At certain times when stocks have tanked, bonds (especially long-term Treasury and high-quality corporate bonds) have rallied, providing comfort to investors when comfort was most needed. See Figure 10-8.

✔ Unlike just about any other kind of investment, bonds provide steady income for people who need it.

✔ Bonds' limited volatility, as compared to many other investments, makes them good bets for people who can't afford to take much short-term risk.

✔ Even though bonds have earned squat compared to stocks, they are virtual money machines compared to keeping your money in a savings account or money market fund. Passbook savings accounts and money

> market funds are generally not going to pay you enough to even keep up with inflation.

> ✔ Because you are going to take my advice on regularly rebalancing your portfolio (see Chapter 12), the "drag" of bonds on total portfolio performance will likely be much less than you think.

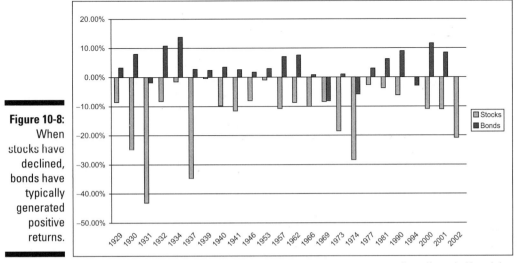

Figure 10-8:
When stocks have declined, bonds have typically generated positive returns.

Source: Vanguard, with permission

Finding Your Risk–Return Sweet Spot

Portfolio A is as volatile as a three-year-old child but offers high return potential. Portfolio B is as volatile as a three-toed sloth (it hangs in trees) and offers modest return potential. Portfolio C is halfway between the two. Without knowing anything else about these three hypothetical portfolios, I'd say that Portfolio A is made up mostly of stocks; Portfolio B is constructed mostly of bonds; and Portfolio C is a more even mixture of both.

Allocating your portfolio correctly

Deciding how to split your portfolio between fixed income (bonds, cash, CDs) and equity (stocks, real estate) is usually going to affect your risk–return profile more than any other decision. For that reason, I have an entire chapter — Chapter 12 — designed to help you make that one crucial decision. Do you want a 70/25/5 (stocks/bonds/cash) portfolio? A 50/45/5 portfolio? A 30/55/15 portfolio? Silly formulas abound. I want you to get it right . . . which you will.

But certainly, what *kind* of equity (large-company stocks, small-company stocks, foreign stocks, dry-cleaning franchise) and what *kind* of fixed income (Treasuries, corporate bonds, junk bonds, munis) you choose for your portfolio will play very much into your risk–return profile as well. In Chapter 13, I ask you to tell me something about yourself so I can help you decide what kinds of bonds are best for you. For now, I want you to start thinking about your risk–return "sweet spot."

Tailoring a portfolio just for you

Your age, your income, your wealth, your expenses, your retirement plans, your estimated Social Security, and your health all come into play when deciding where your risk–return sweet spot should fall.

As far as choosing your bonds, the less volatile bonds (short-term, high quality) will naturally edge your portfolio toward safety but more modest returns. The higher volatility bonds (long-term, high-yield) will move your portfolio toward greater risk but potentially higher return. (Ask Virginia O'Hanlon if this isn't self-evident; she can explain it.)

Ah, but there are times when choosing even a very volatile bond or bond fund may make perfect sense, even for someone looking to avoid risk. You'll understand why after reading about *Modern Portfolio Theory*, which tells us that new investments added to a portfolio must take into consideration existing investments within the portfolio. It's not as complicated as it sounds. Honest! Read all about Modern Portfolio Theory in the next chapter.

Chapter 11

The Science (and Pseudoscience) of Portfolio-Building

No man is an island.

> — John Donne *(Devotions Upon Emergent Occasions, "Meditation XVII")*

No bond is an island, either.

> — Russell Wild *(Bond Investing For Dummies, Chapter 11)*

*P*eople sometimes ask me, "Russell, is such-and-such a good investment?" My response is always the same: "It depends largely on what other investments you have in your current portfolio." Wishy-washy? Nah.

Some investments are so horrible that no one should ever touch them. (Your brother-in-law will be happy to recommend several to you, I'm sure. If he can't, mine will!) Somewhere, I suppose, there may be an investment so perfect that anyone who doesn't jump on it is a fool. (I've never seen such an investment, but presumably there is one somewhere.) Most investments are neither horrible nor perfect; they may be good for you but not good for me, or vice versa.

Take John Hypothetical Investor, whose entire portfolio consists of bonds in the ChickenLickin' Corporation. John needs yet another ChickenLickin' bond about as badly as I need water in my basement. But just because another ChickenLickin' bond isn't right for John doesn't make it a fixed-income pariah. Such a bond may be just the perfect addition to the portfolio of Jane Hypothetical Investor, whose present wealth consists of a few randomly chosen tech stocks and a dozen mayonnaise jars filled with pennies.

Starting with the next chapter, I explain the mechanics of building a portfolio, including which kinds of bonds may fit in best and how to go about buying and selling them. But before we get there, I need to discuss a few of the theoretical underpinnings that can help you understand how intelligent portfolios are constructed. In this chapter, I explain some of the modern science that allows smart investors, like you, to construct the leanest and meanest portfolios possible — portfolios that minimize risk and maximize potential return.

What do such portfolios look like? Here's a hint: Bonds, be they ChickenLicken or any other variety, are an essential ingredient.

Mixing and Matching Your Various Investments

So, what kinds of investments go well together, and which kinds clash?

If you already have a portfolio that looks like John Hypothetical Investor's — a portfolio filled with ChickenLickin' bonds — the last thing you need is another ChickenLickin' bond. That's because putting all your eggs in one basket is the surest way to wind up with scrambled eggs (or fried chickens). You want to include different kinds of investments in any portfolio, preferably investments from different asset classes and, best of all, investments that have little or no correlation.

Dreaming of limited correlation

An *asset class* is a group of investments that share common characteristics. Long-term, investment-grade corporate bonds would be an example. Small cap growth stocks would be another example. United States–based real estate investment trusts (REITs) would be a third.

For a good, basic education on asset-class investing and why it makes so much sense, I highly recommend two books:

> ✔ *All About Asset Allocation* by Richard Ferri (McGraw-Hill)
> ✔ *The Intelligent Asset Allocator* by William Bernstein (McGraw-Hill)

One distinguishing characteristic of an asset class is that it tends to perform in cycles, and those performance cycles tend to be different than the performance cycles of other asset classes. In other words, two distinct asset classes will have *limited correlation:* They won't move up and down at the same time. And so, having them together in a portfolio helps make for smoother sailing.

Let me illustrate how lack of correlation works to lessen a portfolio's ups and downs. Figure 11-1 shows the performance of two investments, which we'll call "Volatile Investment A" and "Volatile Investment B." Both investments offer high returns and equally high volatility; they move up and down like pogo sticks under a hyperactive child. However, notice that they don't move up and down at the same time. In fact, these two investments move in opposite directions. They are said to have *negative correlation.*

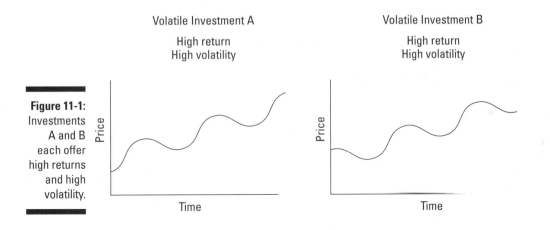

Figure 11-1: Investments A and B each offer high returns and high volatility.

Because of that negative correlation (easy to find in textbooks, very difficult to find in the real world), Volatile Investment A and Volatile Investment B combine to create a portfolio with socko returns but not a wee bit of volatility. Figure 11-2 shows what happens when you put them together into the same portfolio: You get the perfect result of high returns and no price swings! Unfortunately, this is only a model. Finding two high-returning investments with negative correlation is almost impossible in the real world.

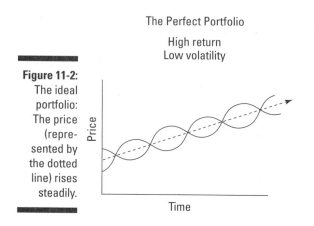

The Perfect Portfolio

High return
Low volatility

Figure 11-2:
The ideal portfolio: The price (represented by the dotted line) rises steadily.

Seeking zig and zag

What I'm talking about is diversification: combining an investment that zigs with another that zags, and possibly a third that zogs. In the investment realm, diversification is your very best friend.

Most investment pros are familiar with something called *Modern Portfolio Theory.* You should be, too. Modern Portfolio Theory is the key to maximizing return with minimal risk. What the theory says is that if you combine asset classes that zig and zag (and possibly zog) in a portfolio, even though each asset class by itself may be quite volatile, the volatility of the entire portfolio can be quite low. In fact, in some cases, you can add a volatile investment to a portfolio and, as long as that investment shows little correlation to everything else, you may actually *lessen* the volatility of the entire portfolio!

Translating theory into reality

Correlation is measured on a scale of –1 to 1. Two investments with a correlation of 1 are perfectly correlated: They move up and down in synch, like two Rockettes. Two investments with a correlation of –1 have perfect negative correlation: When one goes up, the other goes down, like pistons. A correlation of zero means that there is no correlation between two investments: When one goes up, the other may go up or down; there's simply no predicting.

In the real world, negative correlations of two productive investments are hard to find, but you *can* find investments that have close to zero correlation. Perhaps the best example from history is stocks and bonds. Bonds as a whole generally move up and down independent of stock prices. Some bonds — such as long-term Treasuries — tend to have slightly negative correlation to stocks, generally climbing during times of recession (often in response to dropping interest rates). But other bonds, such as U.S. high-yield bonds, tend to move more in synch with the stock market.

When choosing a bond or bond fund, you always want to consider the correlation that your new investment is going to have with your existing investments. High-yield bonds may throw off considerably more interest than Treasuries, but they aren't going to give you nearly the same diversification power if your portfolio is made up mostly of U.S. stocks.

In Figure 11-3, you can see how the performance of the entire bond market (as reflected in the share price of the Vanguard Total Bond Market Index Fund) and the performance of stocks (as reflected in the share price of the Vanguard Total Stock Market Index Fund) exhibit little correlation. Sometimes they go up together and sometimes down together, but often they move in opposite directions.

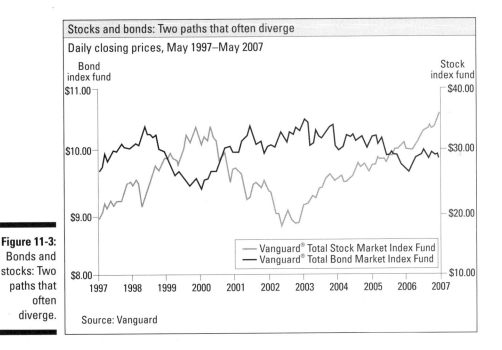

Figure 11-3:
Bonds and stocks: Two paths that often diverge.

Appreciating Bonds' Dual Role: Diversifier and Ultimate Safety Net

Okay, okay, so diversification is a good thing, but why must a diversified portfolio include bonds? After all, there are many, many investments to choose from in this world.

True enough: There are many investments to choose from in this world. And I encourage you, if your portfolio is large enough, to do some *gonzo investing,* as I like to call it. Go ahead, invest in commodities and foreign real-estate funds and emerging-market stocks and stocks in small value international companies and hedge funds and emerging-market debt. All these asset classes are imperfectly correlated, so you will likely get extra return while shaving off some volatility.

But invest with caution. Even when you use sophisticated portfolio-building tools to take maximum advantage of Modern Portfolio Theory, diversification isn't foolproof. It's no guarantee that you won't lose money.

Sometimes, even historically non-correlated asset classes can move in the same direction. We're seeing more examples of increased correlation these days. Thank globalization, which has tied many markets together. Thank hedge funds and certain mutual funds, which have taken previously obscure asset classes, such as coffee-bean futures, and turned them into frequently traded investments.

Protecting yourself from perfect storms

Lately, the markets have seen several *perfect storms:* times when all the economic conditions are lined up in such a fashion that practically everything everywhere loses money. You may recall a few very ugly days on the markets in late February and early March 2007.

Tuesday, February 28, 2007 was one of the worst days the market has ever seen. (I hope that is still true when this book appears in print!) As reported in *The Wall Street Journal* on March 1, 2007, "Tuesday's market drop left few financial assets unscathed. Not only did all 30 stocks of the Dow Industrial Average fall, so did all but two of the stocks in the Standard & Poor's 500-stock index. Of 51 country stock markets followed by MSCI Barra indexes, only two — Jordan and Morocco — didn't fall. Emerging-market and junk-bond prices fell sharply. Even the price of gold, where investors typically run in times of trouble, fell. Treasuries, another haven in times of peril, did rise."

Thank goodness Treasuries and other high-quality bonds are available to provide your portfolio with some kind of cushion!

Eyeing a centuries-old track record

Not only do high-quality bonds, such as Treasuries, have a proven track record of slightly negative correlation to the stock market, but they also have a long history of stability and positive returns. So they provide two vital roles in a portfolio: diversification, and (just in case diversification doesn't work) a solid floor that will keep your portfolio from falling too far in hard times.

You can't say that about many other asset classes:

- ✔ Foreign stocks? With the globalization of markets, foreign stocks, although they still offer somewhat limited correlation to U.S. markets, are beginning to have less diversification power. And foreign stocks, like all stocks, can be very volatile, especially with currency fluctuations.

- ✔ Gold? The precious metal, a hedge against stock market gyrations for generations, has lately lost some its diversifying glimmer. Lately, for a number of reasons, gold has moved in synch with the stock market more often than not. It is also unclear whether gold, silver, oil, or any other nonproductive commodity is going to produce gains in the long run. Over the past 100 years, the price of gold has risen just about the same as the rate of inflation.

- ✔ Hedge funds? They are expensive. Terribly expensive. They are opaque (it's 11:00 p.m. — do you know where your money is?). They are volatile. They are *illiquid* (meaning it's sometimes hard to unload your shares). They may or may not give you the diversification you seek.

- ✔ Cash? Nothing in the short run is as safe as cash. The price of cash is, well, the price of cash! But over the long run, cash is inevitably eaten up by inflation. Keep too much of your portfolio in cash, and you are taking a real risk of losing purchasing power over time.

On the other hand, quality bonds — Treasuries, agencies, and investment-grade corporate bonds — seem to have lost none of their diversifying power. Plus, they earn enough return to stay ahead of inflation, and they are stable. In fact, because bonds offer a steady stream of income, which tends to offset any price depreciation, and because those bond payments are not contingent on company profits (as are stock dividends), quality bonds very rarely lose money. Occasionally, when interest rates rise, long-term investment-quality bonds may lose value for a year or two. By year three, however, you are virtually assured of at least breaking even.

Recognizing Voodoo Science

Although Modern Portfolio Theory has its limitations, the science behind the theory is sound, and its real-world applications are profound. The same cannot be said for other common theories on investing. Now is as good a time as any for me to blow a couple of these common deceits out of the water.

Here's deceit number one: Timing the markets, finding "hidden" bond deals, and predicting changes in interest rates are the ways to manage a bond portfolio. And deceit number two: Successful buying and selling of bonds can boost your portfolio yields considerably.

Comparing actively managed funds to index funds

The Morgan Stanley High Yield Securities mutual fund's latest prospectus explains that the fund's managers, in choosing bonds for the fund, consider "economic developments, rate trends, and other factors it deems relevant." The prospectus goes on to explain that the esteemed fund managers use a slew of very sophisticated and complicated investment strategies — including options, futures, swaps, inverse floaters, and forward foreign currency exchange contracts — to manage the bond portfolio.

The prospectus is downright intimidating, even to someone like me who knows an awful lot about bonds. How can anyone read this prospectus and fail to be dazzled?

Keep reading. And stop being dazzled.

The Morgan Stanley High Yield Securities fund, C Shares (*C shares* means you pay a load or commission when you sell the fund), as of the end of 2006, boasts a ten-year annual return of –2.78 percent. That's a full 3.96 percent lower than the ten-year annualized return for the Lehman Brothers Aggregate Bond Index, a popular index that estimates the return of all bonds in the United States. And it is a full 6.36 percent lower than the ten-year annualized return for the Credit Suisse High Yield index, an index of high-yield bonds in the United States.

According to Morningstar, the Morgan Stanley High Yield fund is one of more than *85 percent* of actively managed bond mutual funds that failed to beat the Lehman Brothers Aggregate Bond Index over the past ten years.

Forecasting the future — and getting it wrong

So few actively managed bond funds succeed at beating the index because timing markets, predicting changes in interest rates, and finding "hidden" bond deals are very, very hard things to pull off. Even the highly educated and handsomely paid managers who run the nation's largest bond funds consistently fail to do it.

Just as is the case in the stock market, bond markets tend to be *efficient*. Because there are so many investors out there, all looking for a good deal, good deals are very, very hard to find.

Fund managers who spend hours and hours poring over company documents (so-called *fundamental analysis*) to find "hidden" deals usually fail to beat the market. Those who read charts that show the price of bonds going up and down and try to predict their future direction (so-called *technical analysis*) usually fail to beat the market. Those who read *The Wall Street Journal* every day and can list all the leading economic indicators, from employment figures to the latest on the trade deficit, usually fail to beat the market.

Those few mutual fund managers who succeed at beating the market often succeed to such a small degree that they typically don't add enough value to offset their high fees and the many costs of constant trading.

Of course, most people buy into the belief that investment professionals, including bond mutual fund managers and bond brokers, know what they are doing — and can pull off miracles. Millions and millions are spent on advertising each year so that people continue to believe. And yet year after year, those who buy and hold *index funds* — funds that simply track stock or bond indexes and charge little in fees — come out ahead.

Ignoring the hype

I'm not saying that a good bond broker or bond mutual fund manager can't be an asset to you. There are a handful of good bond mutual fund managers out there, and I've occasionally invested in their funds.

There are also good bond brokers, to be sure, who can help structure a portfolio, build good bond ladders for regular income, and help you gauge a proper level of risk for your investments. But please don't believe the broker who says that he is privy to information that will help you score big in the bond world. Such inside scoops, legally or illegally obtained, are extremely rare.

Beware especially of the bond broker who pats herself on the back for never having sold you a bond that went into default. No Treasury or agency bond has ever defaulted. Defaults among municipal bonds are as uncommon as penguins in the Caribbean. And defaults in the corporate bond universe are easy to avoid if you select top-rated quality bonds.

Bonds are ballast to a portfolio; they aren't meant to make a killing. How to pick the best individual bonds is the subject of Chapter 15. How to pick the best bond funds is covered in Chapter 16. None of it is magic. None requires secret decoder rings. The best bonds are bought with common sense, frugality, and the knowledge that no bond is an island.

Chapter 12

Dividing Up the Pie: What Percentage Should Be in Bonds?

As a teenager, I had a boat. It was 15 feet from bow to stern, yellow with two white vinyl bucket seats up front and a small bench in the back. I kept it behind my home on Long Island, tied to a floating dock in an inlet that led to the Atlantic Ocean. It was propelled (if you can even use that word) by a 25-horsepower engine. The boat, when it had the currents running against it, moved at a snail's pace. When I had three passengers in the boat, it was lucky to move at all.

Mind you, I am *not* looking for sympathy. I know darned well that other kids growing up had to deal with much, much tougher things in life, but this alleged power boat would lose a race to a paddle boat. Sometimes the other teenage boys on the water would throttle their engines, do vicious circles around me, point in my direction, and scream "Slooow down, Russell!" while laughing themselves sick.

My father, you see, bought that boat from an elderly gentleman who used it for lake fishing. Dad purposely wanted a boat with little horsepower because he figured the severely limited speed might keep his son safe. Dad's motivation was good, but his reasoning wasn't so good. A boat that size with a 25-horsepower engine may be perfect for lake fishing, but out in the ocean it was something of a floating deathtrap, prey to strong currents and the wakes of behemoth yachts.

After such a wake blew me into the side of a concrete bridge and cracked the hull, I was finally able to convince my father to up the horsepower a bit . . . for safety's sake. I wasn't exactly going *vroom vroom* with my new 35-horse-power engine, but I ceased having to listen to "Slooow down, Russell!" from my boating schoolmates. And that felt awfully good.

Funny how some things never change. Many years later, I would become an investment advisor. And my Dad, by then retired from years as a New York City attorney, was living (along with my Mom) off a portfolio of mostly bonds and CDs. It took some doing, but I was finally able to convince them to "up the horsepower" of the portfolio by adding some stocks. Like many retirees I've worked with, especially those who lived through the Great Depression, my parents had the notion that bonds and other slow and steady fixed-income investments, such as bank CDs, mean safety.

True, a bond portfolio, unlike a stock portfolio, tends to move at a steady pace. But as with an underpowered boat in a large ocean, lack of horsepower can be as dangerous as too much horsepower. Bond portfolios lack volatility, but they are easy prey to the currents of the economy and the tides of infla-tion. The truly safest portfolios, as we've seen in both the Great Depression and the hyperinflation of the 1980s, have both the horsepower of stocks *and* the stability of bonds.

Ah, but how much horsepower and how much stability? How do you find that perfect blend? Well, that depends on whether, investment-wise, you are an elderly lake fisherman, a youngster with a hankering for speed, a retired attorney and his wife, or a yachtsman leaving a big wake. In this chapter I ask you some questions about your life and, by examining your answers, help you determine just the proper allocation of bonds for your portfolio. In other words, I help to find just the right *vroom-vroom/slooow-down* ratio.

Why the Bond Percentage Question Is Not As Simple As Pie

I may as well cut right to the chase. Here's how to figure out what percent of your portfolio should be in bonds, in Seven Easy Steps. Simply pull out a blank piece of paper, and pencil in the appropriate numbers. Ready?

1. Start with the number 100. <u>100</u>

2. Subtract your current age from 100. <u>   </u>

3. Divide line 2 by the number of years between now and retirement. <u>   </u>

4. Do you have a pension? If so, add 5. ___

5. Does your boss have freckles? If so, subtract 3. ___

6. Do you have a cousin named Pablo? If so, subtract 6. ___

7. Add the number of feet between you and the closest garbage can. ___

All done? Good! Now wad up the piece of paper and see if you can sink a three-pointer in the basket.

My point?

> *There are no simple formulas.*

A 28-year-old with $2,800 in savings should not be investing his money the same as a 56-year-old with $620,000 in savings. A 67-year-old with a $500,000 nest egg and no pension will want to invest very differently from a 67-year-old with the same nest egg but a generous pension. A gazillionaire with spouse and kids and a desire to leave half a gigillion to charity may want to invest differently than a gazillionaire whose greatest interest is throwing big parties in Morocco with dozens of camels in drag. These are only some of the factors ignored by simplistic formulas.

They will *not* be ignored in this chapter!

Minimizing volatility

If I may recap very, very briefly what I say about bond returns in Chapter 10: The long-term return on all bonds, judging by the past 80 years, is about *half* that of all stocks. The *real* return on bonds (after inflation but before taxes) is about *a third* that of stocks. For the average taxpayer, the after-tax, long-term return on bonds is roughly *a quarter* that of stocks. So what percent of your portfolio do you want in bonds? If there were an easy formula, it would be this:

> *Ideal percent of your portfolio in bonds = The necessary amount — and no more (or less, for that matter)*

The "no more" part, in my book (hey! — this *is* my book!), is the easier part of the formula. The answer is *75 percent.* No kidding. Except perhaps in very rare circumstances, no one needs or wants a portfolio that is more than 75 percent bonds. Why? Because stocks and bonds together provide diversification. With all bonds and no stocks, you lack diversification. Diversification smoothes out a portfolio's returns.

Believe it or not, even though stocks are much more volatile than bonds (see Figure 12-1), a modest percent of stocks added to a portfolio of mostly bonds can actually help lower the volatility of the portfolio. (I discuss this when I explain Modern Portfolio Theory in Chapter 11.) To include less than that (or more than 75 percent bonds) raises volatility and lowers the odds of favorable returns both over the short run and long run. So why would anyone ever want to go there? Unless you have good reason to expect an economic apocalypse anytime soon (you don't), it doesn't make a whole lot of sense to invest only in bonds.

Maximizing return

The highest returning portfolios over the past few decades — over any few decades, for that matter — are made up of predominantly stocks. But those are also the portfolios that go up and down in value like popcorn on a fire. So the question "How much do you need in bonds?" is really a question, in good part, of how much short-term volatility you can or should tolerate.

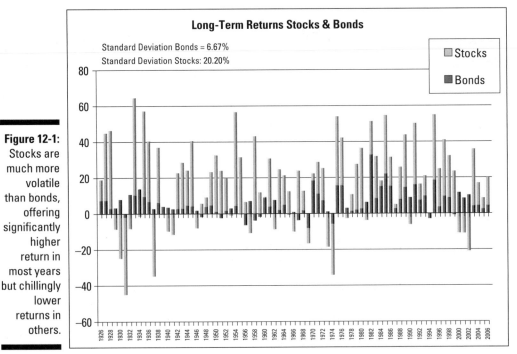

Figure 12-1:
Stocks are much more volatile than bonds, offering significantly higher return in most years but chillingly lower returns in others.

Source: Vanguard, with permission

How much volatility you can or should stomach, in turn, becomes largely a factor of time frame: Are you investing for tomorrow? Next year? A decade from now? Five decades from now? If you run an endowment fund, or if you happen to be immortal, your time frame may be infinite. For most of us human-being types, there will come a time when we want to tap into our treasured nest egg. But when?

To compare the volatility of bonds versus stocks, take a look at Figure 12-2. Bonds' long-term gains pale in comparison to stocks, but when things get rough, bonds don't take it on the chin as stocks do. The figure shows the best and worst returns for stocks and bonds (as measured by the S&P 500 Index and the Lehman Brothers U.S. Aggregate Bond Index) since the Great Depression.

Figure 12-2:
The best and worst years for stocks and bonds since the Great Depression.

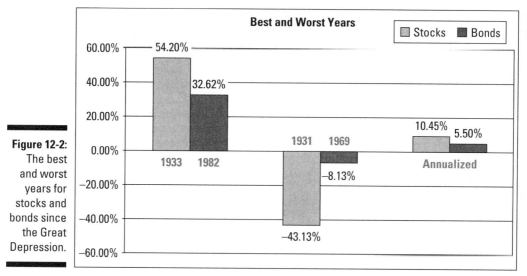

Source: Vanguard, with permission

Peering into the Future

You may be saving and investing to buy a new home, to put your kid(s) through college, or to leave a legacy for your children and grandchildren. For most people, however, a primary goal of investing (as well it should be) is to achieve economic independence: the ability to work or not work, to write the Great (or not-so-great) American Novel . . . to do whatever you want to without having to worry about money.

In Chapters 17 and 18, I discuss in some depth how big a nest egg you'll likely need for economic independence and how much you'll be able to withdraw from your portfolio, should you stop working, without running out of money. I'll save the nitty-gritty for those later chapters (or you can jump ahead and then return here, if you wish). For now, the pertinent question is this: Just how far along are you toward achieving your nest-egg goal?

For reasons I divulge in those two upcoming chapters, please think of how much you will need to withdraw from your nest egg each year when you stop getting a paycheck. Whatever that number is ($30,000? $40,000?), multiply it by 20. That is the amount, at a minimum, I would like to see you have in your total portfolio when you retire. (I'd prefer 25 times, however.) Now multiply that same original-year withdrawal figure ($30,000? $40,000?) by 10. That is the amount, at a minimum, that I'd like to see you have in fixed-income investments, including bonds, when you retire.

I'm assuming here a fairly typical retirement age, somewhere in the 60s. If you wish to retire at 30, you'll likely need considerably more than 20 times your annual expenses (or else very wealthy and generous parents).

Assessing your time frame

Okay. Got those two numbers: one for your total portfolio, and the other for the bond side of your portfolio at retirement? Good. Now how far off are you, in terms of both years and dollars, from giving up your paycheck and drawing on savings?

If you're far away from your goals, you need lots of growth. If you currently have, say, half of what you'll need in your portfolio to call yourself economically independent, and you are years from retirement, that likely means loading up on stocks if you want to achieve your goal. *Vroom vroom.*

If you're closer to your goals, you may have more to lose than to gain, and stability becomes just as important as growth. That means leaning toward bonds and other fixed-income investments. *Slooow down.*

For those of you far beyond your goals (you already have, say, 30 or 40 times what you'll need to live on for a year), an altogether other set of criteria may take precedence.

Factoring in some good rules

As I hope I made clear at the onset of this chapter (with my silly example of the boss's freckles and the cousin named Pablo), there are no simple formulas to determine the optimal allocation of bonds in a portfolio. That being said, there are some pretty good rules to follow. Here, I provide you with a few, and then I ask you to join me for a few case studies to help clarify:

✔ **Rule #1:** You should keep three to six months of living expenses in cash (such as money market funds or online savings bank accounts like www.emigrantdirect.com or www.hsbcdirect.com) or near-cash. If you expect any major expenses in the next year or two, keep money for those in near-cash as well. When I say *near-cash,* I'm talking about very short-term bonds or bond funds, such as those I introduce in Chapter 16.

✔ **Rule #2:** The rest of your money can be invested in longer-term investments, such as intermediate-term or long-term bonds; or equities, such as stocks, real estate, or commodities.

✔ **Rule #3:** A portfolio of more than 75 percent bonds rarely, if ever, makes sense. On the other hand, most people benefit with some healthy allocation to bonds. The vast majority of people fall somewhere in the range of 85/15 (85 percent equities/15 fixed income) to 40/60 (40 percent equities/60 fixed income). Use 60/40 (equities/fixed income) as your default. Tweak from there depending on how much growth you need and how much stability you require.

✔ **Rule #4:** Stocks, a favorite form of equity for most investors, can be very volatile over the short term and intermediate term, but history shows that your risk of loss diminishes with time. Over the course of 10 to 15 years, you are virtually assured that any losses in the stock market will be earned back — at least if history is our guide. (It shouldn't be our only guide! History sometimes does funny things.) Most of the money you won't need for 10 to 15 years or beyond should be in stocks, not bonds.

✔ **Rule #5:** Because history does funny things, you don't want to put all your long-term money in stocks, even if history says you should. Even very long-term money — at the very least 15 percent of it — should be kept in something safer than stocks.

Recognizing yourself in a few case studies

Different strokes for different folks. The following vignettes are all based on real, live clients who have asked me to massage their portfolios. All names and most identifying information have been changed to protect the identities of these good people. Perhaps you will see some similarities between their situations and yours.

Jean and Raymond, 61 and 63, financially quite comfortable

Married in 1982, Jean and Raymond raised three children; the third is just fin-ishing up college. Jean and Raymond are both public school teachers and both will retire (he in two years; she in four) with healthy traditional pen-sions. Together, those pensions, combined with Social Security, should cover Jean and Raymond's living expenses for the rest of their lives. The couple will also likely bring in supplemental income from private tutoring. Jean's mother is 90. When Mom passes away, Jean, an only child, expects to receive an inheritance of at least $1.5 million. Mom's money is invested entirely in bonds and CDs. So what should Jean and Raymond do with the $710,000 they've socked away in their combined retirement plans?

Jean and Raymond are in the catbird seat. Even if they were to invest the entire $710,000 nest egg in stocks, and even if we were to see the worst stock market crash in history, Jean and Raymond would likely still be okay. The couple certainly doesn't need to take the risk of putting their money in stocks because they don't need to see their portfolio grow in order to accomplish their financial goals. But given their pensions, is investing in stocks really that risky? No. If Jean and Raymond desire to leave a large legacy (to their children, grandchildren, or charity), a predominantly stock portfolio would be the way to go. Because equities tend to be so much more lucrative than fixed income in the long run, a greater percentage in equities would likely generate much more wealth for the future generations.

Ignoring for the moment a slew of possibly complicating factors, from the simple scenario above, I would feel comfortable suggesting an aggressive portfolio: perhaps 70 to 75 percent equity (stocks and such) and 25 to 30 per-cent fixed income (bonds and such). I show this breakdown in Figure 12-3. It's not what most people think of as appropriate for an "aging" couple, but to me, it makes a whole lot of sense.

Kay, 59, hoping only for a simple retirement

Kay, divorced twice, earns a very modest salary as a medical technician. She scored fairly well in her last divorce. (Hubby was a condescending jerk, but a well-paid condescending jerk.) Thanks to a generous initial cash settlement, as well as having made a good profit on the sale of her last home, Kay has a portfolio of $875,000. Kay doesn't hate her work, but she isn't crazy about it, either; she would much rather spend her days doing volunteer work for stray animals. After careful analysis, she figures that she can live without the pay-check quite comfortably if allowed to pull $45,000 a year from savings. Her children are grown and self-sufficient.

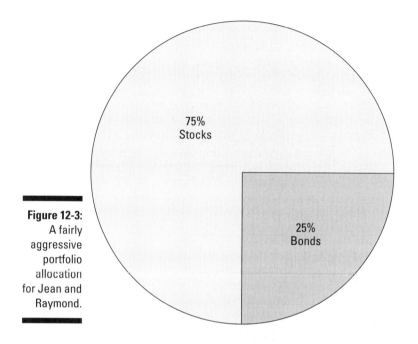

Figure 12-3:
A fairly
aggressive
portfolio
allocation
for Jean and
Raymond.

75%
Stocks

25%
Bonds

I use Kay to illustrate why simple formulas (such as *your age = your proper bond allocation*) don't work. Kay is roughly the same age as Jean in the previous example. And Kay, like Jean, is financially comfortable. But it would be a great mistake for Kay to take the same risks with her money. Unlike Jean, Kay does not have a spouse. Unlike Jean, Kay does not have a pension. Unlike Jean, Kay is not expecting a big inheritance. Unlike Jean and Raymond, Kay cannot afford to lose any significant portion of her nest egg. She is dependent on that nest egg to stay economically afloat.

At her current level of savings and with a fairly modest rate of growth in her portfolio, Kay should be able to retire comfortably within four to five years. In Kay's case, she has more to lose than to gain by taking any great risk in the markets. On the other hand, if things work out as she plans, Kay may be spending 30 or more years in retirement. So an all fixed-income portfolio, which would get gobbled up by inflation, clearly won't work. In Kay's case, I would likely recommend a portfolio of 40 to 45 percent bonds and 55 to 60 percent equities (see Figure 12-4).

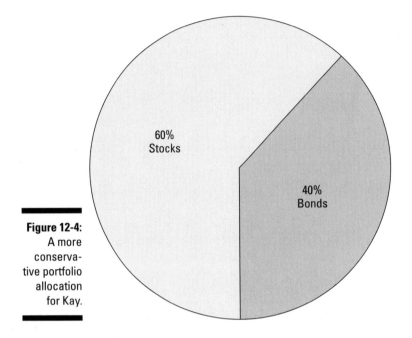

60%
Stocks

40%
Bonds

Figure 12-4:
A more
conserva-
tive portfolio
allocation
for Kay.

Juan, 29, just getting started

Three years out of business school with an MBA, Juan, single and happy in his city condo, is earning an impressive and growing salary. But because he has been busy paying off loans, he has just started to build his savings. Juan's 401(k) has a current balance of $3,700.

Juan — yet another example of why simple formulas don't work! — should probably tailor his portfolio to look something like Jean and Raymond's, despite the obvious differences in age and wealth. Juan is still many years off from retirement and doesn't see any major expenses on the horizon. Juan's budding 401(k) is meant to sit and grow for a very long time — at least three decades. History tells us that a portfolio made up of mostly stocks will provide maximum growth. Of course, history is history, and we don't know what the future would bring. So I would still allocate 15 to 20 percent bonds to Juan's portfolio (see Figure 12-5).

Before moving any money into stocks or bonds, however, I would want Juan to set aside three to six months' worth of living expenses in an emergency cash fund, outside of his 401(k), just in case he should lose his job, have serious health issues, or become subject to some other unforeseen crisis.

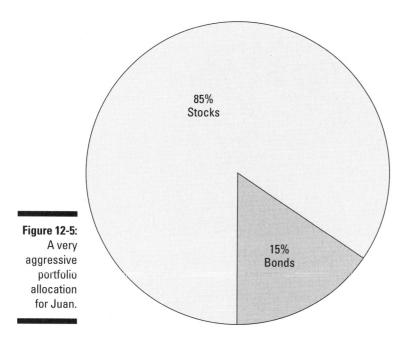

Figure 12-5:
A very aggressive portfolio allocation for Juan.

Miriam, 53, plugging away

Never married, with no children, Miriam wants to retire from her job as a freelance computer consultant while still young enough to fulfill her dreams of world travel. Her investments of $75,000 are growing at a good clip, as she is currently socking away a full 20 percent of her after-tax earnings — about $20,000 a year. But she knows that she has a long way to go.

Miriam is right. She does have a long way to go. To fulfill her dreams of world travel, Miriam will need considerably more than a nest egg of $75,000. In Miriam's case, the bond allocation question is a tough one. Miriam needs substantial growth, but she isn't in a position to risk what she has, either. Cases like Miriam's require delicate balance. I would likely opt for a starting portfolio of mostly stocks and about 20 to 25 percent bonds (see Figure 12-6), but as Miriam gets closer to her financial goal in coming years, I would urge her to up that percentage of bonds and take a more defensive, conservative position.

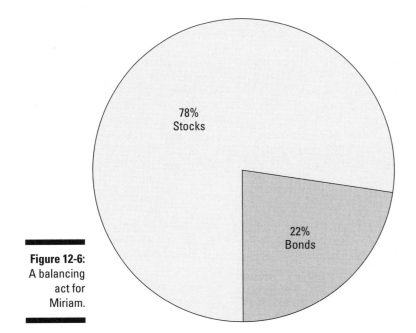

Figure 12-6:
A balancing
act for
Miriam.

Noticing the Many Shades of Gray in Your Portfolio

Although the world of investments offers countless opportunities — and dangers! — all investments qualify as one of these two types:

- ✔ **Equity:** Something you own (such as stocks, real estate, or gold)
- ✔ **Fixed income:** Money you've lent in return for interest (such as bonds, CDs, or money market funds), or possibly money you've given up in return for steady payments (annuities)

For the sake of simplicity, my portfolio discussion thus far has dealt largely with "stocks" and "bonds," ignoring the many shades of gray that define both of these large umbrella terms. I've also ignored other forms of fixed income, such as annuities, and other forms of equity, such as real estate and commodities. It's time now to stop ignoring and start addressing.

Bonds of many flavors

If the point of investing in bonds is to smooth out the returns of a portfolio that also includes stocks (Yes! That *is* the point!), it makes sense to have bonds that tend to zig when stocks zag. By and large, you're looking at either Treasuries, including Treasury Inflation-Protected Securities (see Chapter 5), corporate investment-grade bonds (see Chapter 6), or agency bonds (see Chapter 7). If you're in the higher tax brackets and have limited space in your retirement accounts, you may consider municipal bonds (see Chapter 8). If you have a very large bond portfolio, you may consider a smattering of international bonds (see Chapter 9).

High-yield bonds (addressed in Chapter 6) may also play a role in your portfolio, along with other forms of more exotic bonds (see Chapter 9), but they need to be added with some finesse. As alluring as high-yield bonds can be, they don't offer the same diversifying power as do quality bonds. When stocks sink, high-yield bonds tend to sink as well, for the very same reason: Companies are closing doors.

Whatever your choice in bonds, it is best to seek some diversification: different issuers, different maturities. I make specific recommendations for diversifying the bond side of your portfolio in Chapter 13, again in Chapter 15 where I discuss individual bonds (diversification mandatory!), and yet again in Chapter 16 where I talk about bond funds. You can probably tell that I'm something of a stickler when it comes to diversification!

Stocks of all sizes and sorts

This is a book about bonds, so I won't dwell on what you should do with the stock side of your portfolio. In this chapter on portfolio-building, however, it seems fair to devote at least a few paragraphs to the subject. So here goes:

Because stocks can be so volatile, it is imperative to diversify. The best way to diversify is with low-cost, no-load mutual funds (index funds are often best) or exchange-traded funds.

Just as stocks and bonds tend to poorly correlate, different kinds of stocks and different kinds of bonds similarly have limited correlation. That's especially true on the stock side of the portfolio. Smart investors make sure to have both domestic and foreign stocks, stocks in both large companies and small companies, and both growth and value stocks. (*Growth* stocks are stocks in fast-moving companies in fast-moving industries, such as technology. *Value* stocks are stocks in companies that have less growth potential; you may be able to get these stocks on the cheap, at times making them better investments than growth stocks.)

Just as you get more bang for your buck but also more bounce with stocks versus bonds, you also get more potential return and additional risk with small-company stocks versus large-company stocks. Although international stocks aren't any more volatile than U.S. stocks, *per se,* differences in exchange rates can make them much more volatile to U.S. investors. The greater your tolerance for risk, the more small-company stocks and the more international stocks you may want to incorporate.

After your portfolio grows and you have all the broad asset classes covered, you may consider branching out into narrower (but not too narrow) kinds of investments. Possibilities would include high-yield bonds; small international company stocks; commodities; and certain industry sectors of the economy, especially those that tend to have limited correlation to the market at large, such as real estate and energy.

For more tips on investing in stocks, do *not* go to your local pub or to various and sundry get-rich-quick Web sites! Instead, see *Stock Investing For Dummies,* 2nd edition by Paul Mladjenovic; *Mutual Funds For Dummies,* 5th edition by Eric Tyson; or my own entertaining and highly educational *Exchange-Traded Funds For Dummies.* (All are published by Wiley.) Sure, there are many other good books out there (and lots of bad ones too), but the Dummies series is a darned good place to start.

Other fixed income: Annuities

For some people, sticking an annuity on the fixed-income side of the portfolio makes sense. When you purchase an annuity, you surrender your principal to the issuer of the annuity. In exchange, you receive income at regular intervals — at a rate of return considerably higher than you would receive by buying a Treasury or municipal bond.

Let me be clear: I'm not talking about *variable* annuities, most of which are terrible investment products sold by people who make outrageous commissions. Rather, I'm talking about *fixed* annuities. The difference? With a variable annuity, you receive payments that are largely based on the performance of some piece of the market, such as the S&P 500 or another stock index. A fixed annuity gives you a certain fixed amount of income at fixed intervals (which may be inflation-adjusted). Your payments are not contingent on the performance of the markets or anything else. And the interest earned may be tax-deferred.

With either kind of annuity, the rate of return will usually be largely determined by your age. The fewer years the annuity provider thinks he'll be sending you checks, the more generous he'll be with his payments.

At the time I'm writing this, a 65-year-old man with $100,000 could get about 8 percent on an immediate fixed annuity for the rest of his life. Treasuries are currently paying about 5 percent. But keep this in mind: If the investor dies tomorrow after taking out an annuity today, his estate loses $100,000. He could get an annuity with a death benefit (so his spouse continues to get payments should he die), but that lowers the rate of return.

The best candidates for annuities are generally healthy people with good genes in their 60s or 70s who don't mind dying broke and don't care about leaving behind any chunk of money. It is important to remember that an annuity is only as good as the company issuing it. Don't even consider buying an annuity from anything less than a huge and stable issuer, such as Vanguard or Fidelity. I would generally recommend only inflation-adjusted annuities; otherwise, you risk seeing your income get swallowed up by inflation to the point that your monthly checks will seem like pin money.

Some investment houses, Vanguard and Fidelity included, have begun to offer very modestly priced fixed annuities without the horrible surrender charges that plague this industry. Typically, if you sign up for an annuity and then change your mind and want your principal back, you'll be penalized to the tune of 7 percent if you try to withdraw your money within a year, 6 percent if you try to withdraw within two years, and so on.

For more on annuities, check out *Annuities For Dummies,* written by a friend of mine (and fellow resident of Allentown, Pennsylvania), Kerry Pechter, and being published in 2008 by Wiley.

Other equity: Commodities and real estate

Equity is investment-speak for "something you own." It doesn't have to be a share in a company. You can own real estate, silver, gold, or corn futures. Real estate, if it refers to your own home, should generally not be considered part of your nest egg, simply because you will always need a place to live. Selling your home and downsizing or moving to an apartment may someday add to the size of your nest egg, and you always have the option of a reverse mortgage (although it is expensive), but you should not count on your home as your main retirement fund.

Investment real estate can indeed be profitable, but only if you know what you're doing and are willing to clock some serious hours landlording. It helps to know something about plumbing. And my own personal nightmare a number of years ago involving a property in Maryland tells me that no one should *ever* be a long-distance landlord!

If you want to learn more about buying houses for a profit, check out *Real Estate Investing For Dummies* by Eric Tyson and Robert S. Griswold (Wiley).

Commodity investing was once a sticky business, with high fees and complicated strategies. Lately, with the advent of exchange-traded funds and exchange-traded notes that allow you to buy into commodity indexes, commodity investing is no more complicated than buying a stock or bond fund. Commodities have limited correlation to both stocks and bonds, and I recommend a position of 5 to 10 percent commodities for most people's portfolios.

My favorite vehicle for tapping into commodities is the Barclays iPath Dow Jones-AIG Commodity Index exchange-traded note (ticker symbol DJP), which I discuss at the end of Chapter 9. By the time you are reading this book, however, there may be many more options.

Making Sure That Your Portfolio Remains in Balance

Say you've decided that you want a portfolio of 60 percent equities and 40 percent fixed income (commonly expressed as a *60/40* portfolio). You have $100,000, so you aim to construct a portfolio that is $60,000 in stocks and $40,000 in bonds.

Over the ensuing months, the stock market takes off. At the end of a great year, you count your blessings and realize that you now have not $60,000, but $75,000 in stocks. Your bonds, however, have hardly budged. Let's say you have $41,000 in bonds. Your entire portfolio is now worth ($75,000 + $41,000) $116,000. But it is no longer a 60/40 portfolio. It is now a 65/35 portfolio. Funny how that happens.

What to do? It is time to rebalance.

Rebalancing means getting your investment house back in order. Unless your life circumstances have changed, you probably still want a 60/40 portfolio. That means that your new $116,000 portfolio should be ($116,000 x 60 percent) $69,600 in stocks, and ($116,000 x 40 percent) $46,400 in bonds. In order to get to that point, you're going to have to sell ($75,000 – $69,600) $5,400 in stocks and buy ($46,400 – $41,000) $5,400 in bonds.

It won't be easy. You've seen your stocks go up, up, up, while your bonds have languished. But rebalancing is the smart thing to do. Let me explain why.

Tweaking your holdings to temper risk

The primary reason to rebalance is this: to keep you from losing your shirt. If your personal situation a year ago warranted a 60/40 portfolio, then a 65/35 split is going to be more volatile than the portfolio you want. If you continue to leave the portfolio untouched and stocks continue to fly, you'll eventually wind up with a 70/30 portfolio, and then a 75/25 portfolio. And what happens if the stock market reverses at that point, moving as quickly backwards as it was moving forwards a year or two before? You'll see a much larger loss than you ever bargained for.

Wouldn't you rather lock in some of your profits, and start afresh with the proper portfolio mix?

Savoring the rebalancing bonus

Rebalancing also helps you to realize larger returns over time. Think about it: Most investors buy high, choosing whatever asset class is hot, and sell low, getting rid of whatever asset class is lagging. The financial press is continually pushing us to do this — "10 HOT FUNDS FOR THE NEW YEAR!" inevitably focuses in on ten funds that have risen to new heights in the past months, largely because of the kind of asset class in which they invest (U.S. stocks, foreign stocks, long-term bonds, or whatever).

Studies show that, as a result of continually buying high and selling low, the average investor barely keeps up with inflation. It's sad. But you, by rebalancing regularly, are destined to wind up ahead. Rather than buying high and selling low, you will continually be selling high and buying low. In the example above, you were selling off your recently risen stocks, for example, and buying more of your lagging bonds.

Over the long run, not only will rebalancing temper your risk, but your long-term returns, if we're simply talking about rebalancing stocks and bonds, will tend to be about ½ percent higher.

Need proof?

Consider the ten-year average annual return of the Vanguard Total Stock and the Vanguard Total Bond Index funds. They currently clock in at 8.03 percent average annual return for the stock fund and 6.07 percent for the bond fund. Adding the two together, giving the stocks a 60-percent weighting and the bonds a 40-percent weighting, you would expect the average annual ten-year return of the two to be 7.25 percent. But when you look at the Vanguard Balanced Index fund, which combines the total stock market with the total bond market and continually rebalances, the average annual return for the same period (ending February 28, 2007) is not 7.25 percent — it's 7.64 percent.

If you invest in multiple asset classes (including commodities, foreign and domestic stock, and so on), regular rebalancing may add a full percentage point or more each year to your long-term returns.

Scheduling your portfolio rebalance

With the miracle of modern technology, Excel spreadsheets and whatnot, rebalancing can be easy — too easy! Rebalancing your portfolio every week, or even every month, is most likely going to be counterproductive. There are often transaction costs, and there may be potential capital gains taxes with every sale you make. But another important (and often overlooked) factor is the *momentum* of markets: When an asset class shoots up, all those yokels out there who like buying something that is up will often, by the very fact that they are buying, force the price a bit higher.

The question of how often to rebalance has been studied to death, and those studies show that someone who rebalances as often as he brushes his teeth tends to lose out to momentum — in addition to paying more in transaction costs and taxes.

So, what's the perfect time to rebalance? There is no perfect time. It depends on the volatility of the markets, the correlation of the securities in your portfolio, the cost of your personal transactions, and your tax status. In general, however, rebalancing should be done once every year or two. If you are retired and pulling cash from your portfolio, you may want to rebalance twice a year in order to make sure your cash reserve doesn't dip too low. But do be careful whenever selling securities to watch your trading costs, and monitor your potential tax hit.

The division between stocks and bonds, be it 70/30 or 50/50 or 30/70, is often the most important risk-and-return determiner in your portfolio. Even if you allow everything else to get out of balance, keep your balance of stocks and bonds on an even keel.

Such balance, grasshopper, will keep you afloat and spare you from getting slammed into financial bridges or swamped by the wake of inflation.

Chapter 13

Which Kinds of Bonds Make the Most Sense for You?

*E*ach spring, as the crocuses sprout and the song birds return to my yard, I face the difficult question of whether to call Mike. Mike is a guy in my town with a truck, and for a flat price, often much less than the local nursery charges, he'll drop an entire truckload of mulch — *ka-chunk* — onto my driveway. Given the cost savings, and the fact that I don't particularly enjoy lugging home big plastic, leaking bags of mulch in my car, it seems like a slam-dunk decision.

It isn't.

Most years, I simply can't use as much mulch as Mike's required minimum. So I wind up shoveling mulch on mulch, begging the neighbors to take some, watching the dregs biodegrade on my driveway, and then waiting for the summer rains to flush the rest away.

Of course, the question of how much mulch to buy goes hand-in-hand with what *kind* of mulch to buy. There's hardwood mulch. Pine mulch. Cypress mulch. There are big chips. Little chips. Shredded mulch. And finely pureed mulch. And then there's the more exotic cocoa-bean mulch, which comes largely from The Hershey Company in nearby Hershey, Pennsylvania. Yup, it smells like chocolate.

This chapter is about picking the kinds of bonds you're going to put into your portfolio. It's just like buying mulch. You look first at the quantity of fixed income you need. You then decide on the particular kinds of bonds: Treasuries, corporates, munis, or maybe something more exotic. Finally, you need to decide where and how to purchase them.

Mike the mulch guy doesn't sell bonds (as far as I know), but The Hershey Company sells them by the truckload. Unfortunately, they don't smell like chocolate.

Reviewing the Rationale Behind Bonds

In Chapter 12, I present a plan for dividing a portfolio largely between stocks and bonds. Stocks and bonds are yin and yang, peanut butter and jelly, Fred and Ginger, cookies and milk, tequila and taxi-rides home — they go together perfectly. Stocks are where you're likely to get your growth. Bonds provide predictability and stability.

Any other reasons for having bonds in your portfolio — such as getting a stream of income — are nice, but secondary. (If it seems that I'm too lightly kissing off the importance of bond income, read Chapter 17.)

Some bonds are more volatile than others. That matters, for sure. But what also matters, and perhaps matters more, is the extent to which the price of bonds tends to rise and fall with the price of stocks. The kinds of bonds that historically zig when stocks zag are by and large the kinds of bonds that should dominate most people's bond portfolios. And those kinds of bonds are government and agency bonds, high quality (investment-grade) corporate bonds (like Hershey's), and municipal bonds.

Making your initial selection

In Part II, I outline the different kinds of bonds I mentioned here, and I review their most distinguishing characteristics. But in choosing a type or types of bonds to put in your portfolio, you also need to look at your *personal* characteristics.

For example, what may your need for funds be over the next several years? What is your tax bracket? Are you subject to the sneaky alternative minimum tax? How much room do you have in your retirement accounts? How heavily is the stock side of your portfolio invested overseas? How subject are you to the ravages of inflation? These are some of the things that make me different from you, and may make my "perfect" bond portfolio very different from your "perfect" bond portfolio.

As I do in Chapter 12, here I give you the best rules I can. Then, toward the end of this chapter, I provide a few case studies to help sharpen your sights on what kinds of bonds may best match your investment goals.

Following a few rules

These guidelines should begin to give you an idea of the kinds of bonds you may want. They are quick and a bit dirty. I clean them up — and get more specific in my recommendations — as this chapter rolls along.

✔ **Rule #1:** It's best to keep three to six months of living expenses in cash (a savings account or money market fund) or near-cash for emergencies. For any major expenses you anticipate in the next couple years, you may want to keep that money in near-cash as well. By *near-cash,* I mean very short-term bonds or bond funds maturing in one to three years. Short-term bonds generally pay slightly higher rates of interest than savings accounts and money market funds but less interest than longer-term bonds. Correspondingly, they can be a wee bit more volatile than a money market account but far less volatile than longer-term bonds.

✔ **Rule #2:** Money you won't need in the next few years should be invested in higher yielding securities for greater income and growth. These securities include bonds with maturities of three years and greater.

✔ **Rule #3:** The majority of your bond holdings should be high-quality bonds, be they Treasuries, corporate bonds, agency bonds, or munis. If you're looking for higher return and can take the risk, you're usually going to be better off moving into stocks than into high-yield bonds.

Go with munis if your tax bracket warrants it and if you are investing in a taxable account. See Chapter 8 for all the muni formulas you need. As for the other bonds, it is preferable to mix and match both issuers and maturities.

✔ **Rule #4:** Whatever your allocation to fixed income, about one-third should be inflation-adjusted, either with an inflation adjusted annuity or with special bonds called Treasury Inflation-Protected Securities (TIPS). TIPS are a nice complement to other bonds because they tend not to correlate to other bonds in their price movements. If inflation takes off, traditional bonds tend to suffer, but TIPS tend to flourish. (In 2000, for example, TIPS returned 13.17 percent, while high-yield bonds returned –5.21 percent.)

If inflation is less than expected, however, TIPS won't do as well. (In 2006, for example, high-yield bonds returned 11.92 percent, and TIPS returned 0.41 percent.)

Sizing Up Your Need for Fixed-Income Diversification

As you know, some stocks can double or triple in price overnight, while others can shrink into oblivion in the time it takes to say "CEO arrested for fraud." Unless you are investing in individual high-yield bonds (not a good idea), your risk of default — and your investment shrinking to oblivion — will be minimal. But diversifying your bonds is still a very good idea.

Although you can negate your risk of default by simply buying Treasury bonds, you still incur other risks by having too concentrated a bond portfolio.

Diversifying by maturity

Regardless of whether you invest in Treasuries, corporate bonds, or munis, you always risk swings in general interest rates (which can send bond prices tumbling) and reinvestment risk (the fact that interest or principal invested in a bond may not be able to be reinvested in such a way that it can earn the same rate of return as before). Both risks can be greatly ameliorated with the fine art of _laddering,_ or staggering your individual bond purchases to include bonds of differing maturities. I discuss laddering in Chapter 15. Both risks can also be greatly lessened by investing in bond funds, discussed in Chapter 16.

Diversifying by type of issuer

In addition to diversifying by maturity, you also want to divide up your bonds so they represent different kinds of bond categories, such as government and corporate. This is true with both individual bonds and bond funds. Different kinds of bonds do better in certain years than others. Having various types of bonds helps to smooth out your total bond portfolio returns.

Let's take two years — 2002 and 2004 — as examples.

The year 2002 was an extraordinarily great year for bonds. Interest rates were falling, and investors, bruised by a falling stock market, were looking for safety in fixed income. That helped to drive up demand for bonds, which tends to drive up the price. That year, from January to December, we saw the following juicy returns:

✔ Long-term government bonds: 11.79 percent

✔ Municipal bonds: 9.60 percent

✔ Investment-grade corporate bonds: 8.58 percent

But 2004 was a not-so good year for bonds. Investors were bidding *au revoir* to bonds and moving back into stocks. Interest rates were no longer falling. Government bonds just about kept even with inflation. Munis and corporates fared better:

✔ Investment-grade corporate bonds: 6.25 percent

✔ Municipal bonds: 4.48 percent

✔ Long-term government bonds: 3.54 percent

Generally, investment-grade corporate bonds do better than government bonds when the economy is strong. When the economy is weak (and people flock to safety), government bonds — especially long-term Treasuries — tend to do better. If you think you can tell the future, buy all one kind of bond or the other. If you realize that you are not clairvoyant, it probably makes the most sense to divide your holdings.

Diversifying by risk-and-return potential

The returns on high quality corporate bonds, Treasuries, and munis (after their tax-free nature is accounted for) generally differ by only a percentage point or two in any given year. But some other kinds of bonds, such as high-yield corporates, convertible bonds, and international bonds, can vary much, much more.

In general, because the potential return on stocks is so much higher than just about any kind of bond, I favor stomaching volatility on the stock side of the portfolio.

For some people, however, more exotic, "cocoa-bean" type bonds make sense. High-yield bonds, for example, act like a hybrid between stocks and bonds. They often produce high returns (higher than other bonds, lower than stocks) when the economy is growing fast, and they tend to take dives (more than other bonds, less than stocks) when the economy falters. Because of this hybrid nature, they make particular sense for relatively conservative investors who need the high yield but can't take quite as much risk as stocks involve.

Emerging-market bonds (issued by the governments of poor countries) also can produce very high yields but can be very volatile. Unlike U.S. high-yield bonds, they tend to have limited correlation to the U.S. stock market. For this reason, I often include a small percentage of emerging-market bonds in many people's portfolios.

Diversifying away managerial risk

Where I discuss bond funds in Chapter 16, I suggest that you put most of your bond money into *index* funds: funds run by managers who work on the cheap and do not attempt to do anything fancy. But occasionally, taking a bet on a talented manager may not be such a terrible thing to do. And regardless of what I say, you may turn your nose up at index funds anyway. You may attempt to beat the market by choosing bond funds run by managers who try to score big by rapid buying and selling, going out on margin, and all sorts of other wild and crazy things.

Whenever you go with an actively managed fund (as opposed to a passively managed fund, otherwise known as an index fund), you hope that the manager will do something smart to beat the market. But you risk that he or she will do something dumb. Or that manager may get hit by a train, and the fund winds up getting managed by the incompetent junior partner. That is called *managerial risk.*

Managerial risk is real, and it should always be diversified away. If you have a sizeable bond portfolio and you are depending on that portfolio to pay the bills some day, you shouldn't trust any one manager with that much responsibility. Recall the numbers from the "Diversifying by type of issuer" section, which reflect the differences among returns of different kinds of bonds in a couple sample years? That is *nothing* compared to the differences you find between well-managed and poorly managed active bond funds.

According to Morningstar Principia,

- ✔ The ten-year cumulative return on the well-run Loomis Sayles Bond Fund is **148.65 percent.**

- ✔ The ten-year cumulative return on the not-so-well-run Morgan Stanley High Yield Fund is **–23.40 percent.**

If you're going to take a shot at beating the market by giving your bond money to managers who tinker and toy (yes, even Dan Fuss, the very talented manager at Loomis Sayles — see Chapter 21), do it in moderation, please.

Weighing Diversification Versus Complication

Most individual bonds sell for $1,000. But buying individual bonds (not Treasuries, but most other bonds) can be very expensive. You can't very well build a diversified bond portfolio — different maturities, different issuers — out of individual bonds unless you have quite a few grand sitting around.

Diversifying with funds isn't the easiest thing in the world, either. Most bond funds have minimums, often in the $1,000 to $3,000 range. And exchange-traded funds, even though they have no minimums, carry trading fees. In other words, if you haven't got a fair chunk of change, building a diversified bond portfolio can be a challenge. But I do have a few suggestions for all you non-millionaires.

Keeping it simple with balanced funds (for people with under $5,000)

If you have under $5,000 to invest, you are going to find little choice if you want a balanced portfolio. Forget about individual stocks and bonds. Even building a fund portfolio, given the minimums of most funds, will be tough.

Best solution: Consider a *balanced fund,* a one-stop-shopping fund that allows you to invest in stocks and bonds in one fell swoop. Note that some balanced funds are static; they will allocate, say, 60 percent of your money to stocks and 40 percent to bonds, and that is how it will always be. Others are dynamic; these are often called *life cycle* funds. A life cycle fund has a target retirement date and, as you move toward that date, the fund shifts your money, usually from the stock side to the bond side, to become more conservative.

See my recommendations for the Vanguard STAR Fund in Chapter 16.

Moving beyond the basic (for people with $5,000 to $10,000)

In the ballpark of $5,000 to $10,000, you may be looking to invest several thousand in stocks and several thousand in bonds. Your best bet for building a diversified portfolio would be a handful of low-cost, no-load mutual funds. Perhaps you want one total market bond fund, one total U.S. stock fund, and one diversified foreign stock fund.

See Chapter 16 for my recommendations for total market bond funds.

Branching out (with $10,000 or more)

With $10,000 or more, you can begin to entertain a more finely segmented portfolio of either mutual funds or exchange-traded funds. But you'll probably want more than $10,000 in the bond side of your portfolio before you sell your total market bond fund and start diversifying into the various sectors of the bond market.

I wouldn't suggest dabbling in individual bonds unless you have a bond portfolio of $100,000 or so. Otherwise, the trading costs will eat you alive. The exception would be Treasury bonds because you can buy them at www. treasurydirect.gov without any markup. Even some large brokerage houses allow you to buy Treasuries without a markup.

Finding the Perfect Bond Portfolio Fit

In Chapter 12, I introduce four portfolios, belonging to Jean and Raymond, Kay, Juan, and Miriam. In that chapter, I suggest what percentage of their portfolios should be in bonds. I revisit our friends here to suggest what specific kinds of bonds they might consider.

Case studies in bond ownership

You'll notice that just as there are no hard and fast rules for the percentage of a portfolio that should be in bonds, there are no absolutes when it comes to what kind of bonds are optimal for any given investor.

Jean and Raymond, 61 and 63, financially fit as a fiddle

These folks have a solid portfolio of nearly three-quarters of a million dollars. A fat inheritance is likely coming. They are both still working in secure jobs, and when they retire, their (inflation-adjusted) pensions and Social Security should cover all the basic bills. With their children and grandchildren in mind and having little to risk with any volatility in the markets, Jean and Raymond have wisely decided to invest 75 percent of their savings (all in their retirement accounts) in equities — mostly stocks, with some commodities. The other 25 percent ($177,500) they have chosen to invest in fixed income. What to do with the fixed income? Financially fit as they seem, Jean and Raymond still could use an emergency kitty. Because they are both older than 59½ and are allowed to pull from their retirement accounts without penalty, I would suggest three months' living expenses ($15,000) be kept in cash or in a very short-term bond fund, of the kind I suggest in Chapter 16.

Okay, that still leaves them with $162,500. Chances are this money won't be touched for quite some time — perhaps not until after Jean and Raymond have passed to that great teachers' lounge in the sky, and their children and grandchildren inherit their estate. That being the case, it warrants investing in higher yielding bonds. But just in case the economy takes a real fall and the lion's share of the estate goes with it, these bonds should be strong enough to stand tall.

Tax-free munis make no sense in this case because Jean and Raymond have room in their retirement accounts, and munis, which pay lower rates of interest than bonds of comparable quality and maturity, *never* make sense in a tax-advantaged retirement account.

I would suggest nearly one-third of the pot (approximately $54,200) be put into long-term Treasuries, either in a bond fund or, perhaps better yet, into individual bonds through www.treasurydirect.gov. Another almost one-third should go into Treasury Inflation-Protected Securities (TIPS), again either in a TIPS fund (see my recommendation in Chapter 16) or individual TIPS purchased free of markup on the Treasury's own Web site. The final almost one-third should go either into a fund of investment-grade corporate bonds or a handful of individual investment-grade corporate bonds. The corporate bonds over time will tend to return higher interest than the government bonds but may not do quite as well if the economy hits the skids.

If Jean and Raymond want to place a small percentage of their bond allocation in a foreign bond fund, that money could be worked into the mix (taking away equally from the other categories). It would add a bit more diversification to the portfolio. But foreign bond funds have their pros and cons, as I discuss in Chapter 9. Whether the couple goes with a foreign bond fund or not would depend on how much exposure they had to foreign currencies on the equity side of their portfolio. I present some good international bond funds in Chapter 16.

See Figure 13-1 for a chart that reflects my recommendations to Jean and Raymond.

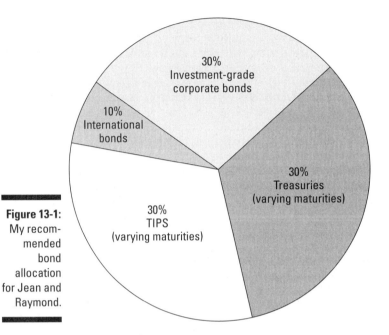

Figure 13-1:
My recom-
mended
bond
allocation
for Jean and
Raymond.

Kay, 59, approaching retirement

Kay, our divorced medical technician, is currently on her own. She needs a larger emergency fund than do Jean and Raymond. Having no pension, she will also be reliant on her portfolio when she retires and can't take quite as much risk as the older married couple. (Simple formulas that say you need to take less risk as you get older simply aren't very helpful much of the time.) Kay's healthy portfolio of $875,000 is divided 60/40 between equities and fixed income. That equates to $350,000 in fixed income.

Where to put it?

Kay needs a somewhat larger cash cushion for emergencies than do Jean and Raymond. She is, after all, on her own, although her adult children could help her in a real emergency. I would allot four to five months of her fixed income to either a money market fund or a very short-term bond fund. That would still leave $330,000 to invest in higher yielding instruments.

Kay doesn't care about leaving an inheritance. Her kids are grown and doing very well. She is also of good genes, eats granola and grapefruit for breakfast, and expects to live a long life. In four or five years, when Kay plans to retire, she will be a good candidate for an inflation-adjusted fixed annuity that will guarantee her an income stream throughout the rest of her life.

I would set up a bond portfolio for her with the intention of making the move to an annuity when Kay is in her mid-60s (provided interest rates at that time are favorable). Kay needs a bond portfolio that will be there for her in four or five years, providing income and, more importantly, providing the cash she'll need to live on in retirement should the other 60 percent of her portfolio — the stocks — take a dive. With $330,000 to invest in bonds, roughly twice what our teacher couple has to invest, I would suggest a somewhat more diversified bond allocation.

Kay may start by taking a third of her bond money ($110,000) and buying either a Treasury Inflation-Protected Securities (TIPS) fund or individual TIPS through `www.treasurydirect.gov`. These bonds offer modest rates of return but adjust the principal twice a year for inflation. If inflation goes on a rampage, Kay will have some protection on the fixed-income side of her portfolio.

With the other two-thirds of her bond portfolio ($220,000), I would suggest equal allocations to long-term traditional Treasuries, intermediate-term Treasuries, long-term investment-grade corporate bonds, intermediate-term investment-grade corporate bonds, international bonds, and high-yield bonds (see Figure 13-2).

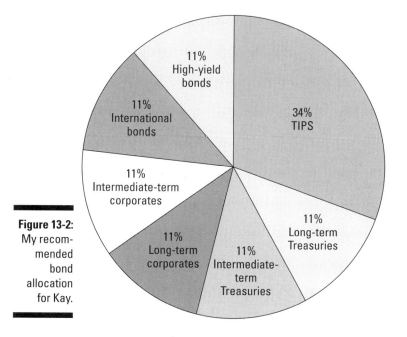

Figure 13-2: My recommended bond allocation for Kay.

Juan, 29, building up his savings

Juan's 401(k) has a current balance of just $3,700, but he's making a good salary.

I would first encourage Juan to save up enough so he can set aside three to six months' living expenses in an emergency cash fund.

Given that his 401(k) money is (we hope) not going to be touched until Juan is at least 59½ (and able to make withdrawals without penalty), he has decided to allocate only 15 percent of his retirement fund to bonds — just about right.

The purpose of those bonds is to somewhat smooth out his account's returns, provide the opportunity to rebalance, and be there just in case of an economic apocalypse. Juan, of course, is prisoner to his 401(k) investment options, be they what they are.

If his employer's plan is like most, he may have the option of one mixed-maturity Treasury fund and one mixed-maturity corporate-bond fund. Because we're talking about only 15 percent of his portfolio, whichever way he goes shouldn't make a huge difference over the next few years. I'd suggest splitting the baby and going half and half (see Figure 13-3).

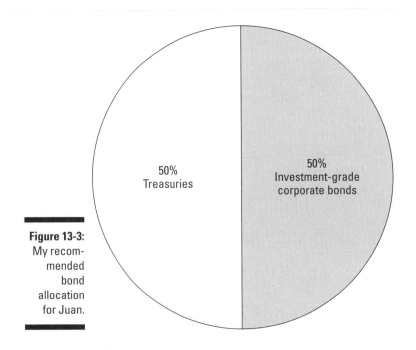

Figure 13-3: My recommended bond allocation for Juan.

50%
Treasuries

50%
Investment-grade
corporate bonds

Should Juan leave his job, he may be able to transfer his 401(k) to his new place of employment, or he may be able to roll it into an individual retirement plan (IRA). I would usually advise the latter because IRAs typically offer better investment choices at lower costs. At that point, should Juan open an IRA, and should the balance grow beyond several thousand dollars, I would encourage greater diversification of his bonds.

Miriam, 53, behind on her goals

With $75,000 in savings and the good majority in stocks, Miriam's 22 percent in bonds ($16,500) must serve two purposes: First, it must provide ballast to smooth out the year-to-year return of her investments. Second, it must help provide cash flow when (within a decade, we hope) Miriam is able to retire and fulfill her dreams of world travel.

Miriam is currently making Trump dollars in her job as a freelance computer consultant — about $160,000 a year. But she lives in New York City, paying high city and state taxes. She rents rather than owns her home, so she gets no mortgage deduction. Being self-employed, Miriam does not have a 401(k) but is socking away about $20,000 a year in her SEP-IRA. The $75,000 in savings is half in her IRA and half outside her IRA.

Given Miriam's relatively high tax bracket and the fact she pays a boatload in taxes, it would make most sense for Miriam to have her $16,500 in her taxable account socked away in high-quality municipal bonds or in a muni bond fund exempt from federal, state, and local taxes (see Figure 13-4).

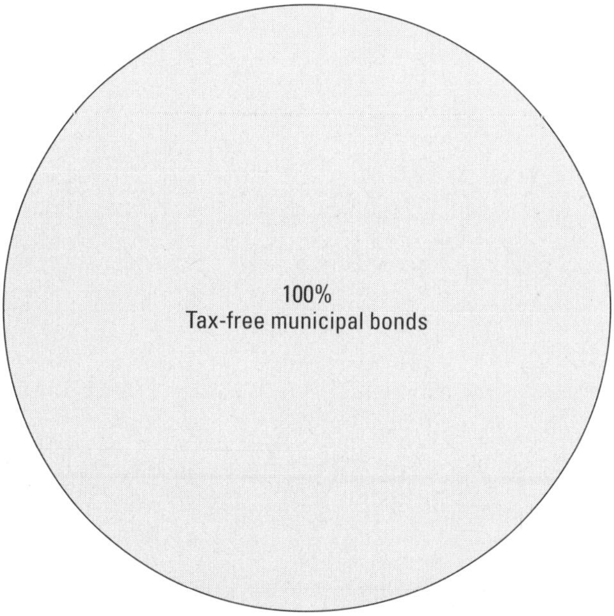

100%
Tax-free municipal bonds

Figure 13-4:
My recommended bond allocation for Miriam.

Seeking out the more exotic offerings

You may have noted that none of these case scenarios calls for more exotic ("cocoa-bean" type) bonds. Sometimes, I like exotic. High-yield bonds from abroad, for example, have very handsome historical returns and, unlike U.S. high-yield bonds, tend to rise and fall *somewhat* independently of the U.S. stock market. That is especially true of so-called *emerging-market* bonds (bonds from poor countries). Because of their extreme volatility, however, I recommend putting emerging-market bonds, in modest allocations, on the equity side of the portfolio.

Ditto for *exchange-traded notes,* bond-like instruments that don't pay a steady rate of interest but rather offer a yield tied to a certain benchmark, such as a commodity index that tracks the fortunes of gold, silver, and corn futures. See further discussion of both emerging-market bonds and exchange-traded notes in Chapter 9.

In Chapter 12, I discuss *rebalancing.* It is crucial, after you set up a properly allocated portfolio, to go in once a year or so and make sure that if you allocated, say, 60 percent to equities and 40 percent to fixed income, those allocations don't go too far astray. At the same time, you want to check once a year or so to make certain that your bond allocations — your division between Treasuries, corporates, munis, and other kinds of bonds — are where you want them to be.

Perhaps you can rebalance your portfolio every spring, just about the same time you spread your mulch. I don't know if Mike-with-the-truck does that, but that's what I do.

Part IV
Bonds Away! Navigating the Fixed-Income Marketplace

In this part . . .

In the following three chapters, I will make you a savvy bond investor. I promise! By the time you finish Part IV, you'll be trading bonds like a pro.

The action starts with Chapter 14. Here, I help you through the crucial first question you need to ask before trading bonds: Are you going to be trading individual bonds, or bond funds? While attacking that question, I also address the issue of investment *containers*: whether it makes more sense to store your bonds or bond funds in taxable accounts or in tax-advantaged retirement accounts. I also touch on the timing of your bond purchases: whether it makes sense to wait for the right kind of interest environment, or whether you should just jump in tomorrow.

Chapter 15 shows you the ropes where it comes to buying and selling individual bonds. You find out how to negotiate the best deals and, using some rather revolutionary new tools, lower your transaction costs greatly.

And finally, Chapter 16 gets you up to snuff on bond funds: Which are the best? Which should you avoid? What is the most you should pay?

Ready to set sail?

Chapter 14

Strategizing Your Bond Buys and Sells

In This Chapter

▶ Appreciating recent changes in the fixed-income marketplace

▶ Deciding whether to invest in individual bonds or bond funds

▶ Keeping an eye on interest rates

▶ Choosing between a taxable account and a tax-advantaged retirement account

▶ Factoring in, and avoiding, the tax hits

*I*n 1497, Vasco da Gama, a man from Portugal with a bushy beard and funny pants, gathered up 170 of his cronies, most of whom also had bushy beards and funny pants, and set sail for India. Along the way, da Gama and company encountered fierce ocean storms, thirst, hunger, disease, and hostile natives who hated the pants.

But the intrepid travelers, in their four rickety vessels, made it to India, did a bit of sightseeing, picked up a few bags of spices, and headed for home. The trip was deemed a great success, and Mr. da Gama was hailed a hero — despite the pants, two years of misery at sea, half of his boats lost, and 116 dead cronies.

The fact that you could sail from Europe to India was seen as a great advance for humankind. As grueling and treacherous as the seagoing voyage was, it was still preferable to doing the 5,500 miles from Portugal to India on foot.

A short number of years ago, if you wanted to invest in bonds, you had a similarly bitter choice. You could either walk into the office of your local bond broker and face fierce markups on individual bonds, or you could sail into the sea of funds and deal with hostile management fees and loads. Whichever option you chose, whatever kind of pants you were wearing, bond investing was often a very perilous journey.

Today's bond market is becoming a friendlier place. Let me introduce you.

Discovering the Brave New World of Bonds

Regardless of which way you decide to invest your money, bond funds or individual bonds, the going is easier and potentially more lucrative today than it was just several years ago. And it is getting easier all the time.

Finding fabulously frugal funds

Expensive bond funds still exist. According to Morningstar, more than 400 of them charge 2 percent or more in annual fees. Imagine. At today's modest interest rates, most bonds pay only about 5 percent a year. That's a *nominal* — before inflation — 5 percent a year. After inflation, you're looking at a total *real* return of about 2 to 3 percent a year. After taxes, you're looking at less than that. And you're going to fork over 2 percent to a fund manager? Lots of people do! They haven't yet read this book.

But paying such fees, once a hard thing to avoid, is now strictly optional. Yes, the times they are a changin'. In 1998, 36 bond funds had expense ratios below 0.50 percent. Today, that number is over 300. In the past ten years, according to Morningstar figures, the number of bond funds charging annual fees of 0.20 percent or less has increased by more than 50 percent.

The lowering of mutual-fund fees is largely due to the recent introduction of exchange-traded funds (ETFs). If you want to know more about ETFs, well, I wrote an entire book about them: *Exchange-Traded Funds For Dummies* (Wiley). ETFs are wonderful investment vehicles in their own right — both inexpensive and tax-efficient. They have also given some serious competition to mutual funds, and that has resulted in a lowering of fees across the board.

A new line-up of ETFs from Vanguard, which anyone with minimal money can buy, allows you to invest in numerous bond index funds, Treasury or corporate, short-term or long-term, for an annual fee of a mere 0.11 percent. A number of bond index mutual funds from Vanguard and Fidelity — the two largest U.S. financial supermarkets — are charging annual fees in the same ballpark (although most of these mutual funds have minimums of at least $3,000).

Dealing in individual bonds without dealing over a fortune

The transaction costs on individual bonds, which have traditionally been way higher than stock transaction costs, have been dropping faster than hail.

Peek-a-boo: Bond trades move out of the darkness, into the light

Once upon a time, you'd go to buy (or sell) a bond, and you'd say to your bond broker, "Hello," and he would say to you, "Hello! How are you? How are the kids?" And you would say, "Good. Good." And then the bond broker would tell you about a real beaut of an A-rated bond, with a maturity of ten years and a coupon rate of 5.46 percent . . . blah, blah, blah. And you would say, "Uh-huh," and you would then fork over $5,000 or so having no idea whether the broker was enjoying a $5 markup, a $50 markup, or even a $500 markup.

Bond trades in those dark but not-so-distant days were done by telephone, one broker to another, and the clients were more or less at their mercy. You couldn't look up bond prices in the daily paper, as you could stock prices. There was no agreed-to commission, as there was with stocks. And there was no Internet. Many bond traders were good people, making a fair living but still looking out for their clients' best interests. Others would never give a sucker an even break, carving off the lion's share of the investor's potential profits and hoarding it for themselves.

Both kinds of brokers still exist, for sure. But thanks to the Trade Reporting and Compliance Engine (and, of course, *Bond Investing For Dummies*, which is clueing people into the Engine), suckers are getting rarer and rarer, and profit-hoarding brokers are having to find new careers.

Known most commonly by its acronym, TRACE, the Trade Reporting and Compliance Engine is a baby of the Securities and Exchange Commission (SEC) and the former National Association of Securities Dealers (NASD), which is now part of the Financial Industry Regulatory Authority (FINRA). TRACE began in July 2002 and was phased in over several years. As of February 2005, every corporate bond trade in the United States — replete with all the information about the trade you could hope for — gets reported into the system and shows up on the Web, in living color. A parallel system for municipal bonds is run by an outfit called the Municipal Securities Rulemaking Board.

So now if a broker says that you can get an A-rated bond with a maturity of ten years and a coupon rate of 5.46 percent, you can immediately go online (to www.finra.org or www.investinginbonds.com) and see the most recent trades made on that particular bond. That will often reveal what that broker paid for the very same bond he is now offering to sell you for $5,000. If you can't find that very same bond, you can find very similar bonds: other A-rated bonds with similar maturity. If you wish to sell a bond, you can see what other people are getting on the open market for bonds similar to yours. In Chapter 15, I walk you through the system, step by step. You'll like it! And you — not some middleman — will profit from it!

One 2004 study from the Securities and Exchange Commission found that the average cost of a $5,000 corporate bond trade back then was $84, or 1.68 percent — equivalent to several months' interest. Smaller trades (less than $5,000) tended to whack investors with much higher costs.

Trade costs of municipal bonds (a favorite flavor of bond among individuals in high tax brackets), according to the same study, averaged 2.23 percent — equivalent perhaps to a full year's return after inflation — for trades of $25,000 or less. For trades from $25,000 to $100,000, the average price spread was 1.12 percent.

Since 2004, the cost of bond trading has dropped considerably. Although I haven't seen any very recent studies, my guess would be that a savvy bond investor willing to do some legwork can now buy a typical corporate or municipal bond for about half the cost that he or she would have incurred in 2004. Bond sales can still be a tougher, and more expensive, game. (That's one reason that I generally recommend buying single bonds only if you plan to hold them till maturity. I discuss individual bond trading in Chapter 15.)

The changing environment, which has actually thrown many bond brokers out of business, is due in part to the advent of Internet trading but more so to something called the *Trade Reporting and Compliance Engine* (TRACE), a government and securities industry–imposed national database that allows bond traders — both professional and amateur — to see what other bond traders are up to. Brokers can no longer charge whatever markup they wish. See the sidebar "Peek-a-boo: Bond trades move out of the darkness, into the light" for more details.

Deciding Whether to Go with Bond Funds or Individual Bonds

Before I get into the nitty-gritty of buying and selling bonds (the next two chapters are nothing but nitty-gritty), you need to make a decision between individual bonds and bond funds. Thanks to the many recent changes in the bond markets that I discuss in the previous sections, either choice can be a good one. My own bias — built on years of experience — is that most investors are better off, most of the time, with bond funds.

Calculating the advantages of funds

I prefer bond funds for a number of reasons, but far and away the largest reason is the diversification that bond funds allow.

Diversifying away certain risks

The obvious appeal of going with a bond fund over individual bonds is the same as the appeal of going with stock funds over individual stocks: You get instant diversification. If you build an entire portfolio of McDummy

Corporation bonds (or stocks), and the McDummy Corporation springs a serious leak, you could take a serious hit on the McChin. With bond funds, you don't need to worry so much about the crash of a particular company.

Just as importantly, bond funds allow you to diversify not only by issuer but by credit quality (you can have AAA-rated bonds and B-rated bonds — see Chapter 6) and by maturity. Some bond funds allow you to diversify even more broadly by including completely different *kinds* of bonds, such as Treasuries, agencies, and corporates, both U.S. and international.

How much money should you have to invest before you forget about bond funds and build a truly diversified bond portfolio out of individual bonds? "We're talking something in the range of $350,000 to $400,000," says Chris Genovese, senior vice president of Fixed Income Securities, or FIS, a nation-wide firm that provides targeted advice on bond portfolio construction to investment advisors.

Making investing a lot easier

Sure, you can own a boatload of individual bonds and *ladder* them (which means to use a diversification technique I discuss in Chapter 15), but owning one or a handful of bond mutual or exchange-traded funds is often a lot simpler. Also, given the numbers that Genovese is talking about, most people don't have nearly enough money to diversify properly with individual bonds.

Individual bonds are also more work than bond funds.

When you own an individual bond, the interest payments generally come to you twice a year. If you reinvest that money rather than spend it, you need to decide how to reinvest. In other words, a portfolio of individual bonds takes ongoing care and maintenance, sort of like an old car that needs to go to the shop every few months. Bond funds, in contrast, can be set up to reinvest automatically and can almost be put on autopilot.

Having choices: Index funds and actively managed funds

If you wish to capture the gains of the entire bond market, bond index funds allow you to do that. If you want to bet (yes, it is always something of a bet) that you can do better than the bond market at large, you can hire an active manager who will try to eke out extra returns for you by looking for special deals in the bond market.

I believe largely in index investing (for both stocks and bonds) because beating the market is very hard to do. Study after study shows that index investors, in both equities and fixed income, wind up doing better than the vast majority of investors. That's largely because index funds tend to be the least expensive funds. Index fund managers take less for themselves, and they incur far fewer trading costs.

Still, if you put the time and effort into finding the right active bond manager, and you pay that manager a modest fee, you may wind up ahead of the indexes. Just know the odds are against it. According to Morningstar, only 28 percent of actively managed bond funds have outperformed the Lehman Brothers Aggregate Bond Index over the past 15 years, while many of them take on more risk than the index.

If you wish to try to beat the market using individual bonds, you may be able to find a really good bond broker who knows the markets inside and out and will charge you only a reasonable markup for each trade or a reasonable flat fee for his or her services. Finding such a broker, however, is a lot more diffi-cult than researching bond-fund managers. And most such talented brokers aren't going to work with you if you have chump change to invest.

Keeping your costs to a minimum

For the savvy investor, the cost of trading individual bonds is cheaper than ever. But so, too, is the cost of investing in bond funds. Treasury bonds can be bought online (`www.treasurydirect.gov`) without any kind of fee or markup. Any other kind of bond, however, will cost you something to trade. Given the volume that bond fund managers trade, they can often trade cheaper than you can.

"Institutional buyers can buy and sell bonds and get much better prices than the retail investor," says Helen Modly, CFP, executive vice president of Focus Wealth Management in Middleburg, Virginia. "Because of that, bond funds, especially bond index exchange-traded funds (ETFs), make a lot of sense."

If you pay a fund manager a pittance per year (such as the 11/100 of 1 percent that a Vanguard ETF manager receives), Modly says (and I agree) that you are nearly always going to get off cheaper with the fund than with building your own bond ladder.

Note that popular wisdom has it that individual bond investing is cheaper than investing in bond funds. Don't buy it. Except perhaps for Treasury bonds, and maybe sometimes new issues on agency bonds or municipals, the small investor is unlikely to wind up ahead dealing in individual bonds.

I should add that many buyers of individual bonds often incur one frequently forgotten cost: the cost of having idle cash. If you collect your semiannual coupon payments and don't spend them, they may sit around in a low-interest money market account. Many of the clients I've seen show me their existing "bond" portfolios, and I immediately notice wads and wads of cash sitting around earning next to nothing. That doesn't happen with bond funds, where the monthly interest can easily be set up to roll right back into the fund, earning money without pause.

Considering whether individual bonds make sense

Individual bonds and bond funds, like politics and money, are even closer than most people think.

Dispelling the cost myth

People who imagine great differences often say that bond funds are more expensive than investing in individual bonds. Often untrue. Bond funds' expenses have traditionally been more *visible* than the expenses of trading individual bonds, but overall, funds tend to be less expensive, unless individual bonds are bought for very large amounts and held till maturity.

Dispelling the predictability myth

There is also a misconception that individual bonds are much more predictable than bond funds. After all, you get a steady stream of income, and you know that you are getting your principal back on such-and-such a date. Technically, these things are true. But they're more complicated than they seem.

Say you had all your money in one big, fat bond worth $100,000 with a coupon rate of 5 percent, maturing in 20 years. You would know that you'd get a check for $2,500 once every six months and that, in 20 years, you'd get a final check for $102,500 (your final interest payment, plus your principal returned).

But that's not how things work in the real world. In the real world, investors in individual bonds typically have bonds of varying maturities. As one bond matures, a younger bond takes its place. Except by rare coincidence, the new bond will not have the same maturity period or the same coupon rate. So the argument that the returns on a portfolio of individual bonds are as predictable as the sunrise is weak.

In addition, consider the effects of inflation. Yes, $100,000 invested in individual bonds today will be returned to you in 10, 20, or however many years, depending on the maturity of the bonds. But what will that money be worth in 10 or 20 years? You simply don't know. Because of inflation, it could be worth quite a bit less than the value of $100,000 today. I'm not arguing that inflation wallops the return on individual bonds any more than it wallops the return on bond funds; I'm only arguing that the effect of inflation renders final bond returns kind of mushy — whether we're talking individual bonds or bond funds.

To look at it another way, individual bond *ladders* (which I describe in Chapter 15) fluctuate — in both interest payments and principal value — just as bond funds do. So you won't convince me that individual bonds (except perhaps for short-term bonds that are not as vulnerable to inflation or interest rate fluctuations) are better than bond funds for reasons of either price or consistency. But that's not to say that individual bonds are never the better choice. They certainly can be, in some cases — most notably, if you plan to hold them to maturity.

Dispelling the tax myth

This one isn't so much a myth: The reality is that bond mutual funds can incur capital gains tax where individual bonds do not. When a fund manager sells an individual bond for more than he bought it, the fund makes a capital gain that gets passed onto the shareholders (if there are no offsetting capital losses). With individual bonds, you never pay a capital gains tax unless you yourself sell the bond for a profit, which is something you have the option of doing or not doing.

But while capital gains on stock funds can be very large, capital gains on bond funds generally aren't. Most bonds simply don't appreciate in price very much. Also, if you are concerned with capital gains on your bond funds, you can always put them into a tax-advantaged retirement account, and your capital-gains tax problems disappear. Or, rather than invest in a bond mutual fund, you can choose a bond exchange-traded fund (ETF), which has a different structure than a mutual fund and is able to dodge capital gains tax. Both ETF investing and putting your bond funds in retirement accounts are strategies that I recommend. I discuss tax-advantaged retirement accounts more in just a few pages. You'll find more on ETFs in Chapter 16.

Embracing the true benefits of single bonds

Neither price nor consistency makes individual bonds a better option than bond funds. What *can* sometimes make individual bonds a better option is control. If you absolutely need a certain amount of income, or if you need the return of principal sometime in the next several years, individual bonds can make sense. For example:

✔ If you are buying a house, and you know that you're going to need $40,000 in cash in 365 days, buying one-year Treasury bills may be the best investment you can make.

✔ If your kid is off to college in two years, and you know that you'll need $20,000 a year for four years, then Treasury bills and bonds may be the ticket. (However, it may make more sense to open a 529 College Plan. See *529 & Other College Savings Plans For Dummies* by Margaret A. Munro [Wiley].)

✔ If you are comfortably retired and your living expenses are covered by your pension and Social Security, but you need to pay out $500 twice a year for property taxes, it may be wise to put away enough in individual bonds to cover that fixed expense, at least for several years down the road. (Beyond several years, you can't be certain what your property taxes will be.)

✔ If you are pulling in a sizeable paycheck and find yourself in the upper tax brackets, and you live in a high-tax city and state, and your reading of Chapter 8 tells you that investing in triple-tax-free munis makes the most sense, then a ladder of triple-tax-free munis may be your best portfolio tool. (*Triple-tax-free* means free from federal, state, and local tax.)

Individual bonds allow for a precise tailoring of a fixed-income portfolio. Quite simply, most people don't need that kind of precision and, therefore, the advantages of funds usually outweigh the advantages of single bonds.

There are perhaps a few other instances, however, when individual bonds make sense:

✔ **You meet a bond broker extraordinaire.** If you find a bond broker who is so talented in the ways of bond trading that he or she can do for you what a bond fund manager can do, only better, then I say go for it. Such bond brokers are very rare birds, but maybe after reading Chapter 15, you'll have the prowess to spot one.

✔ **You plan to become a bond expert.** If you yourself intend to make such an intense study of bonds that you can serve as your own expert, researching individual bond issues and issuers to the point that you feel you have an edge on the market, then individual bonds are for you. My guess is that because you are reading the words on this page, you, Luke, have a *lot* of studying to do before you become a true fixed-income Jedi warrior.

✔ **You have an inside edge.** If you have inside information that allows you to know that a particular bond is worth more than the market thinks it is worth, you may take advantage of it by investing in that bond. Of course, true inside information, such as the information available to directors of a company, is illegal to take advantage of — in stock trading or bond trading. And false insider information, the kind of information available *free* all over the Internet, is worth every penny you pay for it!

✔ **You plan to spend a lot of time and energy on your portfolio.** There are certain strategies to help juice your returns that you can do with individual bonds that you can't do with funds. One strategy, called *rolling down the yield curve,* entails holding long-term bonds paying higher interest until they become intermediate- or short-term bonds, and then selling them and replacing them with other higher yielding long-term bonds, until they become intermediate- or short-term bonds. Such a strategy takes time, energy, a good head for finance, and strong trading skills.

Is Now the Time to Buy Bonds?

After suggesting a bond portfolio — or any other kind of portfolio — to a new client, I often hear, "But . . . is *now* a good time to invest?"

The answer is *yes*.

Predicting the future of interest rates . . . yeah, right

With stocks, the big concern people have is usually that the market is about to tumble. With bonds, the big concern is that interest rates are going to rise, and any bonds purchased today will wither in value as a result.

But interest rates are almost as unpredictable as the stock market. Yes, the government has more control over interest rates than it does the stock market, but it doesn't have complete control, and the actions it decides to take or not take are not for you to know.

And furthermore, I would argue that even if you *could* predict interest rates (which you can't), and even if you *did* know that they were going to rise (which you don't), it still is a good time to buy bonds.

I'm assuming, of course, that you've done the proper analysis (see Chapter 12), and you've decided that more bonds belong in your portfolio, and you have cash in hand. What do you do with it? You have three savings/investing options, really:

- ✔ Keep it in cash.
- ✔ Invest it in equities.
- ✔ Invest it in fixed income.

If you invest in equities (stocks or commodities), you mess with your overall portfolio structure, making it perhaps too risky. If you keep cash (a savings or money market account), you earn enough interest to *maybe* keep up with inflation — but after taxes, probably not. In either scenario, you lose.

Now suppose you choose to go ahead and buy the bonds. And suppose that interest rates, as you feared, do rise. That isn't necessarily a bad thing. Yes, your bonds or bond funds will take a hit. The value of the bonds or the price of the bond-fund shares will sink. But in the long run, you shouldn't suffer, and you may even benefit from higher interest rates.

After all, every six months with individual bonds, and every month with most bond funds, you get interest payments, and those interest payments may be reinvested. The higher the interest rate climbs, the more money you can make off those reinvestments. Waiting for interest rates to fall — which they may or may not do — just doesn't make sense.

Paying too much attention to the yield curve

Another difficult decision for bond investors putting in fresh money occurs at those rare times in history when we see an inverted yield curve. The *yield curve* refers to the difference between interest rates on long-term versus short-term bonds. Normally, long-term bonds pay higher rates of interest. If the yield curve is *inverted,* that means the long-term bonds are paying lower rates of interest than shorter-term bonds. That doesn't happen often, but it happens. The reasons for the yield curve are many and complex, and they include inflation expectations, feelings about the economy, and foreign demand for U.S. debt.

Whatever the reasons for an inverted yield curve, it hardly makes sense to tie up your money in a long-term bond when a shorter-term bond is paying just as much interest or possibly a slight bit more. Or does it?

Some financial planners would disagree with me on this one, but I am not averse to investing in long-term bonds even when the yield curve is a slight bit inverted. Perverted? Nah. Remember that a large reason you are investing in bonds is to have a cushion if your other investments (such as stocks) take a nosedive. When stocks plunge, money tends to flow (and flow fast) into investment-grade bonds, especially Treasuries. Initially, the "rush to safety" creates the most demand for short-term bonds, and their price will tend to rise.

Over time, however, a plunge in the stock market often results in the feds lowering interest rates (in an attempt to kick-start the economy), which lifts bond prices — especially the price of longer maturity bonds. In other words, long-term Treasuries are your very best hedge against a stock market crash. If that hedge is paying a hair less in interest, it may still be worth having it, rather than shorter-term bonds, in your portfolio.

There's another reason for investing in long-term bonds, even if they aren't paying what short-term bonds are paying. What if interest rates drop, regardless of what's going on in the stock market? Sometimes interest rates fall even when the stock market is soaring. If that is the case, once again, you may wish that you were holding long-term bonds, says bond guru Chris Genovese.

"If interest rates are falling when your short-term bonds mature, you may be forced to reinvest at a lower rate," he says. "In the context of an entire bond portfolio, having both short-term and long-term bonds, regardless of the yield curve, may be advisable."

Adhering — or not — to dollar-cost averaging

Instead of throwing all your money into a bond portfolio right away, some people say it makes more sense to buy in slowly over a long period of time. That way, the argument goes, you spread out your risk, buying when the market is high *and* when the market is low. And if you invest equal amounts of money each time, you'll tend to buy more product (bonds or fund shares) when the market is low, potentially adding to your bottom line. This approach to investing is called *dollar-cost averaging*.

Dollar-cost averaging makes some sense if you are taking freshly earned money and investing it. If you have a pool of cash, however, it simply doesn't make sense. The cash you leave behind will be earning too little for the whole scheme to make any sense.

If you have a chunk of money waiting to be invested, and you have an investment plan in place, go for it. Buy those bonds you were planning to buy. There's no reason to wait for just the right moment or to buy in dribs and drabs.

Choosing between Taxable and Tax-Advantaged Retirement Accounts

In yesteryear, when corporations and municipalities were still offering *bearer* bonds — bonds that came with a certificate and were registered nowhere with no one — you didn't have to concern yourself with keeping them in any particular account. You could keep your bearer bonds in your safe, your glove compartment, or your underwear drawer. Today, it's a different matter.

Chances are that you have both a taxable account where you can store your investments and a tax-advantaged account, such as an IRA, a Roth IRA, a 401(k), or a 529 college savings plan. Think of these as *containers* of sorts, which you fill up with your various investments.

In which container do you keep your bonds?

Balancing your portfolio with taxes in mind

Suppose you've decided that you want a 50/50 portfolio: 50 percent stocks and 50 percent bonds. Suppose, in addition, that you have both a taxable brokerage account and an IRA. You've decided to put all your bonds in the IRA, and all your stocks in your taxable brokerage account. Do you really have a 50/50 portfolio?

No, probably not. The IRA bond money, whenever you decide to tap it, will incur income tax. The stocks will be taxable as capital gains — in most cases, 15 percent — only to the extent that they've grown in value.

In other words, $100,000 taken from the stock portfolio in your brokerage account, assuming you originally invested $50,000, will incur a tax of ($50,000 capital gain x 15 percent) $7,500. But $100,000 taken from the bond portfolio in your IRA may incur a tax (assuming you are in the 28 percent tax bracket) of $28,000.

As you can see, your IRA portfolio is worth considerably less (in this case, about 22 percent less) than the same amount of money in your taxable account.

If you are more than five years from tapping your nest egg, don't concern yourself too much with this discrepancy. You don't yet know what your income tax rate or the capital gains rate will be when you start to withdraw from your savings. Nor can you predict very well the appreciation you'll enjoy in your various accounts. But as you approach retirement, or if you are already in the "disbursement" phase of your investor life, it makes sense to factor this tax differential into your portfolio allocation.

In the example above, a *true*, after-tax, 50/50 portfolio might actually have 22 percent more bonds than stocks.

Positioning your investments for minimal taxation

Say you're in the 28 percent federal tax bracket. You'll pay 28 percent tax (plus state income tax) on any bond interest dividends paid from any bonds held in a taxable account — except for tax-free municipal bonds. Plain and simple, tax-advantaged accounts exist to allow you to escape — or at least postpone — paying income tax on your investment gains. It generally makes the most sense to keep your taxable income–generating investments, such as taxable bonds, in your retirement accounts.

Here are some other things to keep in mind:

✔ Treasury bonds are free from state tax. Therefore, if you have room in your retirement accounts for only one kind of bond, it makes most sense for it to be corporate bonds.

> ✔ Foreign bonds often require the paying of foreign tax, which will usually be reimbursed to you by Uncle Sam, but only if those bonds are kept in a taxable account.
>
> ✔ Municipal bonds, usually free from federal tax, always belong in your taxable accounts.

Figure 14-1 illustrates where you want to keep your bond holdings.

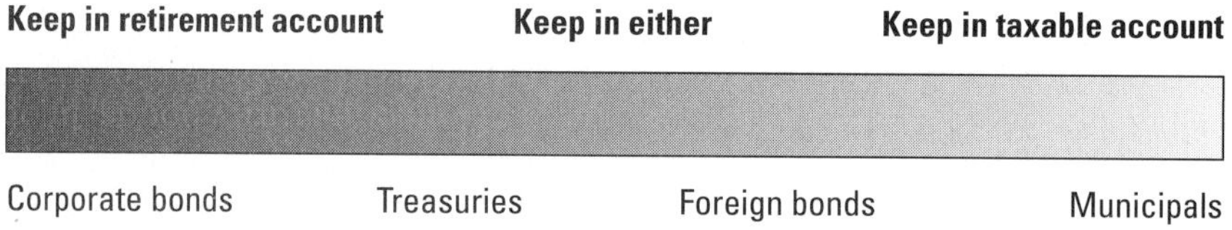

Figure 14-1:
Some bonds
naturally
belong in a
taxable
account,
and some
belong
in a tax-
advantaged
retirement
account.

Keep in retirement account	Keep in either	Keep in taxable account
Corporate bonds	Treasuries	Foreign bonds	Municipals

Factoring in the early-withdrawal penalties and such

Keep in mind that any money withdrawn from an IRA, 401(k), or SEP (self-employed pension) prior to age 59½, except under certain special circumstances, is subject to a 10 percent penalty. (Income tax must be paid regardless of when you withdraw.) So any bonds you are planning to cash out prior to that age should not be put into your retirement account.

On the flip side, at age 70½, you must start taking minimum required distributions from most retirement accounts. That should be figured into your allocation decisions, as well. If your minimum required distributions — the amount the IRS requires you to pull from your account each year after age 70½ — are substantial, it can mess with your balance of investments.

As I discuss more in Chapter 18, Roth IRAs are different animals. There is no tax to pay when you withdraw, and you are not required to withdraw at any particular age. The money grows and grows, tax-free, potentially forever. Imagine. Had Vasco da Gama in 1497 invested a mere $1 in a bond fund that paid 5 percent a year, and if he had held it in a Roth IRA, that $1 would now be worth $64,053,449,900. Think of all the spices *that* could buy!

Chapter 15

Investing (Carefully!) in Individual Bonds

Quit ev'ry surement and ev'ry bond

That ye have made to me as herebeforn,

Since thilke time that ye were born.

Have here my truth, I shall you ne'er repreve.

— Geoffrey Chaucer, *The Canterbury Tales,* 14th century

*U*nless you have a Ph.D. in medieval literature, or you're 620 years old, you probably have no more idea what those words mean than I do. (I chose the particular passage above simply because it has the word *bond* in it, although I don't think it has anything to do with finances.) In any case, I'm afraid that Chaucer has become a bit moldy with age.

Alas, I may come to know the same fate. By the time you read these words, this very chapter may well seem antiquated. That's how rapidly the world of individual bond trading is changing.

Ne'rtheless, um, nevertheless, in this chapter I do my best to get you up to current speed. And, should the tales I tell become faded by time, fear not: I give you a few online resources so that with the tap of a few keys and the click of a mouse, you can access the most modern methods — the most efficient, friendly, and profitable methods — for buying and selling individual bonds.

Understanding Today's Individual Bond Market

You don't pay commissions when you trade individual bonds, as you do when you trade stocks. Instead, bond trading has traditionally been done by someone, usually in a fancy suit, called a *broker*. A broker buys a bond at one price and sells it at a higher price. The difference, known as the *bid/ask spread,* is what the broker brings home. We're sometimes talking *lots* of bacon here. The bid/ask spreads on bonds can sometimes be big enough to make the commissions paid on stocks look like greyhound fat.

Once upon a time, and for many decades, commissions on stocks were as fat as spreads on bonds, sometimes fatter. That began to change shortly after Mary Tyler Moore moved to Minneapolis. (Historians believe the connection is only coincidental.)

In 1975, the Securities and Exchange Commission (SEC) deregulated the stock markets, allowing for open competition and discount brokerage houses. That paved the way for Internet trading, and within a few short years, the money that most people spent to make a stock trade was reduced to a fraction of what it had been. In the 1970s, a typical stock trade cost $100 (about $400 in today's dollars). Today, a stock trade may cost as little as $5, and rarely more than $20.

And how has bond trading changed since 1975? It's changed. But it's changed like men's fashions change — not women's. You have to look hard to notice the differences.

Getting some welcome transparency

Bond trading today is, in a sense, about where stock trading was in the early 1980s. You can still spend $300, $400, or way more on the cost of a single trade. But you shouldn't have to anymore. Thanks to a system called the *Trade Reporting and Compliance Engine* (TRACE), bond trading is becoming a bit more like stock trading.

TRACE is a system run by the Financial Industry Regulatory Authority (FINRA) that can be accessed through many financial Web sites.

Because of TRACE, bond trading no longer has to be a muddied affair in which individual investors are at the mercy of brokers. This system ensures that every corporate bond trade in the United States is reported, and the details appear on the Web. (The Municipal Securities Rulemaking Board runs a similar system for municipal bonds.)

TRACE ensures that trading costs are no longer hidden, bond yields (greatly affected by the bid/ask spreads) are easy to find, and good information is available. Among investment people, access to information is generally referred to as *transparency*. TRACE provides some pretty amazing transparency.

Unfortunately, not everyone knows about the TRACE system, so not everyone realizes that she can find out (for free) the price a broker paid for a bond. In fact, lots of people don't know. The world today is divided more or less evenly, I'd say, between those who know about TRACE and those who don't. Those who don't pay a heavy price.

Ushering in a new beginning

The new transparency, ushered into practice between 2002 and 2005, has removed much of the mystery from bond trading. You can now go online and, provided your Windows system doesn't crash that particular day, quickly get a pretty good idea of how much a single bond is being bought and sold for — by brokers, institutions, and individuals. You'll also see how far a broker — *your* broker — is trying to mark a bond up, and exactly what yield you'll get after the middleman and all his cousins have taken their cuts, should you purchase that bond.

Unfortunately, the cuts taken on bond trades still tend to be too high, and you can't (except in rare circumstances) bypass the middlemen. But with some tough negotiating on your part, you won't make them terribly rich at your expense, either.

Dealing with Brokers and Other Financial Professionals

As I say elsewhere in this book, you are probably better off investing in bond funds (see Chapter 16) rather than individual bonds unless you have a bond portfolio of $350,000 or so. It's hard to build a diversified bond portfolio — diversified by type of bond, issuer, and maturity — unless you have that amount to work with. It's also hard to negotiate good prices on bonds when you're dealing with amounts that brokers tend to sneeze at.

Investing in individual bonds also requires substantially more work than investing in bond funds. With individual bonds, you not only have to haggle, but you need to haggle again and again. After all, with individual bonds, you get interest payments on a regular basis, usually every six months. Unless you spend the money right away, you need to concern yourself with constantly reinvesting those interest payments. It can be a real job.

Then there's the risk of default. With Treasuries, there is (said to be) no risk of default, and with agency bonds and munis, the risk is minimal. With corporate bonds, however, the risk of a company losing its ability to pay you back is very real. Even when corporations don't default, their bonds may be downgraded by the major rating agencies. That can mean a loss of money, too, if you decide that you can't hold a bond till maturity. Don't start dabbling in individual corporate bonds unless you are willing to put in some serious time and effort doing research.

With these caveats in mind, the first thing you need in order to be an investor in individual bonds is a *dealer*: someone or some institution that is going to place the actual trades for you — without robbing you blind or steering your astray.

Identifying the role of the middleman

Most bond dealers are *brokers* who buy a bond from Client A at one price, sell it to Client B at another, leave the office for a few rounds of golf, and then come back to harvest more profits. Sorry, I hate to be cynical, but the money some of these Brooks Brothers cowboys make at investors' expense is truly shameful.

Some bond brokers are very knowledgeable about fixed-income investing and can help walk you through the maze, making good suggestions for your portfolio. Some are very talented at finding the best buys in bonds and using certain sophisticated strategies to juice your fixed-income returns.

Unfortunately, the way brokers are paid creates a system where the traditional broker's financial interests are in opposition to the interests of his clients. The more the broker makes, the less the client keeps. The more the client keeps, the less the broker makes. The more the broker can get you to *flip,* or trade one bond for another, the more the broker makes. Generally, the more you flip, the less likely you are to come out ahead.

I don't wish to say that brokers are bad people, or greedy people . . . no more so than car salesmen are bad or greedy people. I'm only saying that bond brokers are salespeople (some of them fabulously paid salespeople) and need to be seen as such.

Like the car salesman, the bond broker who acts as *principal* (taking ownership of the bond) is not required to reveal what kind of markup he or she is making. And you won't find this information in *Consumer Reports.* (Fortunately, though, you can find it on TRACE; see the section "Getting some welcome transparency" earlier in the chapter.)

The author's prediction for the future of bond trading

Some day — I'm not sure when, but some day — bond brokers will disappear. You want to buy a Spacely Space Sprockets ten-year bond maturing in 2040? You'll get an identifying code for the bond (perhaps the CUSIP, which I discuss in another sidebar in this chapter), and you'll put it in a Web site (something that resembles www.kayak.com, which currently exists for travel deals). People and institutions will offer to sell you their bonds, and you'll be free to pay the lowest price. Want to sell a Spacely Space Sprockets ten-year bond maturing in 2042? You'll advertise it on the same Web site, and people and institutions will bid. You'll take the highest price you can get.

Alternatively, bonds may wind up trading more like stocks. Instead of a bunch of brokers shouting deals to each other on the telephone, as happens today, bonds will be offered on an open exchange, similar to NASDAQ. Financial supermarkets will begin to allow for *conditional trades,* just as they have recently begun to offer with stocks. You want a ten-year bond with an A rating, paying at least 324 percent? (Interest rates are higher in the future!) You'll put the offer into your computer, and it can apply to any number of bond issues. The first to meet the criteria will nail the sale.

Some bond dealers today work as *agents* and charge you a flat fee, an hourly rate, a certain amount per trade, or a percentage of assets under management. A good agent, like a good broker, may know enough about the ins and outs of bonds to help you make the best selections and get the best prices.

Agents, unlike principals, *do* have to reveal exactly what they are charging you. Alas, whereas an agent is generally better to deal with than a broker (simply because there's no conflict of financial interests), a good one is very hard to find. And even if you do find one, agents often must work with brokers to get trades done.

Do you need a broker or agent at all?

You don't need a broker or agent to buy Treasury bonds. You can do so easily and without any markup on www.treasurydirect.gov. You can usually get savings bonds at your local savings bank for no fee.

Municipal bonds and corporate bonds must be purchased through an intermediary; you can't buy these securities directly from the issuers. Sure, you can loan your neighbor or brother-in-law $1,000 and demand the money back with interest (good luck!), and that's a bond, of sorts. But if you want to buy and sell marketable fixed-income securities, you must go through a recognized agent.

Going through a financial supermarket, such as a Fidelity, T. Rowe Price, or Vanguard, is (generally) cheaper than going through a full-service, markup kind of broker. The supermarket's pricing, which is a *concession* or a fee (more or less), not a markup, is perhaps more clean-cut. But the supermarket agents generally hold your hand only so much, and they won't make actual bond selections for you the way a full-service broker will.

You'll note that I inject some qualifiers in the previous paragraph, such as "generally" and "perhaps." I explain why in the upcoming section "Doing It Yourself Online," where I discuss online bond trading. The financial supermarkets often make their way of trading sound easier, cheaper, and more transparent than it really is.

Selecting the right broker or agent

Whether you go with a full-service, markup kind of broker or with an agent, I would ask you to do a few things:

▪ **Find someone who truly specializes in bonds — preferably the kind you're looking to buy.** If you needed hand surgery, you wouldn't go to a gastroenterologist, would you? If your dealing in individual bonds is going to be any more profitable than, say, investing in a bond index fund, you need a broker or agent who truly knows the ins and outs, tracks the markets carefully, and can jump on a good deal. You don't want a broker who deals in bonds, stocks, gold coins, and collector art!

Start by asking people you know and respect for referrals. Make calls. Ask lots of questions about a broker's background, including academic and professional history. Ask for client recommendations. Don't be shy. Ask for numbers: What kind of return figures has this broker been able to garner for clients, and taking what kinds of risks?

▪ **Be on guard.** Always. Whenever you find a broker and agree to buy or sell individual bonds, be certain that you aren't paying an excessive markup. Although different people in the investment business have different concepts of what constitutes "excessive," if you're asked to cough up the equivalent of more than three months' interest, that's excessive, in my humble opinion. Other financial types have their opinions. See the sidebar "Defining 'excessive' in bond markups" later in the chapter.

▪ **Know a broker's limitations.** Most bond brokers I've known are not the best people to build your entire portfolio. They often have limited knowledge of investments beyond bonds. (And that's probably a good thing — see the first bullet in this list.) If they deal in stocks at all, they often deal in pricy stock mutual funds that you don't want — the kind that will earn them a nice commission.

What the heck is a CUSIP, anyway?

All bonds have a CUSIP that identifies the bond in the same way that a license plate identifies a vehicle. CUSIP stands for *Committee on Uniform Securities Identification Procedures,* which is a part of the American Bankers Association. Although it's often referred to as a CUSIP *number,* that is something of a misnomer because a CUSIP typically contains both letters and numbers. The first six characters of the CUSIP identify the issuer, the next two characters identify the issue itself, and the ninth digit is called a *check digit,* its sole purpose to make computer readers happy. Here's a CUSIP for a General Electric bond: 36966RXR2. Here's one for a Fannie Mae bond: 31396CVP2.

Checking the broker's numbers

In a page or two, I discuss online bond trading. If you deal with a full-service broker, you won't have to know the complete ins and outs of trading bonds online. But I would still urge you, at a minimum, to become familiar with www.investinginbonds.com (the Web site of the Securities Industry and Financial Markets Association) and www.finra.org (the Web site of the Financial Industry Regulatory Authority). On these Web sites, you can plug in information on any bond — either by the name of the issuer or the bond's CUSIP — and you'll experience the type of transparency I discuss earlier in this chapter. (If you don't know what a CUSIP is, see the nearby sidebar "What the heck is a CUSIP, anyway?")

On www.investinginbonds.com, click on <u>See Municipal Market At-A-Glance</u> or <u>See Corporate Bond Market At-A-Glance</u>, and then enter the CUSIP number at the bottom of the first page that pops up, under where it says "Bond History." On www.finra.org ... well, just as this book is going the press, FINRA is planning a major overhaul of its Web site, so you may need to poke around a bit. I've been assured that the new Web site will be user-friendly.

You can see on these Web sites how much the bond recently sold for (if it has sold recently), how many bonds have recently been traded, and the bond's current yield and yield-to-maturity (see Chapter 4). You can plug in the price the bond dealer is offering you (which includes his markup) and see if the yield still makes sense given the yield of similar bonds.

Figure 15-1 shows the recent trading history of an everyday bond (from the pharmaceutical company Merck) as seen at www.investinginbonds.com. You can see the price paid for this bond and the resulting yield. This gives you a pretty good idea of what you should be getting, should you wish to buy or sell . . . provided the particular bond you're interested in has seen recent action.

Print | Close Window

Trade Details for CUSIP: 589331AK3

Following are recent corporate bond trades reported to the National Association of Securities Dealers, Inc., through its TRACE system. Eligible securities, participants and other information is available from the NASD on their NASD Bondinfo Web site. Use the menus on the left of the NASD home page to navigate through TRACE >> Corporate Bond Data >> TRACE Corporate Bond Data. Trade reports published here are on a real-time basis. Times shown are EST.

RTNGS INS	ISSUER CUSIP SECTOR/ SUBSECTOR	COUPON MATURITY	CALL DATES	CALL PRICES
AA- S AA3 M AA F	MERCK & CO INC 589331AK3 Industrial/Drugs	4.750 03/01/2015		

Graph Trade Data

1 2 3 4 5 6 7 8 9 10 ...

TRADE DATE TRADE TIME	PRICE	YIELD	SIZE	NOTES	MORE INFO
06/15/2007 13:41:20	93.188	5.860	65K	@	run calculations
06/15/2007 10:19:00	93.290	5.843	30K	@	run calculations
06/15/2007 10:17:29	93.286	5.844	30K	@	run calculations
06/14/2007 15:56:00	93.129	5.870	25K	@	run calculations
06/14/2007 15:56:00	93.129	5.870	25K	@	run calculations
06/14/2007 15:56:00	93.129	5.870	25K	@	run calculations
06/14/2007 15:49:41	93.129	5.870	25K	@	run calculations
06/14/2007 14:49:53	92.980	5.896	5K	@	run calculations
06/14/2007 14:49:51	93.379	5.828	5K	@	run calculations
06/14/2007 14:49:51	92.980	5.896	5K	@	run calculations

Figure 15-1: The recent trading history of a bond, as shown on `www.investinginbonds.com`.

With permission of the Securities Industry and Financial Markets Association (SIFMA)

If you click on Run Calculations, you get something that looks like Figure 15-2.

To get a bird's-eye view of the bond market, go to Yahoo! Finance at `http://finance.yahoo.com/bonds/composite_bond_rates`. The chart you find there gives you a pretty good idea of what various categories of bonds are paying on any particular day. If you're in the market for a bond, compare the composite yield to the yield you're being offered. If you aren't being offered at least as much as the average yield, ask why. The Yesterday, Last Week, and Last Month columns show you which way bond yields are headed. But remember that yield trends, just like the wins and losses of your favorite sports team, can reverse direction quickly.

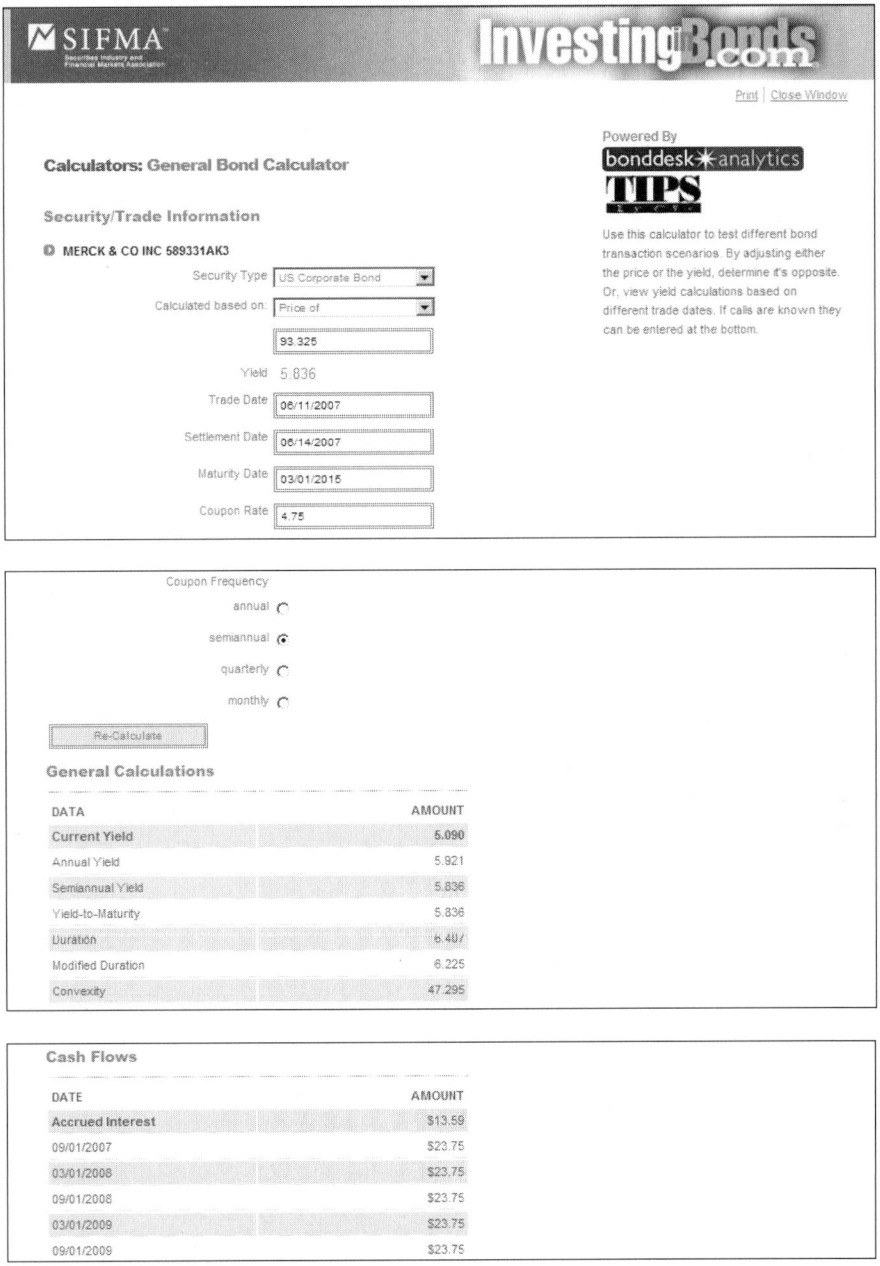

Calculators: General Bond Calculator

Security/Trade Information

MERCK & CO INC 589331AK3

Security Type	US Corporate Bond
Calculated based on:	Price of
	93.325
Yield	5.836
Trade Date	06/11/2007
Settlement Date	06/14/2007
Maturity Date	03/01/2015
Coupon Rate	4.75

Powered By

bonddesk✻analytics

TIPS

Use this calculator to test different bond transaction scenarios. By adjusting either the price or the yield, determine it's opposite. Or, view yield calculations based on different trade dates. If calls are known they can be entered at the bottom.

Print | Close Window

Coupon Frequency
- annual ○
- semiannual ◉
- quarterly ○
- monthly ○

Re-Calculate

General Calculations

DATA	AMOUNT
Current Yield	5.090
Annual Yield	5.921
Semiannual Yield	5.836
Yield-to-Maturity	5.836
Duration	6.407
Modified Duration	6.225
Convexity	47.295

Cash Flows

DATE	AMOUNT
Accrued Interest	$13.59
09/01/2007	$23.75
03/01/2008	$23.75
09/01/2008	$23.75
03/01/2009	$23.75
09/01/2009	$23.75

Figure 15-2:
More detailed information on a bond, as available on www. investing inbonds. com.

With permission of the Securities Industry and Financial Markets Association (SIFMA)

Looking into a broker's record

If you want to make sure that the bond broker you hire isn't going to take your money and buy a one-way ticket to Rio the next morning, check his or her background before you hand over the check. You can get information on the disciplinary record, professional background, and registration and license status of any properly registered broker or brokerage firm by using FINRA BrokerCheck. FINRA makes BrokerCheck available at no charge to the public. Investors can access this service by linking directly to BrokerCheck at www.finra.org or by calling 800-289-9999.

Hiring a financial planner

Lots of people today, including stock and bond brokers, call themselves financial planners. I suggest that if you hire a financial planner, you seriously consider a *fee-only* planner, who takes no commissions and works only for you. To find one in your area, contact the National Association of Personal Financial Advisors (NAPFA) at 800-366-2732, or go online to www.napfa.org. (I'm a member of NAPFA.)

Some NAPFA-certified financial advisors will work with you on an hourly basis. Others will want to take your assets under management. Know that if you hire a financial planner who takes your assets under management, you will typically pay a fee, usually 0.30 to 1.0 percent a year. I think 0.50 percent is plenty; you shouldn't pay more than that unless you're getting help from that planner that extends to insurance, estate planning, and other matters beyond investing.

If you have a sizeable bond portfolio, a fee-only financial planner who is trading bonds for you can potentially save you enough money to compensate for his or her fee. Even though the planner will be dealing with a broker, just as you would, planners with numerous clients can bundle their bond purchases, so the broker will often settle for a substantially lesser markup.

Here's an example of this type of savings. Matthew Reznik, a NAPFA-certified financial planner with Balasa Dinverno & Foltz LLC of Itasca, Illinois, explains that "If an individual investor is buying a $25,000 bond for his or her portfolio, the spread can be as high as 2.25 percent. If that bond is yielding 5 percent, that's a pretty big haircut. If we buy bonds, we buy the same issue in a $1 million piece. In that case the spread would be reduced to 0.10 percent."

Fee-only financial planners may also have access to certain institutional-like (frugal and possibly superior) bond funds that you wouldn't have access to otherwise, should you decide to go the bond-fund route.

Doing It Yourself Online

A growing number of financial supermarkets and specialty bond shops now allow you to trade bonds online, and they advertise that they'll do it for a fixed price.

In the case of Fidelity, the supermarket with which I am most familiar, the price to trade a Treasury bond is 50 cents. The price for a municipal bond is $1.50. And the price for a corporate bond is $2.00.

Whoa, you might say. *That's a great deal!* Well, yes and no. If that were all that Fidelity and the other middlemen were making, it would be a great deal. But what you see and what you get are two different things. The "flat fees" quoted by Fidelity and its competitors are a bit misleading.

"The idea that there are no broker markups is not the case," says financial planner Matthew Reznik. "No matter who sells you a bond, there is always a spread built in to compensate the broker." In other words, Fidelity or Vanguard or whomever may charge you "only $1.50 to trade a bond," but the price you get for your bond, to buy or sell, is marked up from the price that someone else just got to sell or buy. Your particular broker may have marked up the bond itself, or some other broker may have done so. Just don't kid yourself into thinking that $1.50 is all you're paying to trade. It ain't the case.

Proceeding with care

I've traded a good number of bonds online with Fidelity. The trading process there is similar to other financial supermarkets that offer "flat-fee" bond shopping. I explain how it works in a moment. First, I want to let you know that, yes, you can get good buys on bonds online, but you can also get zapped hard. I've talked to many other investment pros who have had very similar experiences at other financial supermarkets, such as Vanguard and Schwab.

You are most likely to get a fair deal online when you're *buying* a bond and dealing in large quantities. You are most likely to get zapped when you're *selling* a bond prior to maturity, especially if you're selling a small number of bonds and if those particular bonds are traded infrequently. In such cases, you may let go of your bonds for one price and (using TRACE) find out that they were sold seconds afterward for 3 percent (or more) higher than the price you just got. Someone is making very quick money in that situation, and it isn't you.

Knowing the cyber-ropes

Here's how online trading generally works.

If you're looking to buy

You first choose a bond category: Do you want a Treasury bond, an agency bond, a corporate bond, or a municipal bond? (For reminders about each category, see Part II of this book.) What kind of rating are you looking for? What kind of maturity? What kind of yield? (Chapter 4 contains the goods on ratings, maturity, and yield.)

Most online bond shops walk you through this process step by step; it isn't that hard. The most difficult piece of the process, and the one I most want to help you with, is making sure that after you know what kind of bond you want, you get the best deal purchasing it.

Here's what I mean by the best deal for a given type and quality of bond, plain and simple: You want the *highest yield.* The yield reflects whatever concession you are paying the financial supermarket, and it reflects whatever markup you are paying a broker. Keep in mind that most callable bonds do get called — despite any contrary messages you've ever heard from a broker. So when weighing yields of callable bonds, look at the yield-to-call, and ignore just about everything else.

A somewhat more subtle yield concept is *yield-to-worst* (or *worst-case basis yield*): the lower of yield-to-call or yield-to-maturity. Whatever that yield is, that's what you're going to get, so you may as well factor that into your bond purchase decisions.

If two comparable bonds — comparable in maturity, ratings, and every other way — are offering yields of 5 percent and 5.1 percent, go with the 5.1 percent bond. Just make sure you've done your homework so you know that the two bonds are truly comparable.

Fidelity has a neat tool on its Web site called the *scatter graph*; it allows you to see a whole bunch of similar bonds on the same graph, and what kind of yield each is paying. You can access it at www.fidelity.com. Click on <u>Investment Products</u> and then <u>Fixed Income</u>. Get into <u>Individual Bonds</u> and then select the type of bond you're interested in purchasing. Enter your parameters to create the scattergraph you need.

To reiterate: The yield reflects the middleman's cut. *Focus on the yield* to get the best deal. Don't over-concern yourself with the bid/ask spread on the bond.

Saving money with a full-service broker?

Many people assume that discount and online brokers allow you to trade bonds more cheaply than with full-service brokers, and that can be true sometimes. But it isn't *always* the case. Kevin Olson, former municipal bond trader for Paine Webber and Bank of America, and the creator of www.municipalbonds.com, says that "Full-service brokers may offer you the best deals on new issues of municipal bonds, especially in those cases where the full-service broker is itself underwriting the bond." If you're going to trade individual munis, Olson suggests having a number of accounts with different brokers, including both discount and full-service brokers. Sometimes, he says, you'll be surprised where you get the best deals. That's true both for new issues of bonds and for the secondary market.

When you go to place your order, use the "Limit Yield" option. You are telling the brokers on the Fidelity network that you'll buy this bond only if it yields, say, 5.1 percent. Anything less, and you aren't interested. If you put in a "Market" order on a bond, you can get chewed up — don't do it.

If you're looking to sell

Selling bonds online can be much trickier business. You have a particular bond you want to dump, and the market may or may not want it.

At Fidelity, you are best off calling a Fidelity fixed-income trader and asking that trader to give you a handle on what the bond is worth. You can then go online, place a "Limit Price" order to sell, and you'll very likely get what the Fidelity trader told you you'd get. But here's the catch: Fidelity itself may wind up buying your bond and selling it to someone else at a large markup. I asked a Fidelity supervisor if perhaps Fidelity couldn't be a better advocate for its clients if Fidelity itself didn't bid on the bonds, and what I got in response was a wee bit Orwellian. The answer is yes. Fidelity could be a better advocate for its clients if it weren't also dealing in the bonds its clients are trading. So be it.

Truth be told, you are likely to pay a high markup anywhere if you sell a bond before its maturity. Charles Schwab is similar to Fidelity in that you tend to pay through the nose when selling, says Dalibor Nenadov, a fee-only financial planner with Northern Financial Advisors in Franklin, Michigan. "The bottom line for the average middle class investor is to build a bond ladder, and hold until maturity. Don't sell before maturity, and don't try to time rates," he says.

Perfecting the Art of Laddering

Bond laddering is a fancy term for diversifying your bond portfolio by maturity. Buy one bond that matures in two years, another that matures in five, and a third that matures in ten, and — presto! — you have just constructed a bond ladder (see Figure 15-3).

Figure 15-3:
A typical
bond ladder.

Why bother? Why not simply buy one big, fat bond that matures in 30 years and will kick out regular, predictable coupon payments between now and then? There are a few reasons laddering makes more sense.

Protecting you from interest-rate flux

The first rationale behind laddering is to temper interest-rate risk. If you buy a 30-year bond right now that pays 5.5 percent, and if interest rates climb over the next year to 7.5 percent, and stay there, you are going to be eating stewed crow for 29 more years with your relatively paltry interest payments of 5.5 percent. Obviously, you don't want that. (You could always sell your 30-year bond paying 5.5 percent, but if interest rates pop to 7.5 percent, the price you would get for your bond would likely be about 70 cents on the dollar you paid for it.)

Defining "excessive" in bond markups

You buy a bond from a broker. You pay $10,000. The broker bought the bond that morning for $9,700. You sell a bond. You get $10,000. You do your research and discover that the broker you sold it to then turns around and sells it for $10,300. Are these fair spreads, or are they excessive?

"There's no hard and fast rule," explains Chris Genovese, senior vice president of Fixed Income Securities, a nationwide firm that provides targeted advice on bond portfolio construction to investment advisors. "As far as what is excessive, spreads tend to get bigger when you are dealing in high-yield bonds, long-term bonds, thinly traded bonds, and small lots. Deciding on what is an excessive spread really depends on the transaction," he says. "In *my* opinion, any spread larger than 4 percent certainly warrants at least a phone call back to the broker for an explanation. I can think of few instances where a spread of 4 percent would be justified."

And what if you call your broker and don't get a satisfactory explanation? "Charges — markups or markdowns — for bond trades must be `fair and reasonable,'" says Richard Wallace, vice president of market regulation for the Financial Industry Regulatory Authority (FINRA). "What constitutes fair and reasonable will change with the nature of the trade, including the kind of bond, the number of bonds traded, and so on. But certainly any markup above 5 percent should be questioned. If you don't get a satisfactory answer as to why you were charged what you were charged, file a complaint with regulators," says Wallace.

FINRA serves as a sort of bond police force. If you wish to make a complaint, go to www. finra.org, click on Contact Us , and then File a Complaint. If you prefer a slightly gentler approach, you can also have your dispute resolved by an arbitration panel. You can get that process going by also logging onto the FINRA Web site and clicking on the Arbitration and Mediation tab on the home page.

Of course, you don't have to buy a 30-year bond right now. You could buy a big, fat two-year bond. The problem with doing that is twofold:

✔ You won't get as much interest on the two-year bond as you would on the 30-year bond.

✔ You are subjecting yourself to *reinvestment risk*: If interest rates fall over the next two years, you may not be able to reinvest your principal in two years for as much as you are getting today.

If you ladder your bonds, you shield yourself to a certain degree from interest rates rising and falling. If you're going to invest in individual bonds, laddering is really the only option. Do it. Do it!

Tinkering with your time frame

Note that as each bond in your ladder matures, you would typically replace it with a bond equal to the longest maturity in your portfolio. For example, if you have a two-year, a five-year, and a ten-year bond, when the two-year bond matures, you replace it with a ten-year bond. Why? Because your five-year and ten-year bonds are now two years closer to maturity, so the average weighted maturity of the portfolio will remain the same: 5.6 years.

Of course, over the course of two years, your economic circumstances may change, so you may want to tinker with the average weighted maturity. That depends on your need for return and your tolerance for risk: topics I discuss in Part I.

A perfectly acceptable (and often preferable) alternative to bond laddering is to buy a bond mutual fund. This option is the heart of Chapter 16. But whether you ladder your bonds or you buy a bond fund, I would caution you that relying only on fixed income to fund your retirement is probably not the wisest path. You should have a bond ladder or bond mutual funds *and* other investments (equity investments) as well. I discuss this subject fully in Part V.

Chapter 16

Picking a Bond Fund That Will Serve You for Life

● ●

● ●

*W*hen I was 11, I found a fan belt in the street, undoubtedly fallen from some car engine. I wiped the grease and dirt off on my T-shirt, and claimed the 9-inch diameter oval piece of rubber as my prize. One of the other boys in the neighborhood, Brian Callahan, decided that he wanted it as *his* prize. So he lunged at me, grabbed the belt, and started to pull. I pulled back. He slugged me. About a dozen other boys were looking on, so what could I do? I returned the punch. Next thing, the two of us were rolling around in the middle of the busy street, cars hurtling by. One of us, or both of us, might have been killed.

Was it worth risking life itself for a piece of old rubber?

Yup.

In the eyes of an 11-year-old boy, at least in the neighborhood I grew up in, getting run over by a two-ton vehicle was clearly preferable to being labeled a wimp.

And so it is with some bond investors. They cling to the notion that if you hire a fund manager, you are something of a wimp. They'd rather get run over trading individual bonds. That is somehow more manly, more intelligent, more sophisticated than buying a bond fund — despite all evidence to the contrary. Yes, even armed with the valuable tips I provide in the previous chapter, a small investor in individual bonds can wind up with tire treads on his back.

I know bonds . . . and I know dumb. I actually have a 40-year-old fan belt in the memorabilia box in my closet (no kidding!) to prove it. So trust me on this: For the vast majority of individual investors, funds are the way to go. There's nothing wimpy about them, and provided you do your homework, they can be as intelligent and sophisticated an investment vehicle as you'll ever find. (Index funds, seen by some as the wimpiest things under the sky, turn out to be mighty tough themselves.)

In this chapter, I introduce you to the many kinds of bond funds — index, active, mutual funds, exchange-traded funds, and unit investment trusts — and reveal that although none are worth dying for, some may well be worth fighting for.

Defining the Basic Kinds of Funds

With more than 2,000 bond funds to choose from, each representing a different basket of bonds, where do you start? That part is actually easy: You start with the kind of bonds you want to own. Treasuries? Corporate bonds? Munis? Long-term? Short-term? Investment-grade? High-yield? A blend of all of the above? The chapters in Part II of this book can help you answer that question. But knowing what kind of bonds you want in the basket isn't enough. You also need to know what kind of *basket* you want.

Bond funds come in four varieties:

- Open-end mutual funds, typically referred to simply as *mutual funds,* are far and away the most common.

- Closed-end mutual funds, usually referred to only as *closed-end funds,* are second most common.

- Exchange-traded funds (ETFs) are the new kids on the block, catching on quickly — for good reason.

- Unit investment trusts are not well known but perhaps worth knowing.

Table 16-1 offers an overview of how these types of funds compare. In the following sections, I provide the details.

Table 16-1	Comparing the Four Kinds of Bond Funds				
Fund Type	*How Many Are There?*	*Do They Offer Diversi-fication?*	*Active Manage-ment or Index?*	*Fee or Commis-sion to Buy or Sell?*	*Average Yearly Expense Ratio*
Mutual funds	1,773	Yes	Most are active	Sometimes	1.08 percent
Closed-end funds	425	Yes	Active	Always	1.16 percent
Exchange-traded funds	40	Yes	Most are index	Always	0.15 percent
Unit investment trusts	Varies	Yes	Quasi-active	Always	0.25 percent

Mining a multitude of mutual funds

When most investors speak of funds, they're talking about mutual funds. And no wonder. According to Morningstar, the total number of distinct mutual funds (ignoring different share classes of certain mutual funds) clocks in at an astounding 6,593. Of those 6,593 funds, 1,773 of them — nearly 27 percent — are bond mutual funds.

Like all funds, a mutual fund represents a basket of securities. You, as the investor, pay the mutual fund company a yearly fee and sometimes a sales charge (called a *load*) to buy the fund. In exchange for your money, the mutual fund company offers you an instant portfolio with professional management.

Most mutual funds are *open-end* funds. This means that there is no limited number of shares. Within reason, as many people who want to buy into the fund can buy into the fund. As more people buy into the fund, more bonds are purchased. The mutual fund shares then sell at a price that directly reflects the price of all the bonds held by the mutual fund. The interest you receive from the fund is a pro-rata portion of the total interest received by all the bonds in the basket.

Mutual fund orders can be placed at any time, but they are priced only at the end of the day (4 p.m. on Wall Street), and that is the price you're going to get.

Choosing between active mutual funds and passive (index) funds

One of the hottest debates among investors — one that will never end! — is whether actively managed investments are any wiser than index fund investments. I'm a huge proponent of index funds. The vast majority of index investors — and I am primarily an index investor — do better than the vast majority of active investors. Although various studies show various results, I know of none that contradicts this basic premise that indexing works, and works very well.

When we look at bond funds specifically, however, things get a bit muddled. On one hand, bond index funds are way cheaper than actively managed bond funds, just as stock index funds are cheaper than actively managed stock funds. But because bond funds tend to yield much more modest returns, costs are more important. A fund made up of bonds yielding an average of 5 percent that costs 1 percent to hold suddenly yields 4 percent; that's a difference in *your* return of one-fifth.

But there's another side to the story, explains Matthew Gelfand, Ph.D., CFA, CFP, and managing director and chief investment officer with Lynx Investment Advisory, LLC, of Washington, D.C. Despite the cost/yield equation, which Gelfand doesn't deny for a second is very important, he argues that active management of bonds makes more sense than active management of stocks. In fact, it makes perfect sense, says Gelfand, because bonds are so much more complicated than stocks.

"There are many, many more bonds and kinds of bonds than there are stocks on the market," says Gelfand. "The analyst coverage is much more sparse. The trading is done mostly over-the-counter. And the spreads can be very large. All this makes for a less 'efficient' market, and allows for good active managers to add real value," he says. "If you can find a reasonably priced, well-managed active bond fund, go for it."

I agree. There's certainly nothing wrong with passively managed (index) bond mutual funds or exchange-traded funds. In fact, Gelfand and I agree that they can, and often do, make excellent investments. Still, handpicking the right actively managed bond fund can potentially juice the returns of your portfolio, with limited additional risk. See the last part of this chapter for some of my favorite funds of both flavors, active and indexed.

Note that certain kinds of bonds, namely muncipals and foreign bonds, have yet to see any indexed options, so in these categories, you have no choice but to go with an actively managed fund.

Most mutual funds are actively managed, which means that the managers try to beat the market by picking certain investments or timing the markets. Other mutual funds are passively run, or *indexed,* which means they are set up to track standard indexes. Index funds tend to cost you a lot less in fees than actively managed funds. Which are better? See the sidebar "Choosing between active mutual funds and passive (index) funds" for my thoughts.

Regardless of whether you go with active or passive, choose only those bond mutual funds that have solid track records over several years and are reasonably priced. The average yearly operating expense of a bond mutual fund, per Morningstar, is 1.08 percent. Because total return on bond funds, over time, tends to be much less than that of stock funds, the cost ratio is a bigger factor. I wouldn't touch anything over 1.0 percent. There's little need to buy more expensive funds; there are many inexpensive alternatives to choose from, and they tend to offer better performance.

Considering the alternative: Closed-end funds

Although most mutual funds are open-ended, some are not. These closed-end funds are a universe unto themselves. Unlike open-end funds, closed-end funds have a finite number of shares. The price of the fund does not directly reflect the value of the securities within the fund. Nor does the yield directly reflect the yield of the bonds in the basket. In investment-speak, the *net asset value* (NAV) of the fund, or the price of the securities within the fund, may differ significantly from the price of the fund itself.

Supply and demand for a closed-end fund may have more bearing on its price than the actual securities it holds. Closed-end funds tend to have high management fees (almost always more than 1 percent a year), and they tend to be more volatile than open-end funds. Closed-end funds are traded like stocks (yes, even the bond closed-end funds), and they trade throughout the day. You buy and sell them through any brokerage house — not directly from the mutual fund company, as you can do with most mutual funds.

All closed-end funds are actively managed. There are 649 closed-end funds, of which 425, or nearly two-thirds, are bond funds. The average yearly fee of these bond funds, per Morningstar, is a relatively chunky 1.16 percent.

Establishing a position in exchange-traded funds

Although relatively new, exchange-traded funds (ETFs) have caught on big in the past several years. If you read my *Exchange-Traded Funds For Dummies,* you'll know that I'm a big fan. ETFs, like closed-end funds, trade on the exchanges like individual stocks. (Yes, even the bond ETFs trade that way.) You pay a small brokerage fee when you buy, and another when you sell. But while you own the fund, your yearly fees are very low; they are, in fact, a fraction of what you'd pay for a typical bond mutual fund or closed-end fund.

Unlike closed-end funds, ETFs maintain a price that very closely matches the net asset value, or the value of all the securities in the portfolio. Unlike both closed-end funds and mutual funds, all bond ETFs are index funds . . . at least at present. As this book was going to print, there were discussions about the launch of the first actively-managed bond ETF. (Oddly enough, the company that may launch it is Vanguard, which is famous for its indexing philosophy.)

There aren't all that many fixed-income ETFs relative to mutual and closed-end funds — only 40 at present. But my prediction is that within a short time after this book is published, that number will double or perhaps triple. Their popularity is in part due to their low expense ratio. The average bond ETF charges only 0.15 percent a year in operating expenses.

Understanding unit investment trusts

A unit investment trust (UIT) is a bundle of securities handpicked by a manager. You buy into the UIT as you would an actively managed mutual fund. But unlike the manager of the mutual fund, the UIT manager does not actively trade the portfolio. Rather, he or she buys the bonds (or in some cases, bond funds), perhaps 10 or 20 of them, and holds them throughout the life of the bonds or for the life of the UIT. A UIT, which may contain a mix of corporate bonds, Treasuries, and munis, has a maturity date — it could be a year, 5 years, or even 30 years down the road. Interest payments (or principal payments, should a bond mature or be called) from a UIT may arrive monthly, quarterly, or semi-annually. There are usually very modest management expenses (0.20 to 0.30 percent) for a UIT, but you pay a commission to buy it (never to sell), usually of 1 to 3 percent. Contact any major brokerage house if you're interested.

Should you be interested?

"A UIT can give you the diversification of a mutual fund as well as greater transparency by knowing exactly what bonds are in your portfolio," says Chris Genovese, senior vice president of Fixed Income Securities, a nationwide firm that provides targeted advice on bond portfolio construction to investment advisors. "They are certainly appropriate for many individual investors, whether in retirement accounts or investment accounts." UITs come and go from the marketplace, explains Genovese. "If you are interested in seeing the currently available selection, talk to your broker. Look at the prospectus. As you would with any other bond investment, weigh the benefits and the risks of the bonds in the portfolio, and determine if it looks like the right mix for you."

Knowing What Matters Most in Choosing a Bond Fund of Any Sort

For years, alchemists tried to turn common metals into gold. It can't be done. The first rule to follow when choosing a bond fund is to find one appropriate to your particular portfolio needs, which means finding a bond fund made of the right material. After all, bond fund managers can't do all that much more than alchemists.

Selecting your fund based on its components and their characteristics

It you're looking for a bond fund that's going to produce steady returns with little volatility and very limited risk to your principal, start with a bond fund that is built of low-volatility bonds issued by credit-worthy institutions. A perfect example would be a short-term Treasury bond fund. If you're looking for kick-ass returns in a fixed-income fund, you can start looking for funds built of high-yield fixed-income securities.

One of the main characteristics you look for in a bond is its tax status. Most bonds are taxable, but municipal bonds are federally tax-free. If you want to laugh off taxes, choose a municipal bond fund. But just as with the individual muni bonds themselves, expect lower yield with a muni fund. Also pick and choose your muni fund based on the level of taxation you're looking to avoid. State-specific municipal bond funds filled with triple-tax-free bonds (free from federal, state, and local tax) will be triple-tax-free themselves.

Pruning out the underperformers

Obviously, you want to look at any prospective bond fund's performance *vis a vis* its peers. If you are examining index funds, the driving force behind returns will be the fund's operating expenses. Intermediate-term Treasury bond index fund X will generally do better than intermediate-term Treasury bond index fund Y if less of the profits are eaten up by operating expenses.

With actively managed funds . . . guess what? Operating expenses are also a driving force. One study conducted by Morningstar, reported in *The Wall Street Journal,* looked at high quality, taxable bond funds available to all investors with minimums of less than $10,000. More than half of those funds charge investors 1 percent or more. Not surprisingly, almost three-quarters of those pricier funds showed performance that was in the bottom half of the category for 2006.

Russell's rule: Don't pay more than 1 percent a year for any bond fund unless you have a great reason. And don't invest in any actively managed bond fund that hasn't outperformed its peers — and any proper and appropriate benchmarks — for at least several years. (By "proper and appropriate benchmarks," I am referring to bond indexes that most closely match the composition of the bond fund in question. A high-yield bond fund, given that you can expect more volatility, *should* produce higher yields than, say, a Treasury index. Any comparison of a high-yield fund's return to a Treasury index is practically moot.)

Laying down the law on loads

An astonishing number of bond funds charge loads. A *load* is nothing more than a sales commission, sometimes paid when buying the fund (that's called a *front-end* load) and sometimes paid when selling (that's called a *back-end* or *deferred* load). My advice? NEVER PAY A LOAD. There is absolutely no reason you should ever pay a load of (not unheard of) 5.5 percent to buy a bond fund. The math simply doesn't work in your favor.

If you pay a 5.5 percent load to buy into a fund with $10,000, you lose $550 up front. You start with an investment of only $9,450. Suppose that the fund manager is a veritable wizard and gets a 7 percent return over the next five years, whereas similar bond funds with similar yearly operating expenses are paying only 6 percent. Here's what you'll have in five years with the load fund: $13,254. Here's what you'd have with the no-load fund: $13,382.

Russell's rule: Buying a load bond fund is plain and simple dumb. Don't. Repeat: Don't buy load funds.

Sniffing out false promises

Although morally dubious, and in some cases even illegal, some brokerage houses and financial supermarket Web sites have been known to promote certain bond funds over others not because those funds are any better but because a certain fund company paid to be promoted. Buyer beware!

"If you see a certain bond fund or funds being promoted as premium choices on your broker's Web site, you might want to ask the broker outright if the firm is being compensated for that promotion," advises John Gannon, senior vice president, investor education, with the Financial Industry Regulatory Authority (FINRA).

Evaluating bond fund advertisements

Some years ago, back in the "wild west" days, bond fund advertisements were often squirrelly tracts of trash. "We don't see as many bad ads as we used to see," says Paul Herbert, senior mutual fund analyst with Morningstar. "The regulators have cracked down to a good degree."

Although we've come a long way, readers are still advised to read bond mutual fund advertisements with a critical eye. Herbert's first piece of advice: "Pay the most attention to everything in small print, and the least attention to everything in large print!"

What he means is that the large print in the ads usually ballyhoos a fund's short-term performance and short-term ranking by the likes of Morningstar and Lipper. There's nothing wrong with casting a quick eye at recent returns. "But

you should be looking more closely at long-term performance and ranking," says Herbert. Anything shy of three to five years' performance, and you have little indication of whether the bond fund manager really has any skill.

A bond fund's performance, which is largely measured by its past yield, can go up or down moving forward. Bond funds are not bonds, and they aren't CDs. Price of the shares and yields will change over time. The riskier bond classes — long-term bonds and high-yield bonds — are especially prone to change.

Of course, you would know that if you read the very small print at the bottom of each advertisement:

Performance data represents past performance, which does not guarantee future results.

My Picks for Some of the Best Bond Funds

And now for the meat . . . In this section I introduce you to bond funds well worth considering for your portfolio. I lay them out in roughly the same order I introduce you to various kinds of bonds in Part II of this book. I start with very short-term, investment-grade bond funds, sometimes referred to as *near cash*. I then proceed to longer-term Treasuries, corporate bonds (investment-grade and junk), agency bonds, municipal bonds, and international bonds.

If you have a somewhat modest portfolio (less than $50,000), I wrap up this chapter with some recommendations for good blend funds that allow you instant exposure to a variety of bonds. If you have an even more modest portfolio (less than $20,000), I suggest you consider a fund that allows you instant exposure to a variety of both bonds and stocks, and I name a great one.

Please note that under each section, I list my favorite funds alphabetically. If you were to see a bond fund called Aardvark Bonds (you won't, but humor me) followed by a bond fund called Zygote Fixed Income, don't assume that I like Aardvark any more than I do Zygote.

Very short-term, high quality bond funds

These funds are going to pay slightly higher rates of interest than money market funds and CDs but less than longer-term bond funds. They carry very little risk of default and have minimal volatility. Sometimes referred to as *near-cash,* these bond funds are often the best investments for money that you may need to tap within one to three years.

Fidelity Short-Term Bond Fund (FSHBX)

Contact: 800-544-8888; www.fidelity.com

Type of fund: Actively run mutual fund

Types of bonds: Short-term government and both high-grade and mid-grade corporate

Average maturity: 2.7 years

Expense ratio: 0.45 percent

Minimum investment: $2,500 ($500 in an IRA)

This is a convenient place to park your short-term money, especially if you're building a portfolio at Fidelity.

State Farm Interim (SFITX)

Contact: 800-447-0740; www.statefarm.com

Type of fund: Actively run mutual fund

Type of bonds: Short-term government

Average maturity: 2.4 years

Expense ratio: 0.19 percent

Minimum investment: $250

Generally, insurance company mutual funds stink; this is a notable exception!

Vanguard Short-Term Investment-Grade (VFSTX)

Contact: 800-662-7447; www.vanguard.com

Type of fund: Actively run mutual fund

Types of bonds: Short-term government and high-grade corporate

Average maturity: 3 years

Expense ratio: 0.21 percent

Minimum investment: $3,000

Vanguard also has a Short-Term Federal fund (VSGBX) and a Short-Term Bond Index fund (VBISX). They are all rather similar, but VFSTX tends to be my favorite.

Intermediate-term Treasury bond funds

U.S. government bonds can be bought on www.treasurydirect.gov without paying a markup. Nonetheless, Treasury bond funds offer instant diversification of maturities at modest cost. Remember that while Treasury bonds are said to carry no risk of default, they do carry other risks, such as interest-rate risk and inflation risk. More on Treasury bonds in Chapter 5.

Fidelity Government Income (FGOVX)

Contact: 800-544-8888; www.fidelity.com

Type of fund: Indexed mutual fund

Type of bonds: Intermediate government

Average maturity: 5.3 years

Expense ratio: 0.45 percent

Minimum investment: $2,500 ($250 in an IRA)

This is an indexed array of government bonds in a mutual fund run by one of the largest U.S. brokerage houses.

iShares Lehman 7–10-Year Treasury Bond Fund (IEF)

Contact: 800-474-2737; www.barclaysglobal.com

Type of fund: Exchange-traded fund

Type of bonds: Long-term Treasury

Average maturity: 7.5 years

Expense ratio: 0.15 percent

Minimum investment: None

As with all ETFs, you pay a commission to buy and sell this fund.

iShares Lehman TIPS Bond Fund (TIP)

Contact: 800-474-2737; www.barclaysglobal.com

Type of fund: Exchange-traded fund

Type of bonds: Treasury Inflation-Protected Securities

Average maturity: 6.5 years

Expense ratio: 0.20 percent

Minimum investment: None

If you want inflation protection in a bond fund, this is perhaps your best choice.

(Mostly) high quality corporate bond funds

Investment-grade corporate bonds have a history of returning about a percentage point higher than Treasuries each year. For more on corporate bonds, see Chapter 6.

Dodge & Cox Income (DODIX)

Contact: 800-621-3979; www.dodgeandcox.com

Type of fund: Actively run mutual fund

Types of bonds: Mostly high-grade corporate, plus a few junkier issues

Average maturity: 6.2 years

Expense ratio: 0.44 percent

Minimum investment: $2,500 ($1,000 in an IRA)

A super track record at a reasonable cost.

iShares iBoxx $ Investment Grade Corporate Bond Fund (LQD)

Contact: 800-474-2737; www.barclaysglobal.com

Type of fund: Exchange-traded fund

Type of bonds: Investment-grade corporate

Average maturity: 10.5 years

Expense ratio: 0.15 percent

Minimum investment: None

This is the low-cost index leader for corporate bond investing.

Loomis Sayles Bond Fund (LSBRX)

Contact: 800-633-3330; www.loomissayles.com

Type of fund: Actively run mutual fund

Type of bonds: Mostly corporate

Average maturity: 11.5 years

Expense ratio: 0.96 percent

Minimum investment: $2,500

This fund keeps outperforming just about every other fixed-income fund on the market. How so, despite its high cost, and whether the outperformance will continue, is something of a mystery.

Junk city: Corporate high-yield funds

High-yield bonds return more than other bonds, but you can lose your money in times of recession when shakier companies start to default on their loans. More on junk bonds in Chapter 6.

iShares iBoxx $ High Yield Corporate Bond Fund (HYG)

Contact: 800-474-2737; www.barclaysglobal.com

Type of fund: Exchange-traded fund

Type of bonds: Corporate junk (average rating BB)

Average maturity: 8 years

Expense ratio: 0.50 percent

Minimum investment: None

This fund opened in April 2007.

Payden High Income Fund (PYHRX)

Contact: 213 625-1900; www.payden-rygel.com

Type of fund: Actively run mutual fund

Type of bonds: Junk bonds, but not crazy junk (average rating BB)

Average maturity: 8 years

Expense ratio: 0.59 percent

Minimum investment: $5,000 ($2,000 in an IRA)

In 2000 — its only year of negative return in the past decade — this fund lost 1.7 percent. The average BB rating is slightly below that of the Vanguard fund's BBB rating.

Vanguard High-Yield Corporate Fund (VWEHX)

Contact: 800-662-7447; www.vanguard.com

Type of fund: Actively run mutual fund

Type of bonds: Junk bonds, but not enormously junky (average Moody's rating BBB)

Average maturity: 7.3 years

Expense ratio: 0.25 percent

Minimum investment: $3,000

This is a long-time leader in junk bond investing. In 2000 — its only year of negative returns in the past decade — the fund lost 0.8 percent.

Agency bond funds

These are almost as safe as Treasury bonds, and you get a bit of extra kick on the coupon payments. For more on agency bonds, see Chapter 7.

American Century Ginnie Mae (BGNMX)

Contact: 800-345-2021; www.americancentury.com

Type of fund: Actively run mutual fund

Type of bonds: Intermediate government agency

Average maturity: 6.2 years

Expense ratio: 0.57 percent

Minimum investment: $2,500

You'll get better return than you'd get on a Treasury bond of similar maturity, and a tad more volatility.

Fidelity Ginnie Mae Fund (FGNMX)

Contact: 800-544-8888; www.fidelity.com

Type of fund: Actively run mutual fund

Type of bonds: Intermediate government agency

Average maturity: 6.0 years

Expense ratio: 0.45 percent

Minimum investment: $2,500 ($200 in an IRA)

This is technically an actively run fund but pretty close to an index fund.

Vanguard Ginnie Mae Fund (VFIIX)

Contact: 800-662-7447; www.vanguard.com

Type of fund: Index mutual fund

Type of bonds: Intermediate government agency

Average maturity: 6.2 years

Expense ratio: 0.21 percent

Minimum investment: $2,000

This fund can't be beat for low cost exposure to this kind of bond.

Municipal bond funds: Taxes be damned

These funds don't give you the yield that taxable bond funds do, but you'll be spared, perhaps entirely, from paying federal income tax. For more on municipal tax-free bonds, see Chapter 8. Note that I've chosen two "high-yield" muni funds as my favorites. "High-yield" does not mean the same in the world of munis as it does in corporate bonds. Municipal bonds rarely go belly up.

Fidelity Tax-Free Bond (FTABX)

Contact: 800-544-8888; www.fidelity.com

Type of fund: Actively run mutual fund

Type of bonds: Municipal tax-free (average rating AA)

Average maturity: 14.5 years

Expense ratio: 0.50 percent

Minimum investment: $25,000

This is a well-run bond fund. All the bonds are exempt from the alternative minimum tax (AMT) so it's a good deal for those in higher tax brackets.

T. Rowe Price Tax-Free High-Yield (PRFHX)

Contact: 800-683-5660; www.troweprice.com

Type of fund: Actively run mutual fund

Type of bonds: Municipal tax-free (average rating BBB)

Average maturity: 18.5 years

Expense ratio: 0.70 percent

Minimum investment: $2,500 ($1,000 in an IRA)

This is a good alternative for people with high incomes but limited wealth.

Vanguard High-Yield Tax Exempt (VWAHX)

Contact: 800-662-7447; www.vanguard.com

Type of fund: Actively run mutual fund

Type of bonds: Municipal tax-free (average rating AA)

Average maturity: 7.2 years

Expense ratio: 0.17 percent

Minimum investment: $3,000

Most, but not all, of the bonds are free from the alternative minimum tax. Although the fund does have high-yield bonds, it also has some higher quality munis.

International bond funds

These are mostly high quality bonds issued in Japan, Western Europe, and Australia. For more on international bonds, see Chapter 9.

American Century International Bond (BEGBX)

Contact: 800-345-2021; www.americancentury.com

Type of fund: Actively managed mutual fund

Type of bonds: High quality international

Average maturity: 9 years

Expense ratio: 0.82 percent

Minimum investment: $2,500

Returns will reflect currency exchange as well as interest payments on bonds, making this a volatile fund by fixed-income standards.

PIMCO Foreign Bond, Dollar-Hedged (PFODX)

Contact: 800-426-0107; www.allianzinvestors.com

Type of fund: Actively run mutual fund

Type of bonds: High quality international

Average maturity: 9 years

Expense ratio: 0.90 percent

Minimum investment: $5,000

As a dollar-hedged fund, this one offers a "pure" return reflecting interest paid on the bonds. Currency flux is factored out. This means less volatility but less potential return as well.

PIMCO Foreign Bond, Unhedged (PFBDX)

Contact: 800-426-0107; www.allianzinvestors.com

Type of fund: Actively managed mutual fund

Type of bonds: High quality international

Average maturity: 9 years

Expense ratio: 0.95 percent

Minimum investment: $5,000 ($2,500 in an IRA)

Returns will reflect currency exchange as well as interest payments on bonds. Watch out for potentially sizeable price swings.

T. Rowe Price International Bond (RPIBX)

Contact: 800-683-5660; www.troweprice.com

Type of fund: Actively managed mutual fund

Type of bonds: Mostly quality international

Average maturity: 7.5 years

Expense ratio: 0.86 percent

Minimum investment: $2,500 ($1,000 in an IRA)

Returns will reflect currency exchange as well as interest payments on bonds.

Emerging market bond funds

If you are willing to deal with the volatility, these bond funds — made up of bonds from Russia, Brazil, Mexico, and Turkey — offer enormous return potential. For more on emerging market bonds, see Chapter 9.

Fidelity New Markets Income Fund (FNMIX)

Contact: 800-544-8888; www.fidelity.com

Type of fund: Actively run mutual fund

Type of bonds: Emerging market bonds

Average maturity: 13 years

Expense ratio: 0.91 percent

Minimum investment: $2,500

1998 was the only year this fund lost money in the past decade, but it lost 22.38 percent that year.

Payden Emerging Markets Bond Fund (PYEMX)

Contact: 213 625-1900; www.payden-rygel.com

Type of fund: Actively run mutual fund

Type of bonds: Emerging market

Average maturity: 11.9 years

Expense ratio: 0.82 percent

Minimum investment: $5,000 ($2,000 in an IRA)

This fund opened in 1999.

Alert! Some really baaaad bond funds

The worst of the worst? They have *loads* (commissions paid to buy and sell), high yearly expenses, and questionable managerial talent. The envelope, please . . .

Morgan Stanley High-Yield Securities A (HYLCX)

Ack! With a 4.25 percent front-end load and 1.30 percent in annual expenses, you wouldn't expect this fund to shine, but still, a ten-year annual return (as of March 31, 2007) of –2.03 is hard to explain, never mind swallow. My condolences to those who invested in past years.

BlackRock High Income (HIS)

Ohmygod! The yearly expense ratio of 1.34 is high, but it still doesn't explain why this closed-end fund, for all the risk it takes with its allegedly "high-yield" bonds, has a ten-year annual return of only 2.24 percent.

Permanent Port Treasury (PRTBX)

Shoot me! A 1.42 percent yearly expense ratio on a Treasury bond fund is incredibly steep. The 15-year annual return of only 3.02 (just keeping even with inflation) reflects the managers' hefty take. Pity the investors.

T. Rowe Price Emerging Markets Bond (PREMX)

Contact: 800-683-5660; www.troweprice.com

Type of fund: Actively run mutual fund

Type of bonds: Emerging market

Average maturity: 14 years

Expense ratio: 1.03 percent

Minimum investment: $2,500 ($1,000 in an IRA)

1998 was the only year this fund lost money in the past decade, but it lost 23.1 percent that year.

All-in-one bond funds

When you don't care to pick and choose, but rather would like to buy up a representative sampling of the total bond market, consider these options.

T. Rowe Price Spectrum Income (RPSIX)

Contact: 800-683-5660; www.troweprice.com

Type of fund: Actively managed mutual fund

Types of bonds: Anything and everything

Average maturity: 7.3 years

Expense ratio: 0.89 percent

Minimum investment: $2,500 ($1,000 in an IRA)

This has been an industry leader since 1990.

Vanguard Total Bond Market ETF (BND)

Contact: 800-662-7447; www.vanguard.com

Type of fund: Exchange-traded fund

Types of bonds: You name it: government, corporate, agency

Average maturity: 6.9 years

Expense ratio: 0.11 percent

Minimum investment: None

Introduced to the market in April 2007, this fund brings new meaning to low-cost, well diversified bond investing. "BND is a great core bond holding," says Ron DeLegge, host of the Index Investing syndicated radio show, publisher of www.ETFguide.com.

All-in-one bond and stock fund

For the total bond market AND the total stock market AND international stocks all rolled up in one, try this.

Vanguard STAR Fund (VGSTX)

Contact: 800-662-7447; www.vanguard.com

Type of fund: Index of indexed mutual funds

Types of bonds: Across the board

Average maturity: 11 years

Expense ratio: 0.35 percent

Minimum investment: $1,000

For those with limited funds (under $10,000), this Vanguard offering allows for an instant 60/40 (60 percent diversified stocks; 40 percent diversified bonds) portfolio. There are other funds that will do the same, but I love this one.

Part V

Bonds As Replacements for the Old Paycheck

"The first thing we should do is get you two into a good bond fund. Let me get out the 'Magic 8—Ball' and we'll run some options."

In this part . . .

Although I do use the word *retirement* in this section, I really prefer to use *retunement*. Today's retirement has changed so much from a generation ago that the difference is almost as great as between *stationary* and *stationery, cats* and *cuts, flies* and *fries*.

A generation ago, most people built a small nest egg, retired at 65, got a pension and Social Security, and lived predictably ever after. Today, the pension has vanished for many. Social Security isn't as secure as it was. Savings rates are negligible.

All this has served to blur the line of retirement. Some older Americans can't retire. Some much younger ones can. Some folks are working part-time and using savings for supplemental income (whether they should or not).

This section is for anyone who has begun to take withdrawals from a portfolio or is thinking about doing so. It's about tapping into that portfolio in the most rational manner. It's about using the portfolio to live the life of your dreams, while keeping your nest egg intact just in case you live to 105.

You won't be surprised to find that bonds are an essential part of the picture.

Chapter 17

Fulfilling the Need for Steady, Ready, Heady Cash

*W*hen I was young, my father would suit up every morning, get into the car, hit the Long Island Expressway, and battle his way into Brooklyn, among the grittier of New York City's boroughs. There, at 50 Court Street, he would take the elevator to his seventh-story office, make himself a cup of coffee, and turn on a big fan that would spit out U.S. dollars, which my father would collect and stuff into his brown leather briefcase.

For years, that's how I thought my family paid the bills.

I realized at some point that my father's story of how he made money wasn't entirely true. (Nor was he a five-star general in World War II, even though my Uncle Sid, also a five-star general, corroborated the story entirely.)

Today, many youngsters believe that money is produced by ATM machines. (That's probably because with air conditioning, they don't see many electric fans anymore.) But, of course, we mature, educated adults don't harbor such silly fantasies about money. Doooweee?

Yeah, right.

There's a particular fantasy about money and retirement, and it goes something like this: *You work hard for many years, you send holiday cards to the creep of a boss, you invest in stocks all the while, and the stocks grow. Then, when your portfolio has grown enough, you move your money to safe bonds, you no longer have to send holiday cards to the creep of a boss, you retire, you live off the interest from the bonds, and you golf.*

In this chapter, I explain why that line of reasoning may be as silly as thinking money comes from fans — maybe more so. I explain why a diversified portfolio that includes bonds *and* healthy doses of other investments makes just as much sense to a retiree as it does to working folk. And I explain — in this chapter and the next — how to use your bonds, in conjunction with other investments, to ride steadily and easily into your financial future long after you've given up the day job in Brooklyn (or wherever you happen to currently toil).

Reaping the Rewards of Your Investments

At this very moment, as I'm typing this very paragraph, I'm feeling rather fortunate. I've had a number of jobs in my life that I didn't particularly enjoy (credit analyst, Maryland National Bank, Baltimore, 1981). But I've also had some that I've enjoyed enormously (yoga instructor, Club Med, Al Hoceima, Morocco, 1978). Luckily, my current job (financial planner and author, Allentown, Pennsylvania) falls into the latter category.

As much as I enjoy my present work, it comforts me greatly to know that in a few more years — fewer if this book sells a lot of copies! — whether I get up in the morning to do work-for-pay, or whether I decide to volunteer my time for a worthy cause, to sleep in, or to phone a friend for a chat, will be completely up to me.

What makes work-for-pay optional (other than being born rich, resorting to crime, or marrying a heart surgeon) is a *freedom* portfolio — a portfolio big enough to produce the income needed to support your lifestyle.

When is a portfolio big enough that employment becomes optional? When it provides enough cash flow to pay the bills: both today's and tomorrow's. The tough part about retirement planning is that you don't know how many tomorrows there are going to be; it's hard to estimate bills that are years off; and certain ongoing expenses, such as medical bills, may be well beyond your control. In addition, Congress keeps toying with "sunset" provisions and such, so you can't even estimate your future tax bills.

And on top of all *that,* even though a predictable cash flow for you could be arranged, total predictability comes at a heavy price.

Estimating your target portfolio

In Chapter 12, I introduce the *20 times rule*: You figure out how much money you need to live on for a year (being realistic — look at your bills) and multiply that number by 20. That is the very *minimum* most financial professionals, including me, would want to see you have in your portfolio before you permanently quit your day job. Anything less, and you can't have any reasonable assurance that you aren't going to be living off baked beans and home-grown parsley someday. But this rough rule doesn't factor in the price of beans, how many beans you can eat, or any number of other variables over the coming decades.

To do a much better estimation and get a firmer idea of what kind of portfolio you should shoot for, you may want to hire a financial planner with fancy software to create a retirement plan for you. Or you can turn to any number of Web sites, some of which do a fairly okay (but not great) job at estimating the size portfolio you'll need. Among my favorites is a Web site called www.firecalc.com. (Click on the <u>Advanced FIREcalc</u> tab, and take it from there.) Just about all brokerage house and financial supermarket Web sites have calculators, as well.

Although they're better than any rough rule (even mine), the problem with all retirement plans — yes, even the fancy ones done by professionals — is that they are static. Over the course of your life, things will change: interest rates, the inflation rate, your portfolio returns, your spending, your health, and those stupid sunset provisions on certain taxes, to name a few. All of which is to say that for the moment, we're going to accept the 20x rule, as splintery rough as it is, and move on to the question of where your cash is actually going to come from after you are no longer getting a paycheck.

Cash flow, dear reader, is the name of the game. Cash is what you need to quit your paid employment, if that is your goal.

After all, you may have $5 million in net worth, but if that $5 million is in the form of a framed Picasso hanging in the hallway or a house atop a hill with an Olympic-sized swimming pool in the backyard, you may be technically a multimillionaire but possibly not have enough in your wallet to buy lunch for one at Taco Bell.

Lining up your bucks

The gods of retirement offer you a number of options for putting cash in your wallet. If you are one of those lucky Americans (retired congressmen, senators, presidents) who can still bank on a solid fixed pension with health benefits, that's great. Social Security, when you're gray enough, can also provide steady cash.

But because this is an investment book, I spend the rest of this chapter, and the next, talking about the money you can tap from your savings. It's money that most of us who are not retired senators will need in order to retire, and it can come from one of three sources: interest, dividends, and the sale of securities. Which of these three options (or what combination of the three) you choose will have a great bearing on how big your portfolio needs to be and how much you can safely withdraw so as to never have to resort to eating dog food.

The best option — *always* — is to adopt a cash withdrawal plan from your portfolio that is flexible and potentially allows for all three sources of cash flow to play into your new paycheckless life. One of the biggest and most common investment mistakes that people make is to lock their sights on one form of cash flow (typically interest income) and ignore the others.

Toward the end of this chapter, I show you how a flexible, sensible, triple-source-of-cash-flow plan works. First, allow me to introduce you to each of the three options just mentioned and explain why the gods of retirement created them, where to find them, and how to maximize them.

Finding Interesting Sources of Interest

All pigs are mammals, but not all mammals are pigs. Bonds are fixed-income investments, but not all fixed-income investments are bonds. Anything that yields steady, predictable interest can qualify as fixed income. That includes not only bonds, but CDs, money market accounts, and a few other not-as-common investments that I address here. Any and all of these may serve as sources of cash, either to boost a pre-retirement portfolio or help mine cash from a post-retirement portfolio.

Certificates of deposit (CDs)

As predictable as the Arizona sunrise, CDs, like zero-coupon bonds, offer your principal back with interest after a specified time frame (usually in increments of three months) up to five years in the future. Like savings-bank accounts, CDs are almost all guaranteed by the Federal Deposit Insurance Corporation (FDIC), a government-sponsored agency, for amounts up to $100,000. Interest rates offered tend to increase with the amount of time you're willing to tie your money up. (If the bank will give you, say, 5 percent interest for six months, you can often get 5.20 percent for 12 months.) Take your money out before the maturity of the CD, and you pay a fine, the severity of which depends on the particular issuer.

Because nearly all CDs are federally insured, they are on par with Treasury bonds as far as your principal being secure. Interest rates vary and may be higher or lower than you can get on a Treasury bond of the same maturity. (Check www.bankrate.com and your newspaper for the highest CD rates available.) FDIC-insured Internet banking accounts, which tend to pay higher rates of interest than the corner bank, are also often on a par with one-year to two-year CDs. Often the three investments — CDs, short-term Treasuries, and Internet banking accounts — hug very closely to the same (modest) interest rate. If all three are equal, the CD, a favorite with retirees everywhere, should be your *last* choice. Here are two key reasons:

- The CD requires you to tie your money up; the FDIC-insured Internet bank account does not.
- The CD, as well as the bank account, generates fully taxable income; the Treasury bond or bond fund income is federally taxable but exempt from state tax.

Even though there can be blips in time when CDs are great deals, by and large, CDs are vastly oversold. If you're going to settle for a modest interest rate, there's generally no reason you need to have your money be held captive.

Compared to bonds: Most bonds provide higher long-term returns than CDs. Only Treasury bonds carry the iron-clad principal guarantee of a CD, however.

Mining the many money market funds

Money market funds are mutual funds that invest in very short-term debt instruments (such as Treasury bills, CDs, and bank notes) and provide a stable price with a very modest return. In essence, a money market is a bond turned inside out. It provides a stable price with a floating interest rate, while a bond provides stable return with a potentially volatile market price (if you sell the bond before maturity). Money market funds are not guaranteed by the federal government, as are most CDs and savings bank accounts, but they are very safe due to the quality of their investments, short-term maturities, and the good name of the issuer. (If a Fidelity, Vanguard, or Schwab money market failed to pay investors, there'd likely be a mass exit out of the brokerage house that same day.)

At rare times in history, when long-term lending pays no more than short-term lending (a *flat yield curve,* as I discuss in Part I), money market funds can offer a yield competitive with, perhaps even exceeding, short-term bond funds. (*Short-term* means that the bonds held by the fund generally mature in one to three years.) At most times in history, however, a money market fund will not pay as much as bond funds. Some money market funds, however, may offer yields as high as you can get on any CD.

Money market funds are often used as the *cash* or *sweep* positions at most brokerage houses. Be aware that when you open an account at a brokerage house, the default, if you fail to specify which sweep account you want, may be a very low-yielding money market fund. And simply for the asking, you can have your money moved to a higher yielding money market fund. But you need to ask: "Which is your highest paying sweep account?"

Compared to bonds: Expect most bonds to provide higher long-term returns than money market funds. Money market funds, however, offer greater liquidity and a very high degree of safety.

Banking on online savings accounts

On the day I'm typing this paragraph, www.bankrate.com, a terrific source of financial information, is listing over a dozen online banks, all FDIC-insured, that are offering interest rates on savings accounts higher than any CD rate available. Some of them are advertising introductory offers of several months' interest no less than a half percentage point above anything I found on a CD. Some, such as ING Direct, are offering a $25 check to anyone opening a new account with at least $250. So why tie up your money in a CD when you don't have to?

Compared to bonds: Expect most bonds to provide higher long-term returns than any savings account. An online savings account, however, may offer fairly handsome rates, with instant liquidity and FDIC insurance.

Prospering in peer-to-peer lending

This is the new kid on the fixed-income block. If you haven't checked out www.prosper.com yet, do so now. Even if you decide not to invest, you'll likely find the cybertrip fascinating. Prosper is something like an eBay for cash. (It has some similarities to Match.com, too.) People go onto the Web site and explain why they need money (often posting pictures of themselves looking as respectable and likeable as possible), and other people choose whether to lend them money or not. Prosper calls it *peer-to-peer* lending. Instead of turning to a credit card company, would-be borrowers can go public with their need for money and perhaps get a better deal. In fact, they often do. And lenders, although charging less interest than Visa and MasterCard (not hard to do), can still get a higher return than they would in another fixed-income investment, like bonds.

I became a Prosper lender a year ago, and I've gotten about 10 percent on my money. Not bad. But I've also been lucky. I've spread my $2,000 investment over 20 loans, and I have yet to experience a default. I know other lenders (through the Prosper forum) who haven't been nearly as fortunate. In fact, some have gotten badly stung. Prosper says it does credit checks on all borrowers, but credit checks aren't perfect. And some of the borrowers are listed as known bad credit risks. You can choose them or avoid them.

All in all, I find this a promising venture, although certainly nothing to bank too much on. Investment-wise, I look at it as the equivalent of corporate junk bonds, but the return may be higher than you can get lending to corporations. Only time will tell.

A few caveats if you want to give Prosper a try:

✔ Spread your loans out. Don't lend too much to any one person, regardless of how good his or her story is. Check out the credit ratings of each individual provided by Prosper. Make sure that all your loans aren't going to deadbeats.

✔ Take Prosper's return figures with a big, fat grain of salt. The statements will tell you that you're earning, say, 14 percent on your money, but they don't factor in the time your cash sits idle. It may take weeks before your loans go through, and Prosper doesn't pay you anything while your money is parked.

✔ Know that you are taking substantial risk with your money. I've lately seen advertisements for Prosper on the Internet, one of which is aimed at potential lenders; it reads "It's Simple, Safe & Secure." BS! It isn't all that simple — it will take you some time to get up to speed — and it isn't at all safe and secure. If you want safe and secure, put your money in an FDIC-insured savings account!

✔ Know, too, that your Prosper money will likely be tied up for at least three years, the term of repayment on all the loans.

Prosper has a competitor, a British company called www.zopa.com, which is reportedly making an effort to enter the U.S. market. Officials from both Prosper and Zopa have promised to look into ways to create a secondary market for their loans. If they succeed, the loans may still be risky, but at least your cash wouldn't be tied up for three years.

Compared to bonds: Expect peer-to-peer lending to generate a yield comparable to high-yield corporate bonds, perhaps higher. The risk also may be comparable (which is to say considerable) and perhaps significantly higher — especially if you choose to lend to high-risk borrowers in search of higher returns. Interest earned will be taxed as normal income.

Considering the predictability of an annuity

A cross between an insurance product and an investment, annuities come in myriad shapes and sizes. The general theme is that you give your money to an institution (an insurance company, a brokerage house, or even a charity), and that institution promises you a certain rate of return, typically for as long as you live. The difference between an annuity and a bond: With an annuity, you don't expect to ever see your principal back. In return for giving up your principal, you expect a higher rate of return.

Some annuities, called *variable* annuities, offer rates of return pegged to something like the stock market. Other annuities, called *fixed* annuities, offer a steady rate of return or perhaps a rate of return that adjusts for inflation. Some annuities charge a small fortune in fees. Most annuities ask for surrender charges if you try to change your mind.

Be careful out there! A majority of annuities are horrific rip-offs, with all kinds of hidden costs and high surrender charges should you attempt to escape (as many people do when they finally figure out the costs). I'm talking about a very steep penalty here. A typical annuity may charge you, say, 7 percent of the total amount invested if you withdraw your money within a year, 6 percent within two years, and so on, with a gradual tapering off up to seven years.

Most annuities are sold with 78-page contracts that no one, not even lawyers, can understand.

There are good annuity products, too. See *Annuities For Dummies* by Kerry Pechter (Wiley, 2008). I have a strong preference for fixed annuities that adjust with inflation. One of the best providers of those is Vanguard. You can get an instant quote online at www.vanguard.com. Do a search for "fixed annuity." Such a product makes more sense for older folks, especially those with no interest in leaving anything to heirs.

Never put an annuity into a tax-advantaged retirement account, such as an IRA. A main advantage to an annuity is the ability to defer taxes. Putting an annuity into an IRA, which is already tax-advantaged, makes about as much sense as donating money to Donald Trump.

Compared to bonds: The return you get on an annuity will be based on your age. The older you get, the higher the return. In almost all cases, you'll get more cash flow than you would investing in bonds, but you give up your principal. The taxing of annuity income can be very complicated. Talk to your tax advisor.

Hocking your home with a reverse mortgage

These babies have been around for years but have exploded in popularity in the past several years. You own a home? You're 62 or over? You can sell it back to the bank over time. Each month, you get a check. Each month, you have less equity in your home. Reverse mortgages are complicated. And, like annuities, there are both good and bad. Do your research. Here are some suggestions:

✔ Order the booklet "Home Made Money" from AARP at 1-800-209-8085.

✔ Talk to a reverse-mortgage counselor. AARP has some on board, or try the nonprofit Consumer Credit Counseling Service in your area. Perhaps your best option is to call the U.S. Department of Housing and Urban Development at 1-800-569-4287 to be referred to a HUD-certified reverse mortgage counselor in your area.

✔ Oh, and read *Reverse Mortgages For Dummies* by Sarah Glendon Lyons and John E. Lucas (Wiley).

Compared to bonds: The cash flow you get from a reverse mortgage will vary tremendously depending on your age, the equity you have in your home, and the terms of the mortgage agreement. Reverse-mortgage income is not taxable.

Recognizing that Stocks Can Be Cash Cows, Too (Moo)

Stocks can generate returns in two ways:

✔ They can appreciate in value.

✔ They can issue dividends.

Historically, dividends have actually accounted for the lion's share of stock returns. In the past couple decades, however, it's been the other way around. Stock returns of late have been pretty darned good, but the dividend yield of an average basket of U.S. stocks, per Morningstar, is now only about 0.76 percent. The average dividend yield of the S&P 500 (500 of America's fattest corporations) currently stands at a lackluster 1.6 percent.

Stock dividends, by definition, are not fixed in stone, as are interest payments on bonds. However, they can, within a diversified portfolio of stocks, deliver a fairly consistent cash flow. And unlike bond interest, which is generally taxed as income, the vast majority of stock dividends receive special tax treatment and would rarely be taxed at anything higher than 15 percent (at least under current laws).

Not all stocks are equally likely to cough up dividends. If you wish, you can add stocks to your portfolio that will do just that. You can grab your dividends with either individual stocks or with any number of mutual funds or exchange-traded funds that offer high-dividend paying stocks.

Focusing on stocks with sock-o dividends

By choosing your stocks selectively, or by picking up a high-dividend stock mutual fund or exchange-traded fund, you can fairly handily up your yearly dividend yield to about 3 percent. A lot of investors have been doing just that of late, for the very same reason that investors usually jump on board any investing style: Dividend stocks have kicked ass of late.

But high-dividend stocks don't kick ass every year, or every decade. High-dividend paying companies, often categorized as *value* companies (categorized as such precisely because they pay out higher dividends), tend to invest less in their own growth. Companies that are more miserly with dividends (often called *growth* companies) tend to shovel more into R&D and such. Sometimes that R&D and such translates into greater profits that result in gangbuster stock performance. (Think of the entire 1990s; growth stocks were definitely the place to be.)

There's certainly nothing wrong with dividends, per se, but by focusing on them you may be giving up on absolute return. The best stock portfolios are well diversified: They have both value and growth stocks. I wouldn't want to see you with a stock portfolio of all high-dividend companies, even though the cash flow would be sweet.

Nor would I want to see you with a portfolio too concentrated in a handful of industry sectors. As fate would have it, most high-dividend paying stocks tend to fall heavily in certain industry sectors, such as utilities, tobacco, pharmaceuticals, and banks. Gear your portfolio too heavily toward high dividends, and you'll be pretty much locking yourself outside of semiconductors, medical equipment, Internet technology, biotechnology, and other sectors that may well turn out to be the superstars of the next decade.

Compared to bonds: The cash flow from interest on bonds will be greater and more predictable than the cash flow from stock dividends. Over the long haul, however, expect the *total* return on stocks (which includes both dividends and price appreciation) to be higher. Stocks are also much more volatile than bonds. Whereas bond interest is typically issued semiannually and bond funds usually pay interest monthly, stock dividends are more commonly posted quarterly, although stock funds may issue dividends quarterly, semiannually, or annually.

Realizing gain with real estate investment trusts (REITs)

One particular sector of the stock market, real estate investment trusts (REITs), offers among the highest dividend yields in the land: currently 3.1 percent, says Morningstar. REITs are also slightly different animals from most stocks, in that REITs *must,* per the law, pay out at least 90 percent of their earnings as dividends. And the dividends that REITs pay are generally not taxed at 15 percent, as are most other stock dividends, but rather at normal income tax rates.

The real estate sector also shows delightfully low correlation to the rest of the stock market. So whether or not you want the dividends, it may not be a bad idea to plunk 10 to 15 percent of the money you have allocated for stocks into REITs — preferably low-cost, indexed REIT mutual funds or exchange-traded funds, both U.S. and foreign.

Caveat: REIT distributions are not only generally taxed as regular income, but they may include return of principal, which can make tax reporting tricky. For this reason, it is best to house your REIT holdings in a tax-advantaged retirement account.

Compared to bonds: Even though REITs pay very high dividends by stock standards, what you get in cash flow probably won't be as much as you could get on interest from bonds of equal principal value. REITs will be much more volatile than bonds but also offer hugely greater potential for appreciation.

Taking a middle ground with preferred stock

Often referred to as a sort of hybrid between a stock and a bond, *preferred stock,* issued by companies both public and private, generally offers greater and more secure dividends than common stock. Preferred stock is also safer than common stock in that if a company goes under, the holders of preferred stock must be paid back before the owners of common stock.

There are many variations of preferred stock with varying degrees of payoff and risk. Generally, preferred stock, like most hybrid kinds of investments, wouldn't be my first choice of investment for most people. I'd prefer to see you have a mix of stocks and bonds, which together will provide the same benefit as preferred stock, with more diversification power. If the concept of preferred floats your boat, however, feel free to discuss it with your broker. There are worse investments.

Compared to bonds. Preferred stocks' dividends usually won't be as much as you'd get in bond interest on a similar amount of money. And preferred stock is riskier. On the other hand, the dividends from the preferred stock will usually be more gingerly taxed than the interest on bonds. And some preferred stock (convertible preferred) offers an opportunity for substantial capital appreciation.

Introducing a Vastly Better Way to Create Cash Flow: Portfolio Rebalancing

I'd like to start this section with two seemingly short and simple questions. Are you ready?

Question #1: You have $100,000 in your portfolio. You withdraw exactly $10,000. How much do you have left?

I know you know the answer.

Question #2: Does it matter whether the money you withdraw — the $10,000 — comes from this past year's interest payments on your bonds or this past year's appreciation in the value of your stock holdings?

Either way, you still have $90,000 left, riiiight?

Yes. Yes. YES. YESSSS.

And yet, despite the simplicity of these two questions, you'd be amazed at how many people get the second question wrong. And then, when I look at them quizzically, they argue with me.

"But . . . but . . . but . . . Russell . . . If I withdraw the money from bonds, since that represents interest, my principal will still be intact. But if I withdraw the money from stocks, I'm then tapping my principal, and then I'm eating into a productive asset," they argue.

No. That's wrong. Your portfolio, after withdrawing the $10,000, will be worth $90,000. Period. End of story. Argue all you want. This is basic math here. The resulting balance is the same. It doesn't matter whether the sum withdrawn comes from bond interest, stock dividends, stock appreciation, selling the Picasso from the hallway, renting out the pool, or unicorn droppings. It just doesn't matter.

I'm not sure where the *bond-interest-is-okay-to-withdraw-but-stock-appreciation-isn't-okay-to-withdraw* myth ever started. But for the record, there is no such thing as leaving your bond principal intact. In truth, more than half the money that you're ever likely to earn in bonds is simply keeping your principal afloat of inflation. If you withdraw those inflation-neutralizing interest payments from your portfolio, the remainder of your bond holdings won't be "intact" at all. Your bond holdings will slowly but surely lose value due to the steadily rising cost of living, otherwise known as inflation.

Table 17-1 shows what $100 today will be worth in the future, assuming an annual inflation rate of 3 percent (the current rate of inflation in the United States). According to these figures, if you have a $100 bond maturing in 20 years and you siphon off all the coupon payments, your "intact" principal will probably be worth only $55 when the bond matures. If you have $100 in stock and you siphon off all the appreciation and dividends over the next 20 years, the stock that remains will probably be worth $55, too.

Table 17-1   The Value of Today's $100 Assuming 3 Percent Inflation

Years in Future	Value of Today's $100
5	$86
10	$74
15	$64
20	$55
25	$48
30	$41

When you can see that withdrawing $10,000 means withdrawing $10,000 — regardless of the source — and that there's no such thing as leaving your principal "intact," you are ready to create a portfolio that can handle withdrawals objectively. By "objectively," I am saying that sometimes it will make sense to take your cash flow from appreciated stock, sometimes from stock dividends, and sometimes from bond interest. As I say in the onset of this chapter, the best option for withdrawing cash from a portfolio — *always* — is to adopt a cash withdrawal plan that is flexible and potentially allows for all three sources of cash flow.

Buying low and selling high

Here is the best method, far and away, for extracting cash from a portfolio. For illustration purposes, I'm going to use a very simple portfolio, consisting of Domestic Stock Fund A, Foreign Stock Fund F, Commodity Fund C, Bond Fund B, and Short-Term Cash Fund S.

Your portfolio allocation today, based on careful analysis of your need for return and your stomach for risk (as I discuss in Part III), looks like this:

Domestic Stock Fund A	26%
Foreign Stock Fund F	25%
Commodity Fund C	5%
Bond Fund B	38%
Short-Term Cash Fund S	6%

You've set up your accounts so that all of your interest, dividends, and capital gains are reinvested in (rolled directly into) each security as they accrue.

Six months pass. During that time, you've been pulling regularly from your short-term cash fund (which, at 6 percent of your portfolio, is enough to cover a year to 18 months' expenses). The world economy is humming, and stocks are sailing, especially foreign stocks. Your allocations have all gone awry. Your portfolio now looks like this:

Domestic Stock Fund A	30%
Foreign Stock Fund F	32%
Commodity Fund C	5%
Bond Fund B	30%
Short-Term Cash Fund S	3%

What do you do? You *rebalance*. That means you sell off some of your stock funds, and you use the proceeds both to boost your cash position and add to your bond position. Your goal is to bring everything back into alignment so you are once again starting with the same allocation (26 percent U.S. stocks, 25 percent foreign stocks, and so on) you had at the beginning of the year. That allocation (your risk/return sweet spot) will only change if your life circumstances change — if, for example, you inherit $1 million from a rich uncle or, conversely, a rich uncle successfully sues you for $1 million.

Rebalancing not only creates cash flow but also puts your portfolio on anabolic steroids. Every six months (it doesn't have to be six months, but I find that is a good time frame for those making regular withdrawals), you are not only providing yourself with living expenses and keeping your portfolio where it should be in terms of your personal risk/return sweet spot, but you are also continually selling high and buying low: the best formula I know — the best formula there is — for long-term investment success.

One more example: Yet six months later. During this half-year, the stock market took a face-dive, commodities soared, and bonds did very well. Your portfolio at year-end again is out of alignment. It now looks like this:

Domestic Stock Fund A	22%
Foreign Stock Fund F	20%
Commodity Fund C	9%
Bond Fund B	46%
Short-Term Cash Fund S	3%

At this point, you're going to sell off the bond and commodity portion of your portfolio. And, after you've gotten your cash position back up to where you need it, you may wind up buying more stocks, which are now selling at bargain-basement prices.

And what about all that bond interest?

In Part I of this book, I explain that bonds' main role in your portfolio isn't so much for the income, nice as income is, but to provide ballast, to keep your portfolio afloat when the waters get choppy. Now you can see why I'm of that opinion.

The coupon payments from your bonds, or the interest payments generated by your bond fund, are to be plowed directly back into the bond side of your portfolio. This practice keeps your bond holdings from getting eaten up by inflation. Historically, stocks have returned much more than bonds. If that holds true in the future (if . . . if . . . if), you'll be skimming much more from the stock side of your portfolio during retirement. If the future turns out to be different than the past, then those predictable bond coupons could spare you from destitution, just as they may have spared your grandparents during the Great Depression.

Bless bonds. Bless bond income. I only ask that you don't become a slave to that income.

Dealing with realities

In the real world, rebalancing can sometimes be a bit tricky. If your portfolio is in a taxable account rather than a tax-advantaged retirement account, you may have to contend with tax consequences when you sell any security. You may also have to deal with trading costs, depending on your choice of securities and the brokerage house you use to house your portfolio. Trading costs and taxes both can nibble away at a nest egg. You've got to be careful.

Perhaps you feel confident factoring those variables into your rebalancing plan. If not, you should see a financial planner, at least for a single visit, to help you orchestrate and fine-tune your rebalancing strategy.

But before you decide whether to handle it alone, read Chapter 18. In this exciting chapter, I discuss your portfolio allocation during retirement and how to sculpt your portfolio — including putting a certain good percentage in bonds, of course — so as to maximize your withdrawal potential without jeopardizing your nest egg.

Chapter 18

Finding Comfort and Security in Old Age

*W*hen it comes to old age, common fears include everything from incontinence and impotence to failing eyesight and loose teeth. But on the financial front, the greatest fear, it goes without saying, is running out of money. For folks who have money in the first place, enough to build a decent portfolio, two things generally can go awry: market volatility (a growly bear suddenly turning investment dollars to dimes) and unexpectedly high inflation (a slow and steady drain of spending power).

If you fear market volatility most, you may tend to err on the side of what is traditionally seen as investment conservatism. You probably love predictable investments, such as CDs, money markets, savings bonds, annuities, and such. People who fear inflation more tend to err on the side of what is traditionally seen as investment aggressiveness. They go for maximum return. They love stocks, commodities, real estate investments, and maybe high-yield or leveraged bonds.

In this chapter, I present the views of both camps — financial liberals and conservatives — blend them together, and present the view that I believe makes the most sense. Together, you and I figure out the best mix of retirement investments to weather both market volatility *and* inflation. As for incontinence, impotence, and loose teeth . . . let's leave all that for another book, shall we?

Looking Ahead to Many Years of Possible Portfolio Withdrawals

Lifespans have increased. There's better than a 50/50 chance that either you or your spouse will still be alive at age 90. If you plan to retire at age 65, that means you need a portfolio that can provide cash flow for about 25 more years. Two and a half decades is a long time. It allows for inflation to eat up a good bit of your savings. (Consider how much gasoline, a chocolate bar, or a loaf of bread cost 25 years ago.)

If you or your spouse are 65 years old right now, Table 18-1 shows the odds that you'll still be alive and kicking at age 80, 90, or 100 (15, 25, or 35 years beyond the traditional age of retirement). It's based on 2005 figures from the Society for Actuaries.

Table 18-1		Your Chances of Living to an Old Age		
Age	*Husband*	*Wife*	*Both of You*	*Either of You*
80	65%	75%	49%	91%
90	24%	37%	9%	52%
100	2%	4%	0.1%	6%

What that added longevity means, all things being equal, is that it behooves you to invest a wee bit more aggressively than did your grandparents. How aggressively? That depends on many factors, and it depends on who you ask. There is, unfortunately, little consensus among financial professionals. Just like the amateurs, we each have a certain bias.

Knowing Where the Real Danger Lies

Most financial pros have moved well beyond the old adage, held dearly for years, that the percent of your portfolio held in bonds should be equal to your age. (By age 60, you should be 60 percent in bonds; by age 70, 70 percent; and so on.) Some say, as do I, that the formula is as antiquated as the cross-bow — and potentially just as dangerous.

"The real risk to most people's portfolios is, paradoxically, not taking enough market risk with higher-returning but more volatile investments, like stocks and commodities," says Steve Cassaday, CFP, president of Cassaday & Company, Inc., an investment management and financial planning firm in McLean, Virginia. "Given what most people have saved by retirement, and the average lifespan today, a more aggressive portfolio is the only choice if people are going to maintain their lifestyles."

Cassaday has researched the returns of various kinds of investments over the past 35 years and has concluded that a portfolio of 15 percent bonds and 2.5 percent cash, with the rest in more aggressive but very well diversified investments like stocks and commodities, actually offers the greatest degree of absolute safety to the average investor. In other words, he opts to put his retired clients in portfolios that are over 80 percent equities, including U.S. stock, foreign stock, REITs, and commodities.

Cassaday's views were published in the September 2006 issue of the *Journal of Financial Planning* and have created quite a stir among professional financial types, many of whom are skeptical, at best, of Cassaday's conclusions.

I know, as the author of a book on bonds, you wouldn't expect me to agree with Cassaday. However, I've seen his number-crunching, and I'm impressed. Although I don't buy into his strategy completely, I don't think the guy is too far off the mark. His aggressive portfolios, when *back-tested* (using computers to simulate how they would have done over history), have held up remarkably well through both bull markets and bears. Sure, they dip when the stock market is down, but they come back.

Finding your comfort zone

The aggressiveness of Cassaday's approach may not be right for all investors. I say that not because I doubt his numbers but for two other reasons:

- ✔ The future of the stock market may be not quite as rosy as the past.

- ✔ A portfolio of more than 80 percent equity is subject to huge dips in bad times. People tend to panic and sell their fallen angels just when they should be holding them the most. The stock and commodity markets are like giant rubber bands: After the biggest down stretches, you tend to see the strongest snap-backs, and vice versa (although giant rubber bands tend to be more predictable than the stock market).

Keep in mind that a portfolio of 80 percent stocks and 20 percent bonds *will* have short-term setbacks. According to data compiled by Vanguard, such a portfolio has seen negative annual returns in 22 of the past 80 years. But the average annual return was a very impressive 10 percent.

For most people, a somewhat less aggressive portfolio than Cassaday's choice portfolio is probably going to work best. (Cassaday himself will amend his portfolio for his clients that can't emotionally handle a lot of volatility.) Another financial-planning colleague of mine, William P. Bengen, CFP, wrote a book for other financial planners called *Conserving Client Portfolios During Retirement* (FPA Press), and in that book he suggests something of a compromise between Cassaday's portfolio and the traditional age-based portfolio.

Most financial planners I know are much, much more in line with Bengen's thinking than with Cassaday's.

Setting your default at 60/40 isn't a bad idea

Bengen, like Cassaday, crunched the numbers backwards and forwards. His conclusion: Yes, tweak your portfolio as you approach retirement to include more bonds and less stock. But after you reach the 60 percent stock/40 percent bond mark, stop right there. Think long and hard before reducing your stock allocation or raising your bond allocation any more than you have already. Given that stock returns have historically creamed bond returns, you may need those stock returns if your portfolio is going to last as long as you do.

Of course, Bengen uses the 60/40 benchmark loosely. Think about your "stocks" as any growth asset, which may also include commodities or investment real estate. Think of your "bonds" as any kind of fixed income, which may also include annuities or CDs. If you err toward riskier growth assets, such as small stocks, or riskier fixed-income investments, such as high-yield bonds, you may tweak your 60/40 allocation to reflect that. In fact, there are many reasons that you may tweak your percentage.

The take-home point: "Don't be wooden," says Bengen.

Choosing your ultimate ratio

Me? Unless my circumstances change, my personal retirement portfolio — which I already have planned! — will be about 70/30: 70 percent stock and 30 percent bonds. (Right now, at age 51, it's just about 75/25.) But I feel that I can emotionally stomach more volatility than most people. I know that I won't sell if the market takes a flop. And I have the kind of career that easily allows me to work part-time to pick up a few bucks if the market sours badly and I feel a need to supplement my portfolio income.

Obviously, retirement planning is a very personal process.

What about the house?

If — and that's a *big* if — you have sizeable home equity *and* you think you'll be able to downsize to something cheaper at a certain point in the future, you can factor your home equity into your retirement portfolio. Most people these days, however, seem to have a hard time downsizing, in which case, your home equity is nice to have but won't provide you with any needed cash. Not now. Not later. If you want to give up your day job, the two empty rooms upstairs won't help you have cash to pay for groceries. Of course, if you're willing to sell the ranch and move into an apartment or retirement facility, the home equity you've built up can play a very important role in your sunset years.

Not only that, but the United States Congress, in its own wisdom, has created a plethora of "sunset" provisions, so that no one, not even the amazing Carnac, not even the editors of *Moolah* magazine who pretend they know which way the markets are going, can come very close to constructing a retirement plan with any great precision. The sunset provisions are temporary changes in our tax codes that may or may not revert back to their original standing. They affect everything from the estate tax to taxes on capital gains and dividends.

Bottom (mushy) line: Most people living off their portfolios are advised to have very well diversified portfolios (U.S. stock, foreign stock, small cap and large cap stock, value and growth securities) with 25 percent to 45 percent bonds (the majority of which should be investment-grade bonds). A very conservative investor may want 50 percent bonds. If you go beyond that, your hankering for safety may very well backfire and your "safe" portfolio will wind up risking your lifestyle as inflation takes its steady toll.

Calculating How Much You Can Safely Tap

Earlier in the book, I present the *20 times rule*: a thumbprint that gives you a *very rough* guide of how big a portfolio you need before you retire. In short, figure out how much you need in a year, subtract whatever retirement income you have outside of investment income (such as Social Security), and multiply the remainder by 20. So if you need $50,000 a year and Social Security will provide $20,000, you should build a portfolio of ($30,000 x 20) $600,000 before you kiss your office colleagues goodbye forever.

That rough rule, like all rough rules, is the product of a few assumptions. Foremost, it assumes that you have a diversified portfolio returning enough so you can not only keep up with inflation but withdraw 4 to 5 percent a year without denting your principal.

That allowable withdrawal amount will depend on a whole slew of factors, such as the actual rate of inflation, your tax hit, market conditions, and — a biggie — your life expectancy and your current age. (At age 97, it is probably okay to see a slow dwindling in your portfolio size.) A lot of those variables, such as your lifespan, you can control only to a limited extent (eat carrots). What you can control *entirely* — and what will have great bearing on how much you can withdraw — is the allocation of your portfolio, especially the ratio of stocks to bonds.

Revisiting risk, return, and realistic expectations

How realistic is a 4 to 5 percent withdrawal rate in the real world? According to figures from Vanguard, a retirement portfolio with an allocation of 50 percent bonds and 50 percent stocks has about a 75 percent chance of lasting 30 years, provided the initial withdrawal is limited to 4 percent and then adjusted for inflation. I don't know about you, but I find that number a bit depressing. It means that you will need $1 million to generate $40,000 a year, and even then, you could go broke before you die.

With a portfolio that is 60 percent stocks and 40 percent bonds, and provided you regularly rebalance your portfolio (as I describe in Chapter 17), that same 4 to 5 percent withdrawal rate gives you about a 95 percent chance of getting through 30 years of retirement — unless the markets take an unprecedented dive. That figure is much less depressing than the previous one!

According to Steve Cassaday, if you are willing to deal with the volatility that comes with a portfolio of 80 percent equities, you should be able to withdraw up to *7 percent* a year and be safe for 30 years and beyond. However, there will likely be times that your portfolio sinks, and sinks hard, and you'll be wondering whether you're going to run out of money next month. I like Cassady's figure best of all (who wouldn't?). But again, I'm not sure how many people could sit tight and deal with the kind of volatility that would be inevitable with such a market-risk laden portfolio.

Basing your retirement on clear thinking

History rarely repeats although, I'm not the first to say, it often echoes. The long-term return on large stocks — at least over the past century or so — has been about 10 percent a year. Small stocks (prone to greater price sways) have returned about 12.5 percent a year. The long-term return on bonds has been about 5 percent. And the inflation rate moving forward, most economists agree, will probably stay somewhere close to its present 3 percent. Based on these numbers, and based on the final portfolio allocation you decide, you can best judge whether your portfolio can long sustain a 3 percent withdrawal, a 7 percent withdrawal, or something in between.

My 70 percent equity/30 percent bond retirement portfolio, after I have it in place and start withdrawing from it, should safely allow me to withdraw 5 percent a year for at least 30 years. And, when I die, there should still be something left for my kids.

But that's me. You need to devise your own plan based on your own longevity, stomach for risk, and the other factors I describe earlier in this chapter. I would only ask you not to think pie-in-the-sky and, as William Bengen says, "Don't be wooden." Allow yourself some flexibility to adjust your cash flow after you begin to withdraw. No retirement plan should be fixed in stone.

Of the many books and articles I've read on retirement planning, one that makes particular sense is *Work Less, Live More* by Bob Clyatt (Nolo). The author suggests something he calls the "95% Rule." It starts with a retirement plan that incorporates a reasonable rate of withdrawal: Clyatt conservatively says 4 percent, maybe 4.5 percent of your initial portfolio ($24,000 to $27,000 a year on a $600,000 portfolio), adjusted each year for inflation. However, if the markets turn sour in any particular year or years, you economize a bit that year or years by withdrawing no more than 95 percent of what you withdrew the previous year. "You'll tighten your belt somewhat, but you won't turn your world upside down," writes Clyatt.

Clyatt's number-crunching tells him that if you follow the 95% Rule, a 50 percent stock and 50 percent bond portfolio, starting with an initial year withdrawal of 4.5 percent and adjusting for inflation, has a 92 percent chance of lasting 30 years. Those aren't bad odds.

Making the Most Use of Uncle Sam's Gifts

The Internal Revenue Service, in cahoots with Congress, gives the U.S. investor two basic kinds of tax-advantaged retirement accounts:

- ✔ Plans that allow for the deferral of income tax until the money is withdrawn (IRAs, SEP-IRAs, 401k plans).
- ✔ Plans that, provided you follow certain rules, allow for tax-free withdrawals after reaching age 59½ (Roth IRAs, Roth 401k plans).

I won't get into the many rules and regulations and the amount that you can stash in each kind of account. That information is readily available elsewhere, and it strays a bit from the focus of this book. Instead, I want to discuss in which account you should place your bond allocation and, should you be in the withdrawal phase of your investing career, from which account you should yank your cash.

Minimizing income is the name of the game

Interest payments from bonds or bond funds (other than municipal bonds, as I discuss in Chapter 8) are generally taxable as normal income. In contrast, the money you make off stocks, whether dividends or capital gains, is usually taxed at 15 percent. It makes sense, especially if you are in a higher-than-15 percent tax bracket, to keep your bonds in a tax-advantaged retirement account. Even if you are in the 15 percent bracket, this plan still makes sense because bond income, regular and steady, is taxed regardless of whether you withdraw it or not. Stock appreciation (capital gains) is taxed only when you sell, although stock held in mutual funds may incur capital gains when the fund sells, even if you don't.

When allocating your portfolio, keep in mind at all times that money in your 401(k) or IRA will eventually be taxed as regular income. Say you decide that you want a 30 percent allocation to bonds, and all of those bonds are in your IRA. If you are within four or five years of withdrawing some of that money, you may want to make the actual allocation of bonds somewhat higher. I can't give you an exact figure because I don't know your tax bracket and I don't know what kind of capital gains taxes you'll pay when you cash out of your taxable accounts. But you may, for example, allocate 35 percent or 45 percent of your portfolio to bonds.

Missing the minimum required distribution — don't!

I'm very happy to live in a country where people who break the law are given due process and, if found guilty of a crime, neither have their limbs removed nor are stoned to death. And yet we have the minimum required distribution (MRD) on 401(k) plans and regular and rollover IRAs, and woe is you if you miscalculate! You won't be stoned, but your finances will certainly be pummeled hard.

Of course, the calculation is easy, says the IRS! You simply take your retirement account's starting balance as of December 31 of the prior year, and you divide that number by your "life-expectancy factor," which is found in IRS publication 590, available on the IRS Web site

(www.irs.gov). Don't get it wrong! The penalty for taking less than your minimum required distribution is brutal. If you withdraw less than the minimum required amount, the IRS can nail you for a sum equal to 50 percent of the amount of the MRD not taken.

MRDs generally begin at age 70½ If you feel uncomfortable doing the calculation yourself, a retirement specialist at the brokerage house where you have your retirement account will help you, or you can ask your tax guru.

Caution: There is an entirely different table for MRDs on inherited IRAs. Lots of people mess up there, with potentially expensive consequences.

If you have various retirement accounts with more space than you need for just your bond allocation, put the bonds in the tax-deferred accounts and put potentially higher-yielding assets, like stocks, in your tax-free accounts, such as your Roth IRA. That's because the Roth IRA does not require you to start taking minimum required distributions at age 70½, so you might as well fuel up your Roth with assets that can really grow over the years.

Lowering your tax bracket through smart withdrawals

At age 70½, you have to start taking something from your 401(k) or your regular or rollover IRA; it's the law. (See the sidebar "Missing the minimum required distribution — don't!") But prior to that age, and to a certain degree after that age, where you take your cash from — whether from your 401(k), IRA, Roth IRA, or taxable account — will be up to your discretion.

How to best use that discretion?

Balance, Grasshopper, balance. Most likely, you want to pull from your tax-deferred retirement accounts only to the point that doing so doesn't push you into a higher tax bracket. At that point, supplement that cash with money from your Roth account or from your taxable brokerage account.

For example, if you are a single guy or gal withdrawing $40,000 a year from your portfolio, consider taking the first $30,650 from your 401(k) or IRA. That amount (according to the 2006 federal tax schedule), and no more, keeps you squarely in the 15 percent tax bracket. Show any more income, and your incremental income will be taxed at 25 percent — a two-thirds increase in tax! Solution: Withdraw the remaining $9,350 ($40,000 – $30,650) from either your Roth or your taxable brokerage account, and you'll keep yourself in the 15 percent bracket.

Having retirement money that is both taxable and tax-free is known in the financial planning world as *tax diversification*. It makes a lot of sense.

Caveat: If you have mucho bucks — more than the federal estate tax exemption (which varies year to year) — the rules change. Your heirs will generally fare much better inheriting money outside of your IRA or 401(k) than money within. It may make sense, in your case, to well exceed your minimum required distributions, take the tax hit, but spare your heirs from having to pay a hefty estate tax plus income tax. Talk to an estate planning attorney, tax accountant, or financial planner before setting up your withdrawal strategy.

Oh, and Roth money is a great gift for your heirs.

Part VI
The Part of Tens

The 5th Wave   By Rich Tennant

"There goes the profit I made on junk bonds last year."

In this part . . .

You have now arrived at The Part of Tens, a classic feature in all *Dummies* books that offers fun and practical lists chock full of takeaway information. I begin with the ten most common misconceptions about bonds — some of them rather huge misconceptions that I've seen carried even by some very experienced investors. I then present ten mistakes that bond investors often make, some potentially quite costly. And I wrap up this section with ten Q&As with Dan Fuss of Loomis, Sayles & Company, without any question one of the most successful bond managers of our age.

Chapter 19

Ten Most Common Misconceptions about Bonds

A scoop of lake water in your hands, clear and cloistered, unmoving, looks like the very essence of simplicity. And yet, a dab under the high-powered microscope reveals an entire world of complex organisms wiggling and squiggling about in your palms.

A bond selling for 100 and paying 5 percent looks like the clearest, most easy-to-understand investment possible. Yet it is, in reality, a much more complex organism. Scoop through these ten common bond misconceptions and you'll no doubt see what I'm talking about.

A Bond "Selling for 100" Costs $100

Welcome to the first complexity in bonds: *jargon!* When a bond broker says that he or she has a bond "selling for 100," it means that the bond is selling not for $100, but for $1,000. If that same bond were "selling for 95," it would be on the market for $950. If it were "selling for 105," it could be bought for $1,050.

Ready for more jargon?

The *par value* or *face value* of a $1,000 bond is $1,000. But the *market value* depends on whether it is selling for 95, 100, 105, or whatever. In addition, that $1,000 face bond may be said to "pay 5 percent," but that doesn't mean you'll get 5 percent on your money! It means you'll get 5 percent on the par value: that is, 5 percent on $1,000, or $50 a year, which may mean a return of greater or less than 5 percent to you. If you paid 105 for the bond (that's called a *premium*), you'll actually be making less than 5 percent on your money. If you paid 95 for the bond (that's called a *discount*), you'll be making more than 5 percent on your money.

Confused? Turn to Chapter 4.

Buying a Bond at a Discount Is Better Than Paying a Premium, Duh

Duh, yourself. Sometimes, you get what you pay for.

Discounted bonds sell at a discount for a reason; premium bonds sell at a premium for a reason. Here's the reason: Those premium bonds typically have higher coupon rates than prevailing coupon rates. Discount bonds, in contrast, typically have lower coupon rates than prevailing coupon rates. In both theory and in practice, two bonds with similar ratings and similar maturities, all other things being equal, will have similar yields-to-maturity (the yield that really matters) whether sold at a premium or a discount.

Example: Bond A, issued in 2000, has a coupon rate of 4 percent. Bond B, issued in 2007, has a coupon rate of 8 percent. Everything else about the bonds is the same: same issuer, same maturity date (let's say 2020), same callability. Currently, similar bonds are paying 6 percent. You would fully expect Bond A to sell at a discount and Bond B to sell at a premium. In both cases you would expect their yields-to-maturity to be roughly 6 percent.

A Bond Paying X% Today Will Pocket You X% Over the Life of the Bond

A bond paying a coupon rate of 5 percent may (if the bound is purchased at a discount) be yielding something higher, like, say, 6 percent. But each six months, as you collect that 6 percent on your money, you'll either spend it or reinvest it. If you reinvest it at an even higher rate of interest (suppose interest rates are going up) — say 8 percent — then your *total return* on your money, over time, will be higher than both the coupon rate of 5 percent and the current yield of 6 percent. If you sell the bond before maturity, the price you get for it (the market value of the bond at the time) will also be factored into your total return.

In sum, the total return on the money you invest in bonds is often unknowable. Bonds are not at all as predictable as they seem at first glance!

Rising Interest Rates Are Good (or Bad) for Bondholders

In general, rising interest rates are good for *future* bondholders (who will see higher coupon payments); for those who *presently* own bonds, rising interest rates may not be so good, because rising interest rates push bond prices down. (Who is going to want to buy your bond paying 5 percent when other bonds are suddenly paying 6 percent?)

On the other hand, rising interest rates allow present bondholders to reinvest their money (the coupon payments that arrive twice a year) for a higher return.

In the end, however, what matters most for bondholders both present and future is the *real* rate of interest, after tax. The real rate of interest is the nominal rate minus the rate of inflation. You'd rather get 6 percent on a bond when inflation is running at 2 percent than 10 percent on a bond when inflation is running at 8 percent — especially after taxes, which tax the nominal rate and ignore inflation.

Certain Bonds (Such as Treasuries) Are Completely Safe

Our national government has been spending money like a drunken sailor on payday. But the U.S. government can also print money and raise taxes. So there isn't much chance of Uncle Sam defaulting on his debt — that's true. Treasuries are not completely safe, however. They are still subject to all the other risks that bonds face. I'm talking about inflation risk and interest-rate risk.

Don't know what those risks are? You'd better read Chapter 10 before plunking your entire savings in Treasury bonds.

Bonds Are a Retiree's Best Friend

Rely on an all fixed-income portfolio to replace your paycheck, and you'd better have an awfully big portfolio or you risk running out of funds. Bonds, unfortunately, have a long-term track record of outpacing inflation by only a modest margin. If you plan on a long retirement, that wee bit of extra gravy may not be enough to get you through the rest of your life without resorting to an awfully tight budget. The retiree's best friend is a *diversified* portfolio that has both stocks (for growth potential) *and* bonds (for stability), with maybe some real estate and a smattering of commodities.

For further discussion on shaping your post-paycheck portfolio for maximum longevity, see Part V.

Individual Bonds Are Usually a Better Deal than Bond Funds

Some of the newer exchange-traded funds offer an instant diversified bond portfolio with a total expense ratio of peanuts — in the case of Vanguard bond ETFs, we're looking at 0.11 percent per year. These ETFs are excellent ways to invest in bonds. Many other bond funds offer professional management with reasonable expenses and impressive long-term performance records.

Buying individual bonds may be the better route for some investors, but the decision is rarely a slam-dunk, especially for those investors with bond portfolios of, oh, $350,000 or less. Less than that, and it may be hard to diversify a portfolio of individual bonds, and the markups you'll pay on your modest buys and sells may be significantly more than you would pay for a bond fund — especially if you wind up not keeping the bond till maturity.

Chapter 14 provides greater insight into the question of individual bonds versus bond funds.

Municipal Bonds Are Free of Taxation

Most income from municipal bonds is free from federal income tax. But the income from many municipal bonds is taxed at the local and state level, especially if you buy bonds that were issued outside of your own backyard. If you see a capital gain on the sale of a muni or muni fund, that will be taxed the same way any other capital gain would be. And some municipal-bond income is subject to the Alternative Minimum Tax (AMT), designed so that those who make six figures and more can't deduct their way out of paying any tax.

Do municipal bonds make sense for you? The tax question is the primary one. Unfortunately, it isn't as straightforward as it looks.

Don't invest in munis, which pay much lower rates of interest than do taxable bonds, without having the entire picture. Crunch the numbers. Talk to your tax guru. Read Chapter 8.

A Discount Broker Sells Bonds Cheaper

Sometimes — often — a discount broker will have the best deals on bonds, but sometimes not. That's especially true for new offers on municipal bonds and corporate bonds where a full-service broker may actually be packaging the bond for the public. It always pays to shop around.

The Biggest Risk in Bonds Is the Risk of the Issuer Defaulting

Even in the world of corporate junk bonds, where the risk of default is as real as dirt, I'm still not sure if actual default qualifies as the biggest risk that bondholders take. Maybe sometimes. But investors in general focus too much on default risk. A bond can also lose plenty of market value if the issuing company is simply downgraded by one of the major credit ratings agencies. Most commonly, however, a bond's principal crashes if interest rates soar. No matter how credit-worthy the issuer, a swift rise in interest rates will cause your bond's value to dip. That's not a big issue if, however, you hold an individual bond till maturity.

Chapter 20

Ten Mistakes That Most Bond Investors Make

*I*nvesting in bonds is easy. Investing well in bonds is hard. The hard part, in good measure, is that there are some very hungry middlemen out there more than willing to share in your profits. In addition, bonds, by their very nature, can be more complicated than they appear. It's easy to get bamboozled, easy to make dumb mistakes. But if you watch out very carefully for the following ten do's and don'ts, you'll be far ahead of the game.

Allowing the Broker to Churn You

Bond brokers generally make their money when you buy and sell bonds. They rarely make anything while the bonds are simply sitting in your account, collecting interest. Largely for that reason, your broker may find many reasons to call you with special deals, and perhaps reasons that a bond issue he sold you last year is — ooops! — no longer worthy of holding.

In truth, it rarely, rarely happens that a bond you were sold last year is no longer worth holding. Company was downgraded by the major ratings agencies? You probably already lost whatever money you're likely to lose; selling the bond now will result in your locking in that loss. Why not hold the bond till maturity, if that was your original plan? Interest rates have risen or fallen? Yeah, so? Don't they always? Bond B has a more favorable tax status than Bond A? Well, why weren't you told that when you bought Bond A?

I won't say that there is *never* a good reason to swap one bond for another. But you are almost always going to be better off as a buy-and-hold-till-maturity investor than you are riding the bond merry-go-round. If your broker calls with reasons to buy or sell, ask lots of questions and make sure you get clear answers as to why it is to *your* benefit, not his, to start trading.

Not Taking Advantage of TRACE

Buying and selling bonds is more transparent than ever before. That means that lots of information is available, if you know where to look. Up till just a few years ago, a bond broker could charge you any kind of markup her heart desired, and you would have no idea what that markup was. Now, with a system called TRACE (the Trade Reporting and Compliance Engine), you can go online and within moments see how much your broker paid for the bonds she's now offering to sell you. Conversely, if your broker sells some bonds for you, you can find out how much she sold them for. You have a right to know.

At the same time you're checking TRACE to see what the broker is looking to score, you'll be able to compare the yield on a prospective bond purchase with the yields of comparable bonds. In fact, the better yield on comparable bonds will often result from a lesser markup by the middleman. The two are closely intertwined.

See Chapter 15 for complete instructions on checking a bond's price history and the yield on comparable bonds.

Choosing a Bond Fund Based on Short-Term Performance

A mutual fund's performance figures, especially going back for any period of less than, say, three years, can often look very impressive, but it may not mean squat. In most cases, a mutual fund's performance, especially over such a short time period, has more to do with the kind of mutual fund it is rather than any managerial prowess. If, for example, high-yield bonds have had a great year, most high-yield bond funds will see impressive performance. If foreign bonds have had a great year, foreign-bond funds will rally as a group. If interest rates have recently taken a nosedive, *all* bond funds will likely look good.

What matters most isn't raw performance but performance in relation to other similar funds and, even more so, performance over the long haul — five years and beyond. See Chapter 16 for more tips on choosing the best bond fund or funds for your portfolio.

Not Looking Closely Enough at a Bond Fund's Expenses

Bonds historically haven't returned enough to warrant very high management expense ratios on bond funds. But that certainly hasn't stopped some bond-fund managers from slapping on high fees. If you look at the performance of bond funds in the long run, the least expensive funds typically do the best. Don't pay a lot for a bond fund.

Going Through a Middleman to Buy Treasuries

Through the U.S. government's own Web site — www.treasurydirect.gov — you can buy any and all kinds of Treasury bonds without paying any markup or fees whatsoever. You don't need a broker. The Web site is easy to navigate, and everything (including the bond holding itself) is electronic. See Chapter 5 for more on investing in Treasury bonds.

Counting Too Much on High-Yield Bonds

High-yield (*junk*) bonds look sweet. Historically, they offer higher returns than other bonds. But the return on high-yield bonds is still much less than the return you can expect on stocks. It may not be worth the added risk of getting an extra couple of percentage points to hold high-yield bonds.

The main role of bonds in a portfolio is to provide ballast. That's not to say that the interest payments from bonds aren't important — they certainly are. But, above all, bonds should be there for you if your other investments, including stocks, have a bad year or few years. Unfortunately, junk bonds don't provide that ballast. When the economy sours and stocks sink, junk bonds typically sink right along with all your other investments. Investment-grade bonds, such as Treasuries, agency bonds, most munis, and high-quality corporates, usually hold their own and often rise in value when the going gets rough.

Paying Too Much Attention to the Yield Curve

There are times when short-term bonds, even money market funds (built on very short-term debt instruments), yield as much as intermediate or long-term bonds. During these times, the yield curve is said to be *flat*. Flatness in the yield curve entices many people to move their money from long-term to short-term bonds. In a way, it makes perfect sense. Why tie your money up and take the greater risk that comes with long-term bonds if you aren't getting compensated for it?

But I would argue that longer-term bonds still belong in your portfolio, even when the yield curve is flat. Remember that the main point of bonds in your portfolio isn't to provide kick-ass returns. That's the job of stocks. The main job of bonds is to provide your portfolio some lift when most of your holdings are sagging. If the economy hits the skids and stocks suddenly plummet, chances are good that long-term, high quality bonds will be the place a lot of money goes. Interest rates will drop. Long-term, investment-grade bonds will soar, and you'll wish you were there.

Buying Bonds That Are Too Complicated

Mortgage-backed bonds, reverse convertible bonds, catastrophe bonds . . . there are bonds and bond products out there that promise far more than simple interest. But in the end, many retail investors who get involved wind up disappointed. Keep it simple. Really. There's no such thing as a free lunch, and any bond or bond product that pays you more than plain vanilla bonds is doing so for a reason. There is risk involved that you may not see unless you squint.

Ignoring Inflation and Taxation

If you're making 5 percent on your bonds, and you're losing 3 percent to inflation, you're about 2 percent ahead of the game . . . for a brief moment. But you'll likely be taxed on the 5 percent.

Inflation and taxation can eat seriously into your bond interest payments. That's not a reason not to invest in bonds. But when doing any kind of projections, counting your bond returns but ignoring inflation and taxation is like visiting Nome in winter and trying to ignore the snow.

Relying Too Heavily on Bonds in Retirement

If this were a chapter on the ten most common mistakes that *stock* investors make, I would advise readers that they must invest in bonds as well as stocks. But this is a chapter on the ten most common mistakes that bond investors make, so I must caution that an all-bond portfolio rarely makes sense.

Stocks offer a greater potential for long-term return and a better chance of staying ahead of inflation than bonds. They also tend to move in different cycles than bonds, providing delicious diversification. They help dampen volatility and smooth out a portfolio's long-term returns, thereby potentially boosting long-term returns. Stocks and bonds complement each other like spaghetti and sauce.

Chapter 21

Ten Q & A's with Bond Guru Dan Fuss

In This Chapter

▶ Explaining his strategy for successful investing

▶ Revealing the most common mistakes he sees

▶ Considering what may be on the horizon for bond investors

▶ Offering tips for individual bond investors and fund investors

My Morningstar Principia software describes more than 3,700 taxable bond funds, of which the number one fund in total return for the past 15 years — with roughly *11 percent* return a year, more than twice that of the average taxable bond fund — is the Loomis Sayles Bond Fund. At the helm of that fund since 1991 (joined by co-manager Kathleen Gaffney in 1997) sits Dan Fuss, who is also vice chairman of the Boston-based Loomis, Sayles & Company. He has been managing investments for nearly half a century. I thought it appropriate that this final chapter of *Bond Investing For Dummies* offer a few words from a guy who obviously knows fixed income . . . perhaps better than anyone.

Q. Dan, to what do you attribute your incredible success as a bond investor?

A. As you drive to work in the morning and you look around you, you get a sense for what season it is. Just as the calendar has seasons, there are also seasons of the economy, what one can also refer to as "cycles." These can greatly affect bond returns. One advantage I have is being older than the hills . . . I've seen a good number of seasons, and I can perhaps recognize them a little better or quicker than most. While I'm looking out for changes in the seasons, I also look at individual bond issuers and how the change of seasons is likely to affect them. "Breezy-Weezy Widget Company," for example, might do better in a hot season than cold.

Q. What would you say is the most common mistake that bond investors make?

If we're talking about investors in individual bonds, the most common mistake is not diversifying enough. I don't think it is even *possible* to diversify adequately unless you have a bond portfolio of considerable size . . . $100,000 for Treasury bonds, $200,000 for municipals, and if you're investing in corporate bonds, you'd better have at least $1 million to invest — *and* lots of time to invest in research, *and* a broker you really know and trust. Otherwise, you're bound to take too much risk on individual issues, and you're going to get eaten alive with fees.

Q. And what about investors in bond funds? What do you see as their most common or most fatal mistake?

There, I'd say the greatest mistake is buying an undifferentiated, general market–correlated fund — almost a "closet" index fund — with high expense ratios. If you're going to be paying a bond manager to manage your bond portfolio, you want that manager to really *manage*. You don't want that manager simply buying the market, because the market is full of terrible bonds that might make perfect sense for the companies issuing them and the brokerage houses selling them, but make no sense for investors.

Q. What is your prediction as to what the total return on bonds and stocks will be over the next ten years?

Prediction? Let's not use that word! My *guess* is that both bonds and stocks will return about 6 percent a year over the next decade, but stock returns will bounce around a lot more than bonds.

Q. So you're saying that bond returns are likely to be slightly higher than their historical average, and stock returns will be considerably lower. On what are you basing those predictions, er, guesses?

Mostly on the growing U.S. federal deficit. That will require greater borrowing by the Treasury, which will tend to force up interest rates. In the long term, such as ten years, rising interest rates will be a good thing for bond investors and not such a good thing for stock investors. But I'm looking at other factors, too, including the currently high valuations of most U.S. companies, and the prospect of a higher corporate income tax.

Q. So if you reckon that stocks and bonds are going to return about the same in future years, and bonds are going to be much less volatile, are you then advocating all-bond portfolios?

I like bonds, but a diversified portfolio with both bonds and stocks still makes sense! First, my guesses about returns could be totally wrong! Second, stock and bond returns will likely continue, as they have in the past, to move up and down in different cycles. Third, if you know what you're doing, you can add a whole lot more return on the stock side by focusing on specific risks.

Q. What about the *yield curve,* the relationship between long-term bond interest rates and short-term bond interest rates? It's been awfully flat lately, which means that a lot of people have been putting their money in short-term bonds. Does that make sense?

It's true that short-term bonds are less volatile than long-term bonds. So if they are paying relatively the same rate of interest, it may *seem* logical to restrict your investments to the short-term. But that would be a mistake. Look at all the people who invested short-term in the early 2000s. Interest rates started to go down, down, down, and their returns spiraled down to almost nothing. There's something to be said for locking in longer interest rates, because you never can tell which direction interest rates will move. If interest rates move up instead of down, you're not going to want everything tied up in long-term, either. *Laddering* — buying both short-term and long-term fixed income — makes sense in any kind of interest-rate environment.

Q. What is the best place to invest right now for people who are most concerned with safety?

There are no completely safe places in the bond market. The risk of capital loss is minimal if you invest in short-term Treasuries, but you have maximum reinvestment risk. If you invest in 30-year Treasury zero-coupons, there is no reinvestment risk, but there is certainly a lot of risk to the value of your principal. With corporate bonds, of course, there are all kinds of additional risks. The greatest safety, now and always, can be found in diversification.

Q. What tips do you have for someone shopping for a bond fund . . . other than choosing Loomis Sayles, of course!

The expense ratio needs to be reasonable: Less than 0.50 percent for a Treasury fund . . . not much more than 1.0 percent for anything else. There should be limited turnover. Turnover costs you money — I'd be wary of any kind of flipping over 80 percent a year. Look for a fund with a long-term positive track record, and make sure that the same manager or team that earned that track record is still the one running the show. Perhaps most importantly, make sure you know what you're buying. For most investors, multi-sector bond funds will make the most sense. Beware that there are many so-called "strategic income" funds out there that sound like multi-sector bond funds, but they may really be balanced funds with exposure to equity as well as fixed-income investments. Read the prospectus!

Q. You've talked of diversification and you've used the word "multi-sector." How diversified should investors be? And how "multi" is "multi" where bonds are concerned?

A diversified portfolio will have both equity investments and bonds. If munis make sense from a tax vantage point, I like to see a good array of municipal issues. If taxable bonds make more sense, I like to see a mix of Treasuries, corporate bonds, agencies, mortgage-backed, and international. Each category will do better at different times. As much as everyone likes to make predictions, you never know what's coming around the corner.

Part VII
Appendix

The 5th Wave   By Rich Tennant

INVESTMENTS

THE BOZO FUND

"All right, ready everyone! We've got some clown out here who looks interested."

In this part . . .

I tried my best to make this book as up-to-date as possible, but some things inevitably grow stale with time. That's why I include this list of Web sites to check whenever you are in need of the latest info on bonds. There are also Web sites that can help you make the essential connections for getting started in serious bond trading. I even include some of the best sites on the Web for general investment guidance.

Appendix

Helpful Web Resources for Successful Bond Investing

• •

1 designed this book so that much of the information is perennial, but some of it will certainly go out of date. Following are a number of Web sites that will change with the times and help to keep you up to speed on changes in the world of bond investing.

Of course, there are many, many Web sites you can turn to for financial information — and misinformation. I handpicked the ones listed here as the best of the lot. Nearly all are entirely free, and they're chock full of good stuff. Some serve as portals that allow you to buy and sell bonds. Others provide you with data unavailable anywhere else.

Bond-Specific Sites

http://finance.yahoo.com/bonds/composite_bond_rates: A great snapshot of the entire bond market, and a logical place to start any bond-shopping expedition.

www.bondbuyer.com: Would you believe there's a daily newspaper about municipal bonds?

www.bondtalk.com: Only for the very serious bond investor.

www.investinginbonds.com: Scads of information on bonds and bond investing from the Securities Industry and Financial Markets Association.

www.municipalbonds.com: Everything you want to know about tax-free investing.

General Financial News, Advice, and Education

`http://finance.yahoo.com`: Navigate your heart away . . . tons of information on financial markets.

`www.bankrate.com`: Compare rates on all sorts of fixed-income investments.

`www.bloomberg.com`: Rather hardcore financial data.

`www.cnnfn.com`: Get your daily fix of everything money related.

`www.dinkytown.com`: Calculators of all sorts.

`www.moneychimp.com`: For the more advanced investor.

`www.morningstar.com`: Exclusive ratings of funds, and more.

`www.riskgrades.com`: A novel way of looking at investment risk and return.

`www.sensible-investor.com`: A huge gateway to other financial Web sites.

`www.socialinvest.org`: A wealth of information on socially responsible investing.

Financial Supermarkets

Otherwise known as large brokerage houses, here are some places where you can buy, sell, and house your bonds or bond funds — as well as other investments, such as stocks.

`www.fidelity.com`: Or telephone Fidelity at 1-800-544-8888.

`www.schwab.com`: Or telephone Charles Schwab at 1-866-232-9890.

`www.tdameritrade.com`: Or telephone TD AMERITRADE at 1-800-454-9272.

`www.troweprice.com`: Or telephone T. Rowe Price at 1-800-638-5660.

`www.vanguard.com`: Or telephone Vanguard at 1-800-662-7447.

Bond Issuers and Bond Fund Providers

If you're in the market for Treasury bonds (see Chapter 5), go to www.treasurydirect.gov.

To check out agency bonds (see Chapter 7), start with these sites:

- ✔ www.fanniemae.com
- ✔ www.fhlbanks.com
- ✔ www.freddiemac.com

If a bond fund is in your future, check out these sites:

- ✔ www.allianzinvestors.com
- ✔ www.americancentury.com
- ✔ www.barclaysglobal.com
- ✔ www.dodgeandcox.com
- ✔ www.fidelity.com
- ✔ www.loomissayles.com
- ✔ www.paxworld.com
- ✔ www.payden-rygel.com
- ✔ www.pimco.com
- ✔ www.schwab.com
- ✔ www.troweprice.com
- ✔ www.vanguard.com

Best Retirement Calculator

How large a portfolio are you going to need to retire in style? How much are you going to have to sock away, and what kind of rate of return do you need to get there?

www.fireseeker.com: *Fire* stands for *financial independence/retire early.* If you didn't realize it, there is an entire movement out there devoted to financial independence. Use this Web site as your entry point. You find what is arguably the best retirement calculator on the Web, along with an Early Retirement Forum where other *Fire* fans passionately discuss their strategies.

Regulatory Agencies

www.sec.gov: The United States Securities and Exchange Commission. Click on "check out brokers and advisors" to make sure a financial planner is fully licensed. You'll also find out if your candidate has any disciplinary history for unethical conduct.

www.finra.org: This is the Web site of the Financial Industry Regulatory Authority (FINRA), formed in July 2007 when the National Association of Securities Dealers (NASD) merged with the New York Stock Exchange Member Regulation. Find scores of information on bond yields, prices, and trends, as well as — naturally — all kinds of regulatory stuff.

Where to Find a Financial Planner

www.cambridgeadvisors.com: A national network of *fee-onlies* (financial people who work for a straight fee rather than commissions) who are eager to work with middle-class folk.

www.cfainstitute.org: CFA Institute is where you want to go to find a Chartered Financial Analyst (CFA), which is not as well-known but very similar to a Certified Financial Planner (CFP).

www.cfp.net: The Certified Financial Planning Board of Standards lists Certified Financial Planners (CFPs) nationwide. The CFP designation assures that the person has a fair amount of education and experience, and passed a wicked 10-hour exam.

www.fpanet.org: The Financial Planning Association is the nation's largest organization of financial planners. It doesn't take much to join.

www.garrettplanning network.com: A network of 250 financial advisors who charge for services on an hourly, as-needed basis.

www.napfa.org: The National Association of Personal Financial Advisors is the association for *fee-onlies,* financial people who don't take commissions but, rather, work for a straight fee. About four out of ten financial planners are fee-onlies.

Yours Truly

www.globalportfolios.net or **www.russellwild.com:** Both URLs will take you to the same place: the author's own fashionable Web site.

Index

● J ●

• *S* •

Notes

BUSINESS, CAREERS & PERSONAL FINANCE

0-7645-9847-3

0-7645-2431-3

Also available:

- Business Plans Kit For Dummies
  0-7645-9794-9
- Economics For Dummies
  0-7645-5726-2
- Grant Writing For Dummies
  0-7645-8416-2
- Home Buying For Dummies
  0-7645-5331-3
- Managing For Dummies
  0-7645-1771-6
- Marketing For Dummies
  0-7645-5600-2

- Personal Finance For Dummies
  0-7645-2590-5*
- Resumes For Dummies
  0-7645-5471-9
- Selling For Dummies
  0-7645-5363-1
- Six Sigma For Dummies
  0-7645-6798-5
- Small Business Kit For Dummies
  0-7645-5984-2
- Starting an eBay Business For Dummies
  0-7645-6924-4
- Your Dream Career For Dummies
  0-7645-9795-7

HOME & BUSINESS COMPUTER BASICS

0-470-05432-8

0-471-75421-8

Also available:

- Cleaning Windows Vista For Dummies
  0-471-78293-9
- Excel 2007 For Dummies
  0-470-03737-7
- Mac OS X Tiger For Dummies
  0-7645-7675-5
- MacBook For Dummies
  0-470-04859-X
- Macs For Dummies
  0-470 04849-2
- Office 2007 For Dummies
  0-470-00923-3

- Outlook 2007 For Dummies
  0-470-03830-6
- PCs For Dummies
  0-7645-8958-X
- Salesforce.com For Dummies
  0-470-04893-X
- Upgrading & Fixing Laptops For Dummies
  0-7645-8959-8
- Word 2007 For Dummies
  0-470-03658-3
- Quicken 2007 For Dummies
  0-470-04600-7

FOOD, HOME, GARDEN, HOBBIES, MUSIC & PETS

0-7645-8404-9

0-7645-9904-6

Also available:

- Candy Making For Dummies
  0-7645-9734-5
- Card Games For Dummies
  0-7645-9910-0
- Crocheting For Dummies
  0-7645-4151-X
- Dog Training For Dummies
  0-7645-8418-9
- Healthy Carb Cookbook For Dummies
  0-7645-8476-6
- Home Maintenance For Dummies
  0-7645-5215-5

- Horses For Dummies
  0-7645-9797-3
- Jewelry Making & Beading For Dummies
  0-7645-2571-9
- Orchids For Dummies
  0-7645-6759-4
- Puppies For Dummies
  0-7645-5255-4
- Rock Guitar For Dummies
  0-7645-5356-9
- Sewing For Dummies
  0-7645-6847-7
- Singing For Dummies
  0-7645-2475-5

INTERNET & DIGITAL MEDIA

0-470-04529-9

0-470-04894-8

Also available:

- Blogging For Dummies
  0-471-77084-1
- Digital Photography For Dummies
  0-7645-9802-3
- Digital Photography All-in-One Desk Reference For Dummies
  0-470-03743-1
- Digital SLR Cameras and Photography For Dummies
  0-7645-9803-1
- eBay Business All-in-One Desk Reference For Dummies
  0-7645-8438-3
- HDTV For Dummies
  0-470-09673-X

- Home Entertainment PCs For Dummies
  0-470-05523-5
- MySpace For Dummies
  0-470-09529-6
- Search Engine Optimization For Dummies
  0-471-97998-8
- Skype For Dummies
  0-470-04891-3
- The Internet For Dummies
  0-7645-8996-2
- Wiring Your Digital Home For Dummies
  0-471-91830-X

* Separate Canadian edition also available
† Separate U.K. edition also available

Available wherever books are sold. For more information or to order direct: U.S. customers visit www.dummies.com or call 1-877-762-2974.
U.K. customers visit www.wileyeurope.com or call 0800 243407. Canadian customers visit www.wiley.ca or call 1-800-567-4797.

SPORTS, FITNESS, PARENTING, RELIGION & SPIRITUALITY

0-471-76871-5

0-7645-7841-3

Also available:
- Catholicism For Dummies
  0-7645-5391-7
- Exercise Balls For Dummies
  0-7645-5623-1
- Fitness For Dummies
  0-7645-7851-0
- Football For Dummies
  0-7645-3936-1
- Judaism For Dummies
  0-7645-5299-6
- Potty Training For Dummies
  0-7645-5417-4
- Buddhism For Dummies
  0-7645-5359-3

- Pregnancy For Dummies
  0-7645-4483-7 †
- Ten Minute Tone-Ups For Dummies
  0-7645-7207-5
- NASCAR For Dummies
  0-7645-7681-X
- Religion For Dummies
  0-7645-5264-3
- Soccer For Dummies
  0-7645-5229-5
- Women in the Bible For Dummies
  0-7645-8475-8

TRAVEL

0-7645-7749-2

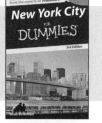

0-7645-6945-7

Also available:
- Alaska For Dummies
  0-7645-7746-8
- Cruise Vacations For Dummies
  0-7645-6941-4
- England For Dummies
  0-7645-4276-1
- Europe For Dummies
  0-7645-7529-5
- Germany For Dummies
  0-7645-7823-5
- Hawaii For Dummies
  0-7645-7402-7

- Italy For Dummies
  0-7645-7386-1
- Las Vegas For Dummies
  0-7645-7382-9
- London For Dummies
  0-7645-4277-X
- Paris For Dummies
  0-7645-7630-5
- RV Vacations For Dummies
  0-7645-4442-X
- Walt Disney World & Orlando
  For Dummies
  0-7645-9660-8

GRAPHICS, DESIGN & WEB DEVELOPMENT

0-7645-8815-X

0-7645-9571-7

Also available:
- 3D Game Animation For Dummies
  0-7645-8789-7
- AutoCAD 2006 For Dummies
  0-7645-8925-3
- Building a Web Site For Dummies
  0-7645-7144-3
- Creating Web Pages For Dummies
  0-470-08030-2
- Creating Web Pages All-in-One Desk
  Reference For Dummies
  0-7645-4345-8
- Dreamweaver 8 For Dummies
  0-7645-9649-7

- InDesign CS2 For Dummies
  0-7645-9572-5
- Macromedia Flash 8 For Dummies
  0-7645-9691-8
- Photoshop CS2 and Digital
  Photography For Dummies
  0-7645-9580-6
- Photoshop Elements 4 For Dummies
  0-471-77483-9
- Syndicating Web Sites with RSS Feeds
  For Dummies
  0-7645-8848-6
- Yahoo! SiteBuilder For Dummies
  0-7645-9800-7

NETWORKING, SECURITY, PROGRAMMING & DATABASES

0-7645-7728-X

0-471-74940-0

Also available:
- Access 2007 For Dummies
  0-470-04612-0
- ASP.NET 2 For Dummies
  0-7645-7907-X
- C# 2005 For Dummies
  0-7645-9704-3
- Hacking For Dummies
  0-470-05235-X
- Hacking Wireless Networks
  For Dummies
  0-7645-9730-2
- Java For Dummies
  0-470-08716-1

- Microsoft SQL Server 2005 For Dummies
  0-7645-7755-7
- Networking All-in-One Desk Reference
  For Dummies
  0-7645-9939-9
- Preventing Identity Theft For Dummies
  0-7645-7336-5
- Telecom For Dummies
  0-471-77085-X
- Visual Studio 2005 All-in-One Desk
  Reference For Dummies
  0-7645-9775-2
- XML For Dummies
  0-7645-8845-1